Radio Mastery for VFR Pilots

Everything you need to know to talk to
Air Traffic Control

Jeff Kanarish

All aircraft call signs and individual identities used in this book are completely fictitious. Any similarity to real aircraft call signs or individual identities is purely coincidental. The names of most air traffic control facilities used in this book are real, but the conversations and stories involving those facilities are fictional, except where noted.

All maps, charts, and illustrations in this book are for demonstration purposes only and are not intended for use in actual navigation.

In memory of Air Force Captain Steve "Syph" Phillis. Syph was the consummate A-10 pilot who first showed me that as the radios go, so goes the mission.

CONTENTS

Acknowledgements

Although I received a great deal of assistance from friends, acquaintances, and experts in producing this book, any errors it contains are entirely my own.

I would like to thank the following people for their generous support and advice. From the St. Louis TRACON, retired air traffic controller and certified flight instructor, Jack Bowers. Jack gave me tremendous perspective on the relationship between pilots and air traffic controllers. Ronnie White, air traffic controller at the Indianapolis ARTCC (Indy Center). Ronnie provided valuable insight on the safety aspects of air traffic control. M.T., an administrator and air traffic controller at an ARTCC in the southern U.S., knows the standards for air traffic control like no one else. He helped me understand why using standard phraseology on the aviation radio band is absolutely critical to flight safety.

Thank you to the many pilots, on six continents, who have generously added to the conversation at my website, ATCcommunication.com. Ladies and gentlemen, your thoughtful questions and comments helped steer the direction of this book, and for that I am deeply grateful.

To the finest air traffic controllers on the planet: the men and women of Atlanta Tower and Atlanta TRACON. Thank you for setting the highest standard in air traffic control worldwide.

My good friend and confidante, Robin Maiden provided the encouragement and guidance I needed to jumpstart ATCcommunication.com and this book. Thank you, Robin.

Finally to my wife and pillar of strength. Thank you for making what I do better, and for putting up with me.

Introduction

I know why you are here. I really do. You are here because you are worried. You know you will need to talk to air traffic control at some point in the future and you are worried you won't be able to do it right. You are worried you are going to say the wrong thing to ATC, and an air traffic controller is going to hammer you for your mistake. You are worried you are going to get brain lock when you key the microphone to speak and nothing is going to come out of your mouth. You are worried ATC is going to rattle off a clearance to you at light speed and you aren't going to understand any of it. You worry about all this, but you don't know how to fix it without having to get on the radio and sound stupid.

Guess what. I'm going to help you fix it. I'm going to show you how take a bunch of little steps that, when added all together, produce an intelligent conversation on the aircraft radio. I'm not saying it's going to be easy, because it won't be. I will say it's going to work. You will feel a lot better about your radio skills. It all begins with clearly defining the problem. Let's do that.

If you have surpassed your third birthday, you probably know how to string more than a couple of words together. You probably can create whole sentences, in your native language, and produce a message that can be understood by another member of your native community. I'd even wager, if you are a certified pilot, or have met the minimum requirements to work toward your pilot's license, you are intelligent and well-spoken.

If all that is true, why is it so hard to put an intelligible sentence together when you key the microphone of your aircraft radio? I'll tell you why. Communication on the aviation radio band is damned complicated. It's complicated because:

- The language of air traffic control is specialized.

- You must speak precisely and efficiently, without all the filler and extra words we use in everyday conversation.

- Every time you key your microphone, the government and your peers listen to--and evaluate--everything you say.

- You have to fly and navigate while talking. Any one of those 3 items takes a lot of concentration, and you are expected to do all 3 simultaneously, with little or no tolerance for error.

When you look at that list, it's no wonder so many student pilots, and even certified pilots, become brain locked when they key the microphone. The mental, and even physical demands of speaking on the aircraft radio are ridiculously high. Learning how to meet those demands takes training, patience, and practice; a lot of hands-on practice.

I have to warn you, learning a new language is not easy if you happen to be older than 8-years old. We adults have a harder time hanging on to new language. I do have tips and tricks up my sleeve that should make the learning process a little bit easier for you, even if you have already graduated from primary school.

If you follow me at ATCcommunication.com, you have heard me say, "You can't learn how to talk on the aircraft radios by reading a textbook." So what did I go and do? I wrote a textbook on how to talk on the radios.

Make no mistake, you will not become proficient at talking on the aircraft radios by only reading this book. To become very good at aviation communication, you will need to practice aviation communication, in real time, in real or simulated flying.

Why bother reading a book about how to talk on the aircraft radios? A book--this book--can guide your live practice so you learn quickly, and with less goofy mistakes than you would make without guidance.

Think of it this way. How much sense would it make for me to give my Aunt Shirley the keys to the family Cessna when good old Shirl has never touched a control yoke in her life? "Hey Aunt Shirley, here's the keys to our single-engine aerospace transportation device. Take her up for a spin and teach yourself how to fly." By the way, I don't have an Aunt Shirley, and our family doesn't own a Cessna, but you get the idea. Before Shirley turns a wheel, she needs someone to lay a foundation for learning.

This book lays the foundation for good radio work in your airplane. Read it to build some airmanship before you spin a prop or crank a turbine. Just don't expect the book to key the microphone and make radio calls for you. You'll have to do that yourself.

Humor Me

Before we move on to the actual headwork, here's a few pointers, disclaimers, definitions, and bits of background information.

First, I'm going to do my best to keep this from being another one of those dry, boring, shoot-me-now, oral-surgery-would-be-more-enjoyable, death-by-monotony textbooks. To do this, I'll use something called h-u-m-o-r.

Please be aware that humor is not a standard practice endorsed by the FAA, the NOAA, the NASA, or the NTSB. Furthermore, while humor can make reading more enjoyable, it has no place in actual radio communication. I'll explain why in a very serious discussion later. (I'm not kidding about the serious discussion.) The difference between humor in this book and humor on the radio is so important, I've created an illustration that explains the difference. (See humor illustration, next page.)

If you are like me, you probably dread reading academic texts. I find instruction, delivered in a friendly conversational style, much more approachable and appealing. Let's park the "indeeds," the "therefores," and the rest of the vocabulary of haute academia on the sideline. If you don't appreciate my loosey-goosey style of writing, drop me an email. In response, I'll produce a second edition of this book that would gladden the heart of any erudite Ivy League scholar.

HUMOR ON
AIRCRAFT RADIO: BAD

HUMOR IN BOOKS: GOOD

Before we launch into the meat of this book, let's define a few terms. Having been raised on the military doctrine of flight training by fear, sarcasm, and ridicule, I will be using the following terms interchangeably: Knucklehead, chucklehead, bonehead, knothead, pinhead, meathead, slugmeat, sluggo, pultroon, maroon, dimwit, half-wit, nitwit, nimrod, ninny, dolt, dodo, doofus, goofus, numbskull, numbnut, lamebrain, all thrust and no vector.

The following words mean the same thing: Ace, slick, jock, hotshot, maestro, guru, meister, shark, whiz.

These may also be used to mean the same thing: Student, studley, stud, trainee, the downtrodden and forlorn.

A flight instructor may be called: Instructor pilot, supreme being, master of all he/she surveys, torturer, tormenter, all-knowing one, flight hours prostitute.

In two-person flight crews, I may refer to the captain, or pilot-in-command, as Skippy. The co-pilot/first officer/second-in-command may be called Bubba. In this book, these are not gender-specific names.

The following words may be used in lieu of "going fast": Speed of stink, mach snot, zorch, re-entry, hot, glowing heat shield, light speed, warp speed, dropping like a manhole cover.

In all other cases, any term used in this book that is

uncommon will be defined when used.

Standards vs. Techniques

A humongous portion of the practices in this book is technique derived from my experience and the experiences of other pilots and air traffic controllers. Whenever I'm talking about standard procedure, I'll make it clear by referring to the U.S. Aeronautical Information Manual (AIM); the International Civil Aeronautic Organization's (ICAO) Air Traffic Management Manual; or, the U.S. Air Traffic Controller Manual. If I don't cite one of those manuals, what I'm talking about at the moment is technique, which you can use or reject at your discretion.

Speaking of manuals, the intent of this book is not to re-create everything in the manuals written about air traffic control. If you want a line-by-line analysis of the Aeronautical Information Manual, you will have to look elsewhere. The goal here is to draw information from the various manuals and build a big picture that makes sense to pilots.

Finally, a word about the standards as they are written in the various air traffic manuals. Some of these standards are regulatory, meaning they are rules that pilots and controllers are required to follow to the letter. Some are best practices, meaning they are strongly recommended, but not required. All of the content in the Aeronautical Information Manual, for example, is a collection of best practices and techniques. The AIM is not regulatory. It says so in the manual's introductory section:

AIM Flight Information Publication Policy

d. This publication, while not regulatory, provides information which reflects examples of operating techniques and procedures which may be requirements in other federal publications or regulations.

You are not required, by law, to follow the guidance in AIM. In most cases it would be foolish to ignore the guidance. However, it's your birthright to behave as foolishly as you choose, so do as you see fit.

Most of the content in the AIM is written in the blood or adrenaline of pilots who have gone before you. To avoid future bloodshed or heart palpitations in similar situations, the feds decided it would be a good idea to write some guidance for staying out of trouble. That is what is at the heart of the AIM.

The AIM and the ICAO Air Traffic Management Manual are the government's and the aviation community's attempt to compile standard practices that reduce risk. We simply cannot afford to have each pilot out there doing his or her own thing. When you and I adhere to a standard practice, we can fly along side each other in a predictable manner.

On the radio, the standards allow you and me to communicate in a common language. It doesn't matter if you are from Senegal and I am from Poughkeepsie. We can understand each other on the radio.

Since the AIM is not regulatory, pilots are not bound by law to follow the communication standards. That may be why you'll hear nimrods on the radio making up their own rules for communication. I'll have plenty of examples of this type of buffoonery in this book.

My advice to you would be, ignore the style of these numbnuts and stick to the standards, including the standards for radio communication. If another pilot lacks the self-discipline to follow the standards, it does not mean you should too. As your parents used to tell you, "When your friend jumps off a cliff, you don't have to follow."

Even if you follow the standards to a T, communication by aircraft radio is not perfect. It has its limitations. For example, when one pilot is talking on the frequency, no one else can speak. All communication is filtered through a single person-- an air traffic controller--who is subject to work overload. There are many other limiting factors on the aviation band, and we'll look more closely at some of them in this book.

For all its limitations, there's no doubt, radio communication makes aviation safer. It allows a controlling agency to coordinate the flight paths of aircraft sharing the same airspace.

Unlike driving, which is the transportation equivalent of the Wild West, air traffic communication puts the civil in civil aviation.

Not that radio communication between car drivers would work anyway. Can you imagine what the conversations would sound like if you let car drivers coordinate their progress by talking to each other on the radio?

"Hey you #*@^! #(%!! Get the #@&! out of my way!"

"You talking to me %&@*!? you &%*#! I was in this lane first! You get the $@(!#! out of my way!"

To summarize, if you have avoided controlled airspace as much as possible so you don't have to talk to the big bad air traffic controller, I'm going to help you fix that. If, when talking to ATC is unavoidable, you rehearse your lines like they are your last words before the executioner throws the switch, I'm going to help you fix that. If, when keying the microphone, your behind has a firm grip on the seat cushion, I'm going to help you fix that. If, your rehearsed speech on the radio sounds like it is being spoken by a six-year old reciting his one and only line in a first grade play, I'm going to help you fix that.

Flying is supposed to be fun. If talking on the radio makes you miserable, you can find less demanding, less expensive ways to be unhappy. It's time to liberate yourself from the tyranny of the aircraft radio! It's time to take charge, and learn the language so it rolls off your tongue without getting stuck in your teeth.

Let's begin by going back to pre-school, when your language skills were not fully formed. In the next chapter, we are going to look at pilots who are essentially stuck in pre-school. We are going to see how a lack of radio training early on, leaves pilots in the same place they were 20 years ago. We are going to look at pilots who used to suck on the radio, currently suck, and will suck until the day they retire. Then, I'm going to give you the recipe to bypass the sucking stage.

Take Action

At the end of each chapter in this book you will find this section. Here, I'll list exercises and other steps you can perform immediately to improve your performance on the radio right away. For the introductory section of this book, your one and only action step is to turn the page and begin the first chapter.

Chapter 1: Let's Make Some Very Bad Radio Transmissions

ATL Tower: "Airliner 271, Atlanta Tower, cross Runway Two Seven Left. Hold short of Runway Two Seven Right at Sierra."

High-Time Pilot: "Airliner 271, crossing Two Seven Left."

ATL Tower: "Airliner 271, cross Runway Two Seven Left. Hold short of Runway Two Seven Right at Sierra."

High-Time Pilot: "We'll hold short of Two Seven Right."

ATL Tower: "Airliner 271, I need you to say your call sign and the runway you are going to hold short of."

In a voice filled with disgust, the high-time pilot says, "Airliner 271, will hold short of Two Seven Right at Sierra." (Completely true, re-created dialogue between an airline pilot and an air traffic controller at the Atlanta Hartsfield-Jackson International Airport. The name "Airliner 721" was substituted for the actual call sign of the offending party.)

How many ways can you screw up a radio call? I'd say, about 50 ways, but only because that number reminds me of the Paul Simon song, "There Must Be 50 Ways to Leave Your Lover." The truth is, there is an infinite number of ways to destroy a radio call. I'm not trying to be flip about this. (Yes I am.) There is a valid reason why you hear so much garbage when listening to the aircraft radio.

Consider the following:

In the United States alone, air traffic controllers handle approximately 50,000 aircraft flights per day. (Source: www.faa.gov press release, July 6, 2011. "FAA Celebrates 75th Anniversary of Air Traffic Control.") Although there are no reliable statistics on this, let's assume, for argument's sake, about 20% of those flights are flown as multiple legs by the same pilot. That means an estimated 80% of the flights are one leg per day operations, flown by an individual pilot. That adds up to 40,000 individuals talking on the aviation band every day. Even if I'm off by a few percentage points either way, that's a lot of certified and student pilots adding their own voice to the air traffic control system.

To receive pilot certification in the United States, a person is not required to receive any formal training in how to communicate on the aircraft radio. Granted, all student pilots will receive some training in radio communication, but that training will be delivered by a flight instructor or ground instructor who also did not receive formal training in radio work.

Let me be clear about that. By no means am I saying instructors are neglecting radio training. Nor am I saying instructors are incompetent in the area of radio communication. Most instructors are very diligent when guiding and correcting their students' performance on the radio.

I am saying there is no specific, FAA-mandated curriculum to guide instructors who teach radio communication. There are no regulations requiring a minimum level of competence on the radios. Heck, there are almost no regulations covering radio work in general!

I'm not a great lover of regulations. It does seem odd, in the ultra-regulated world of aviation, the FAA has almost no regulations about how pilots must conduct themselves on the radio. As a result, the quality of training a pilot receives in radio work is hit or miss. Instructors try to teach good radio habits, but those habits are open to interpretation and modification by each individual who instructs.

Some may argue the Aeronautical Information Manual (AIM) contains everything a pilot needs to communicate accurately and consistently on the radio. It's the gold standard for instructors who wish to teach radio work. As we will see in the coming chapters, there are gaps and inconsistencies in the AIM that leave a lot of radio communication open to guessing and interpretation. Further, some of the guidance for radio communication is scattered among different references, including the Air Traffic Controllers Manual, and the ICAO Air Traffic Services Manual.

You may argue, "What's the big deal? As long as I am understood on the radio when I speak, I'm doing okay." I would agree, right up to the point where you say something nonstandard that gets misinterpreted.

The Real Value of Experience

There are those who argue that experience is the best teacher. All we have to do is listen to the pros on the radio and we'll pick up the habits we need for good communication. We don't even have to fly to learn something new. All we have to do is go to the internet and listen to live air traffic control transmissions on our web browser. That's good training, right? Give me a minute to stop laughing.

Being a pro usually does not extend to radio professionalism, if you equate professionalism with accuracy and consistency. As we will see a little later, most professional pilots are simply pilots who have more experience making radio calls incorrectly.

It's these kinds of arguments that make the strongest case for formal, standardized training in radio work. The gaps and inconsistencies in the manuals, the free-form training, and the habits we pick up by listening to the pros, are all strong reasons why we need formal training. These are also the reasons why you hear so much crap on the radios.

Given the number of ways pilots fill the airwaves with garbage, it would take an eternity to completely cover the subject. Our time together is limited. Let's review a handful of the most glaring errors, and acknowledge we will have only scratched the surface.

Wait a minute, you say. This book is supposed to be about how to make radio transmissions correctly. Why should we have to cover how to screw up a radio call? I'll answer that with a short story.

During the most recent downturn in the airline industry, which began in the early 2000's, many airline pilots had to develop a way to supplement their dwindling income. My wife and I started a dog grooming and boarding shop. It seemed like a good idea at the time.

One of the dog groomers we hired, while generally very competent, was receiving many complaints about his grooming results on one particular breed of dog. Although he knew the basics of how to groom the breed, the standard he applied at the grooming shop in his old neighborhood did not meet the higher expectations in our neighborhood.

Exasperated, he sought the help of another dog groomer in the shop to improve his skills. His decision to seek help took a lot of courage. Most professionals take pride in their accomplishments. It takes a certain amount of humility for an expert to admit he doesn't know everything in his field of expertise.

As he put it, "I don't get it. I've been grooming dogs for 15 years. Fifteen years! I can't believe I'm just now discovering I don't know how to groom this breed of dog." The good news was, the other groomer gave him a few pointers and critiqued his work until it improved. The customers who had been complaining soon began to compliment his work. It was a good outcome, and everyone was relieved.

Getting back to the airline industry. I fly with pilots who have been working in professional cockpits for 20, 25, 30 or more years. I'm talking about pilots with tens of thousands of hours of flying experience. Many, if not most, make terrible radio calls.

Why? They never learned how to make a correct radio call early in their training. As I said, there is no requirement to formally learn radio work.

If you never learned correct radio procedure in the first place, then it's likely whatever you learned, early on, was a grab bag of correct and incorrect procedure. They say, "What's learned first is learned best." It's likely, if you learned bad radio habits early in your career, you will make bad radio transmissions for the rest of your life.

What about experience? It stands to reason, as a pilot gains more experience in the field, that pilot will learn better radio procedure. Not necessarily.

If a pilot believes he has the program wired, he is not going to recognize or absorb different ways of speaking on the radio. Unless he can recognize his own mistakes, and is willing to learn from others, experience isn't going to count for jack. To a pilot who learned bad habits on the radio in his formative years, and then said, "That's good enough," all experience equals is proficiency in making bad radio calls. Like the dog groomer I talked about earlier, "good enough" may work at a small, uncontrolled airpatch. "Good enough" doesn't cut the mustard when moving to a new neighborhood where a higher standard is expected and enforced.

Experience aside, radio work can suffer from something called the "Ivory Tower Effect." When learning a new skill in an academic environment, we are usually taught according to some standard. The standard is the ideal. Often, our instructors will acknowledge that the standard is not what holds up in the real world. Or, maybe the instructor won't admit this in front of his class, but the student in-the-know will whisper to the newbies, "Just you wait until you get out in the real world. You'll see how it's really done."

When you learn something inside the walls of the Ivory Tower--the sterile learning environment where it's assumed some things have nothing to do with the real world--you build an expectation. That expectation is, you will learn how adapt your new skills to the real world once you get out there.

While pilots usually attempt to maintain a very high standard for flying, the standards don't seem to hold up for radio work. In the so-called real world, pilots expect to learn jargon and shortcuts on the radio that work better than the standards. The truth is, when it comes to radio calls, there is no Ivory Tower. The standards are the safest way to communicate.

While the Ivory Tower Effect--as it applies to radio work--is a load of crap, there remains a large group of pilots who have convinced themselves there is a real-world way to do business on the radio: Let the standards be damned. The result is a lot of nonstandard radio calls which are fundamentally incorrect.

Which brings us back to why we are going to spend so much time discussing bad radio calls. I want you to know the difference between a correctly made radio call and a bad one. Unlike my colleagues, who never had the difference explained to them when they were young pilots, or who believe the real world requires something other than the standards, I want better for you. I want you to become an old pilot who spent a career knowing good from bad when you pick up a microphone.

A Recipe for Bad Radio Calls

What makes a bad radio call? There are two categories:

- Bad content.

- Bad technique.

Number 2 is easier to nail down, so let's attack that one first. I wrote an article at ATCcommunication.com called "50 Ways to Screw Up a Radio Call," that summarizes bad microphone technique. You can check it out at:

http://ATCcommunication.com/fifty-ways-to-screw-up-an-aircraft-radio-call.

Microphone technique is how you project your voice onto the radio frequency. We don't need to get into microphone physics to understand that when it comes to voice input, it's "garbage in, garbage out." Basically, if you mumble, spit, or puff into the microphone, the microphone will faithfully reproduce mumbling, spitting, or puffing on the radio.

Microphone dynamics also require a certain volume of voice input to accurately convert your voice into electrons. Talk too softly and the microphone will do the electronic equivalent of, "Huh?" So will the person at the other end of the radio who is trying to hear you.

Shout into the microphone--a favorite technique of cell phone users everywhere--and the microphone will over-modulate your transmission. That's a fancy way of saying the person at the other end of the radio will hear loud noise, but nothing understandable.

Even if you speak at the perfect volume, it won't add up to bupkis if the microphone is not positioned correctly near your mouth. Notice I said, "near your mouth." I didn't say, "in front of your mouth."

Poofta

Placing the microphone directly in front of your mouth

works against you. (See photo, next page.) Doing so puts the microphone directly into the main stream of the breath it takes to produce sound. Air blowing on the mic registers as something called a "plosion."

Plosions are the pops of noise that happen when you pronounce certain breathy consonants, such as the letters p, f, and t. For example, the word "Poofta" is filled with plosions. Plosions are annoying to anyone who has to listen to them, and they may make all, or part of your radio transmission unintelligible.

Hissing is another sound effect related to plosions. If you have the mic positioned directly in front of your mouth when you say a word containing the letter s, your voice will produce an ugly hiss on the radio.

"Kansas City Center, we'd like to continue VFR to the north along the Mississippi."

"Aircraft calling Center, that last transmission was disgusting and unreadable."

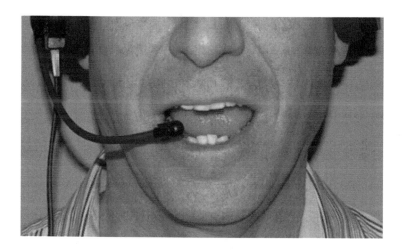

Placing the mic in front of your mouth will cause plosions in your transmissions.

The best position for your microphone is just above your breath stream or slightly off to one side of it. (See photo below.)

The best mic position: To the side of and above your upper lip. (Yes, that's me.)

That means, place the microphone so the top of the mic lines up just outside of the corner of your mouth (first choice), or, place the microphone just above the edge of your upper lip (second choice). Either technique should keep the mic out of your breath stream.

Some instructors recommend placing the mic just below the bottom edge of your lower lip, but that doesn't work for microphones attached to headsets by a boom. When you speak, your jaw moves down, and your lips open up, The boom mic, when placed in a fixed position below your breath stream, comes into the line of fire as your mouth opens to speak.

Holding a hand-held mic below your lower lip works, if you brace the mic against your lower jaw and let your jaw guide it up and down as you speak. This movement keeps the microphone clear of your breath stream as your mouth opens and closes.

If you choose to position a boom mic just above your upper lip, make sure it isn't in the line of fire of your nose. (See photo below.) Nose-breathing into the microphone is no better than mouth-breathing into it.

Microphone incorrectly placed below nose.

Another way to eliminate the noise of your breath as you talk is to place a soft foam mitt or muff over the microphone. (See photo, next page.) A microphone mitt allows voice sounds through but acts as a barrier to your breath stream. You can huff and puff all you want into a mic mitt and your bad breath will not hit the microphone's diaphragm.

A mic mitt prevents your breath from hitting the mic.
Keep the mic off to one side of your mouth even if you
use a mitt.

Even when using a microphone mitt, it's still a good idea to position the microphone above, or to one side of your breath stream. Almost everyone projects tiny droplets of spittle when they say certain words. When that moisture accumulates on the microphone mitt over time, the mitt can become a biohazard. And don't even talk to me about what happens to that mike mitt if you eat while you fly. Disgusting, I know; but trust me, you are better off keeping your mic mitt out of harm's way.

WWII is Over!

Before we move on, I have a news flash. Throat microphones--ones that capture your voice by making contact with your throat--were discontinued in general aviation aircraft shortly after World War II concluded. (See the photo of a U.S. Navy pilot wearing a throat mic.)

Carry the throat mic forward a couple of years for argument's sake. That means, the throat mic has been out of fashion for what, 58 years, give or take?

A U.S. Navy pilot's throat mic.

Back in the Big One, military pilots were taught to speak in a low, rumbly voice because that type of sound transmitted the clearest vibrations from the larynx (voice box) into the throat mic. Today, there are remote cell phone microphones that operate on a similar principle. These cell phone mics rely on bone conduction to carry the sound of your voice from your larynx to the microphone as it rests in your ear.

Here's the second part of the news flash. Modern aviation microphones pick up sound as vibrations in the air. They do not detect vibrations in your throat, or vibrations in your skull. When you attempt to make a radio transmission in a low rumbly voice, the way Army Air Corp pilots were taught to speak into throat mics, your modern microphone can barely hear you.

That cool fighter jock voice you are making low in your throat? It may sound terrific to your ears because your ears are picking it up through bone conduction. It creates a barely audible, sorry excuse for a radio transmission. Whenever I hear another pilot doing the fighter jock thing on the radio, I want to key the microphone and say, "I hope your laryngitis clears up. Get well soon!"

While a low-pitched, low volume voice performs very poorly over the radio, higher pitched voices come through crystal clear on the radio. Most women can beat the daylights out of men when it comes to a clear, intelligible voice on the radio. Don't believe me? Pay attention to the clarity of the transmission the next time you hear a female speak on the radio. I guarantee, you won't misunderstand a single word of her radio transmission.

Sir, I'm not asking you to speak in a high-pitched voice. I am asking you follow the lady's lead and speak the hell up. Ma'am, keep doing what you are doing on the radio. It's working.

Marble Mouth

Even if you do speak at the proper pitch, it's still possible to wreck a radio transmission by mumbling. Mumbling is what happens when you limit the movement of your jaw as you speak. Clear communication, also known as enunciation, demands that you exercise your entire mouth when you speak.

Your larynx only produces basic, guttural sounds. The hard work of converting the basic sounds from your larynx into clear, intelligible words is produced by the tongue and lips. If you doubt this, try saying "She sells sea shells by the seashore" with your lips mostly closed and your tongue pressed against the roof of your mouth. Sounds pretty stupid, doesn't it?

If your lips and tongue play a key role in pronouncing words, then they have to have room to work. Jaw movement

gives your lips and tongue the vertical space to move freely.
Think of it this way: If you have ever injured your writing
hand, you know how difficult it is to write legibly with your
hand in a cast or even a tight bandage. In order to write well,
your fingers need freedom of movement to operate a pen.

It's the same with words. In order to create clearly
understood words, your jaw has to move freely to allow room
for your lips and tongue to shape sound. When you talk on the
radio, move your mouth. Enunciate each word as clearly and
succinctly as possible by fully exercising your jaw, lips and
tongue. Mumbling may be cool if you are a disenfranchised
teenager and you are speaking to other disenfranchised
teenagers. Mumbling is not cool on the aircraft radio. It's just
unintelligible.

Boomer, Baby

If you fly in a noisy cockpit and you aren't using a noise-
reducing headset with an attached boom microphone, kick
yourself three times, right now. Go ahead, I'll wait. Humor me,
otherwise I'll come to your house and kick your ass for you.
(Ass kicking is a free public service I offer, but you'll have to
pick up the cost of my transportation, lodging, and meals.)

You might say, "I wear ear plugs and use a regular hand-held,
noise-canceling mic. That's good enough for me." To which I
say, "You are as wrong as someone who wears a parka in the
Amazon Basin in the middle of summer." Here's why:

A radio headset does four things for you that a hand-held
mic and ear plugs cannot do for you.

1. A headset holds the boom microphone in the correct
    position near your mouth no matter where you turn
    your head.

2. The headset directs incoming transmissions directly
    into your ears. The quality of the sound you hear will
    be much better than listening to a cockpit loudspeaker
    blasting through cockpit noise and the filtering effects
    of your ear plugs.

3. The headset leaves one of your hands free to do things

other than hold a microphone. I don't need to explain why this is important to a pilot.

4. You get truer feedback on the quality of your own transmissions because you can hear the side tone of your voice better through a headset than a cockpit loudspeaker.

Of the four advantages I just listed, you can still ruin correct microphone positioning near your mouth, even if you initially place the microphone boom correctly. Since we are talking about how to botch a radio call, let me give you the recipe for ruining the advantage of using a radio headset:

1. Loop your headset's cord over the microphone boom.

2. Lean or turn away from the point where the headset cord plugs into the headset jack on your airplane's console. Be sure to lean or turn far enough so the cord comes under tension and pulls the headset boom away from your mouth.

3. Without noticing the change in the position of your headset boom mic, make a radio transmission.

4. Wait for the reply from the person you were talking to on the radio. It should sound something like this: "Last aircraft calling, that transmission was weak and unreadable."

Alternately, if you have a headset with a loose microphone boom, simply put the headset on with the cord already looped over the boom. The cord will slowly and steadily pull the boom away from your mouth without any further effort on your part. This will ensure weak and unreadable transmissions until you discover the problem.

By the way, pilots are not the only ones who make this mistake with a headset cord. Air traffic controllers will do it too from time to time. More than once, I've had to tell a controller his transmissions were weak and unreadable. The controller repositioned his mic. Problem solved.

Which brings up a quick point I'll cover in greater detail later. It amazes me how many pilots tolerate weak and barely readable transmissions from ATC. I'll hear a controller making weak transmissions on a frequency and no one will speak up to tell the controller about the problem. When it comes my turn to take a call from the controller, I won't hesitate to tell her I can barely hear her. She fixes her microphone and the transmissions get better. One controller, down in Miami, even jokingly told me, "I forgot to read the step in the checklist where it says to turn the microphone towards my mouth, not away from it."

Why don't other pilots speak up and complain about weak transmissions from ATC? I think it may be a fear of correcting a representative of the FAA. As I said, I'll cover this problem later, but keep the idea in your hip pocket for now.

Timing is Everything

Even if you speak with a level of clarity that would draw admiration from a commercial radio announcer, you can still destroy a perfectly good radio call with the microphone button. They say timing is everything, and if you don't time the pressing of the microphone key just right, you are going to create a lousy transmission. Here are some examples:

"-er 47 Foxtrot, descending to 7,000."

"Cessna 312 Lima Charlie, 128 point --"

"-- four zero, Westwind 55 Echo."

"Your total is four, seventy--. Please drive through to the second win--."

You've heard of hand-eye coordination. In the world of radio transmissions, there is something called thumb-mouth coordination. (I made that term up.) It has nothing to do with thumb sucking. It has everything to do with just plain sucking.

It takes a bit of practice to get the coordination right between activating the transmission machinery in your radio and sending your voice into the machine. Done right, the radio's carrier wave, the magic that carries your voice, should be activated with the microphone switch a half-second or less before you speak. I'm not asking you to get out your stopwatch and time this interval. I just want you to develop an awareness of activating the radio before you speak. I also want you to maintain pressure on the push-to-talk switch until your voice finishes producing sound at the end of your transmission. The only way to get this timing right is to practice, with a critique from a friend.

It's very difficult to analyze your own timing with the microphone switch. If you start speaking before you press the mic switch, you will hear your voice, but it will be unclear whether the sound is coming directly from your mouth or from the radio's sidetone. You need someone to listen to your transmission and tell you whether or not you chopped off the beginning or ending. I'll cover how to practice radio transmissions, with useful feedback, next. First, let's do a recap.

Let's Break it Down

Here's where we are, so far. You can screw up a radio transmission by:

1. Talking too loudly or too softly into the microphone.

2. Spitting or puffing into the microphone.

3. Using a low, rumbly voice.

4. Mumbling.

5. Intentionally positioning the microphone directly in your breath stream.

6. Allowing your headset cord to pull the microphone away from your mouth.

7. Chopping off the beginning or end of your transmission with bad mic button timing.

We just covered a baker's half-dozen of very bad radio techniques. All of these influence the quality of the sound that reaches your microphone. You and I know it's not enough to simply put your finger on the problem. You have to work on correcting or avoiding these problems in actual practice.

Speak into the Book

Since you cannot talk to this book--you can, but it won't impress the book--you must have a way to practice good voice technique on the radio. You can't just switch on your aircraft's radio, pick a random frequency and start transmitting radio calls into the vapor.

Here in the U.S. the Federal Communications Commission (FCC) frowns upon people who make false transmissions on discrete aviation frequencies. Maybe "frowns upon" doesn't convey the right message. The FCC will send somebody to arrest you if you make phony radio transmissions on, say, New York Approach's frequency. (It's happened.) Given this restrictive environment, how are you going to practice decent voice quality on the radio if you can't practice on the radio?

I suppose you can schedule a real flight and practice. It's doubtful ATC is going to let you practice your base leg radio call 15 times in one minute. Nor will ATC tell you if your radio transmission quality is bad unless it is completely unreadable. As I've said, I have flown with pilots with 20-plus years of experience who stink up the radios in all kinds of ways, and ATC never tells them how badly they suck.

Fortunately, I have some options for you. Here they are:

Option 1: Go to ATCcommunication.com and sign up for access to the Aircraft Radio Simulator. (This assumes you haven't already done so. If you have registered, then sign in to ATCinsider.com to use the sim. The beta version of the sim, which is user-record-and-play-back-only, is free.) The Aircraft Radio Simulator has an option to record and play back your radio transmissions. Speak, then listen to the result. I would suggest, if you go this route, using a computer-compatible headset with a boom mic, similar to one you would use in an airplane. With this type of setup, you can practice and refine your radio transmission technique until your tongue cramps and falls out.

Option 2: If you have access to 2 aircraft radios in separate locations, there is a way to practice radio calls without bringing down the wrath of the FCC. The frequency 122.75 is available for air-to-air communication for private fixed wing aircraft (AIM Table 4-1-3). You may use the frequency 122.75 to blab almost anything you care to, as long as it is not profane or threatening. Do not practice giving or receiving ATC clearances on 122.75. Use this frequency to practice microphone technique only.

For example, don't hop onto 122.75 and say, "American 348, descend and maintain flight level two four zero." That kind of transmission will confuse the daylights out of anyone else on the frequency because 122.75 is not used for air traffic control. Telling an airliner to descend, on the chat frequency, might also earn you a visit from serious government types wearing dark suits.

If 122.75 is already occupied by other pilots, wait until their conversation ends before you begin yours. Once you start, don't hog the frequency. Take a break so others can use it. The frequency is used around the world, so it may be congested when you tune in. Wait your turn and don't monopolize radio time.

Let's say you go for this option. You may get two airplanes parked on the ground and ask a friend to work the radio in one of the airplanes. You get on the radio in the other airplane, dial up 122.75 and talk back and forth with your friend. Your friend can critique your radio work, staying alert for the seven deadly sins of lousy radio work we just covered. Remember this is an exercise in microphone technique. Practice by making casual conversation with your practice partner.

If you don't have two airplanes to work with, you might have access to an airplane and one portable aviation radio. Or, you might have two portable radios. Any combination works.

If you don't have a friend to work with you on the radio, you can buy an inexpensive digital sound recorder at any office supply or electronics store to record your transmissions from the second radio. Simply position the recorder so it can pick up the sound from the other radio's speaker. Listen and critique your transmission by playing back the session on the recorder.

Option 3: Buy a set of inexpensive, short-range walkie-talkies at an electronics store or big box retailer. Try to get a set that accepts a headset with a microphone. With walkie-talkies in hand, you can do the same radio practice described in Option 2. Since the walkies use a frequency that has nothing to do with aviation, and because they are very short-range, you can even practice giving and answering ATC clearances. Your emphasis, at this stage, should be on quality, not content.

When it comes to radio transmission quality, I've saved the worst for last. The problem can be summarized in two words: speed kills. It's such a widespread and insidious problem that it's worth an entire chapter all by itself. It's a short chapter, but it is important. Turn the page to see why.

Take Action

Find a partner to work with you on your radio technique. Ideally, your partner would be another pilot or student pilot. If you cannot find a partner, buy an inexpensive digital audio recorder to record your radio transmissions for self-critique. Or, use the free Aircraft Radio Simulator at ATCinsider.com to record and play back your practice transmissions.

Set up a 2-radio communication channel using any of the following:

* Two aircraft radios.

* An aircraft radio and a portable aviation radio.

* Two portable aviation radios.

* Short-range walkie-talkies.

If using aviation radios, communicate on 122.75. If using walkie-talkies, communicate on a preset frequency.

Practice your microphone technique, and critique the following:

* Voice volume.

* Voice pitch, taking care not to speak in a low, rumbly tone.

* Enunciation.

* No plosions.

• Making sure no part of your transmission gets cut off by mis-timed microphone keying.

Chapter 2: Speed Kills

"Cessna Nine Four Uniform, Fort Meyers Approach, say your request," the air traffic controller said.

"NineFosursusiddswlmblwwysodhy, goglwotiyq," the pilot answered on the radio.

I was listening to this exchange as we descended our Boeing 757 between Captiva Island and the Florida mainland on a gorgeous Friday morning. It was an absolutely beautiful day. Scattered puffy clouds cast shadows on the ocean. There were a dozen boats powering around the bay between Fort Meyers proper and the barrier islands nearby. On days like this, flying definitely does not suck. At least, it didn't suck before the radio started squawking.

"Cessna Nine Four Uniform, say again," said the approach controller.

"Cessna Nine Four Uniform, requesswoeh dooe ytiwe wosls Runway 6." The pilot was talking at light speed. He was babbling so fast, I couldn't understand him. The approach controllers couldn't either. At the time, it was just us and the fast-talking pilot on the frequency.

"Airliner 2378, turn left, heading one four zero. Descend and maintain 3000," said Fort Meyers Approach to us.

I replied, slowly and evenly, "Airliner Two-Three-Seven-Eight. Left, heading one, four, zero. Descend and maintain three thousand." Maybe the other pilot would hear my transmission and get a clue. Not that I'm a gift to aviation, but setting a good example might help another pilot.

"Cessna Nine Four Uniform," Fort Meyers approach said again, "Understand you want another approach to Page?"

"Cessna fksjjf djfoe soguy, ILS ajfdj to Page. Then sljfslfdj boa eoe Sarasota."

C'mon guy, I thought. It's just you, me and the approach controller. There's no rush. Get a clue and slow your transmissions down! He can't understand you when you speed talk. I'm surprised you can understand yourself because your words are so slurred and run together.

When talking on the radio, speed kills. It's not likely you are going to end up in a shallow grave because you talked too fast on the radio. It's more likely talking too fast on the radio will kill your conversation with ATC.

Bad things happen when people talk too fast on the radio. Misunderstanding tops the list of bad things. Obviously, when it comes to pilot-controller communication, understanding is fairly important. The Aeronautical Information Manual (AIM) agrees. Look at the introduction in the AIM chapter about radio communication. The second paragraph begins:

> b. The single, most important thought in pilot-controller communications is understanding. . . controllers must know what you want to do before they can properly carry out their control duties. And you, the pilot, must know exactly what the controller wants you to do.

If you are able to spit out a radio transmission at light speed, hurray for you! Here's your trophy for linguistic dexterity. We are all impressed. (Not really.) Now, take that trophy and cash it in at the pawn shop for something that really matters: useful, intelligent radio work that lets the other person know your intentions.

Why do pilots--and controllers, for that matter--have a tendency to talk so fast? There are two reasons, according to my non-existent PhD in Psychology. One or both reasons may be in play at any given time:

- A sense of urgency.

- Machismo. (The TV show, Saturday Night Live had a

funny skit about this in which there was a game show called "Quien es Mas Macho?," translated as "Who is More Macho?")

Reason one—a sense of urgency--is probably the most prevalent. As the radio frequency gets more congested with transmissions, both pilots and air traffic controllers feel the need to get on the radio, speak quickly, and get off the radio. The aviation radio band is a time-share platform. I can't talk while you are talking, and you can't talk while I'm talking. Let's both get through what we have to say so others can use the communication band.

Twisted logic follows: If time on the radio is a precious commodity, then I better not waste time. I'll speak as fast as possible so I can stop transmitting as quickly as possible.

Here's the problem with that logic. If you speak so fast that your transmission cannot be understood, you are going to have to say it again. Worse still, if your first attempt is not understandable, then there is actually going to be three or more transmissions to clear up the problem.

Pilot: "Cessna234IndiaAlphadescendin't'fithsand."

ATC: "Cessna 234 India Alpha, say again."

Pilot: "Cessna234IndiaAlphadescendin't'fithsand."

ATC: "Cessna 234 India Alpha, you're unreadable. Say again slower."

Pilot: "Cessna 234 India Alpha, descending to five thousand."

ATC: "Cessna 234 India Alpha, Boston Center copies you're descending to five thousand."

If the pilot in Cessna 234 India Mike had spoken at a steady and understandable rate in his very first transmission, his point would have been made in one attempt. Instead, it took 6 transmissions to get the controller to understand the pilot was descending to 5000. Explain to me how 2 fast-spoken transmissions, plus 1 evenly-paced transmission, plus 3 responses from ATC, all for the same bit of information, equals speed on the radio. If we applied the same standard to stall recoveries--6 recovery attempts to fly out of one stall--we would probably fly every stalled airplane into the dirt. It's odd how the regs hold us to a certain standard for aircraft control, but no regulated standard for radio control.

Sometimes a sense of urgency on the radio is nothing more than a bad habit. The never-ending driving nightmare in Atlanta is always a good place to illustrate lousy habits, so let's go there for a sec.

Driving Me Crazy

It's 5:30 on a Sunday morning in Atlanta. I'm driving to the airport for an early check-in to fly a trip. I'm driving the speed limit of 35 mph on a side street leading to the highway. A car catches up to me from the rear and begins to tailgate. The driver in that car then crosses the double-yellow, no-passing line and enters the opposite direction lane to pass me. Huh. He must have some sort of emergency.

I get to the highway and enter. I speed up to just over the speed limit. In Atlanta, if you drive the speed limit on the highway, you are likely to get hit, at fairly high velocity, from the rear by another car. (I'm not kidding about that.) On the highway, I notice other drivers are passing me like I'm standing still. Bear in mind, again, it's pre-dawn on Sunday morning! You cannot convince me everyone has an emergency at this hour. Sometimes, speeding addresses no practical need. It's just a bad habit.

It's the same with speed-talking on the radio. For some, it's just a bad habit. The story about the speed-talking pilot near Fort Myers, in the beginning of this chapter, is one example.

Then there's the problem of machismo. Machismo is, supposedly, the collection of behaviors that demonstrates a person is an absolute master of the situation. Maybe it would be more accurate to say machismo is the delusion that a person is an absolute master of the situation. If it could be put into spoken words, it would sound like this: "Hey, look at me. I'm a badass."

Some pilots have gotten it into their heads that speed-talking on the radio is a sign of mastery. They think it says, "I've got this aviation thing wired. I'm so good, I can whip through a radio transmission at light speed and not even break a sweat."

They can think that--while most of us old heads in the aviation business are thinking, "What a pultroon." Real competence in aviation is not demonstrated by speed, it's demonstrated by accuracy and efficiency. If a lightning-quick radio transmission gets mis-understood, it's neither accurate, nor efficient. We are neither amused, nor are we impressed. If you speed talk as a demonstration of your advanced aviation skills, that doesn't make you a badass. It might make you an ass. (Actually, I'm fairly convinced it makes you an ass.)

As I write this, I realize speed-talking is probably not a big concern for you right now. Sure, you are worried an air traffic controller may speak to you faster than you are comfortable hearing. At this stage, you would probably be happy to get a radio call off without stumbling. Speed-talking has not made it onto your to-do list.

I think it's important to address speed talking because I want you to realize it is not a goal. You have not reached the summit of aviation when you can fart out a radio call at the speed of stink.

Relax and Enjoy the Conversation

Now, and in the future, I want you to concentrate on making every radio call count the first time you make it. The only way to do it right is to speak at a slow to moderate pace. Think "relaxed conversation" when you think of your talking pace. If you are going to err on speed, err in the direction of speaking slower than normal, not faster.

Actually, you don't have to worry about pacing if you enunciate each word in your transmission. Speed-talking almost always produces slurred or incomplete words. If you care to prove this point to yourself, tune in one of those auto auction shows on TV. Listen to the auctioneer and tell me, honestly, that you understand every word he says when he cranks up his auction patter. When you deliberately say each word crisply and succinctly, it's darned near impossible to speak quickly.

Before we move on, let's get back to that issue of an air traffic controller who speaks faster than your ability to understand her. The solution is simple. Ask her to repeat her transmission more slowly.

"Tower, can you say your last a little slower, please?"
Courtesy helps.

ATC will always--I mean always--comply. The controller has
no choice. If she doesn't slow down, and you end up doing
something wrong because you misunderstood an instruction,
guess who is going to hang for that. She is, maybe. (I can't say
for certain on this one. I'm an airline pilot, not a lawyer. It may
depend upon what you did to bring wrath upon your license.
My best advice? Don't follow through on a clearance until you
clearly understand it.)

Why? Two reasons. First, you put your request for slower
instructions on an audio recording. All ATC facilities record
every radio transmission. Any investigation into an aviation
incident that involves radio work will include a review of the
audio tapes. If you ask a controller to slow down, and she
doesn't comply immediately, her non-compliance will be on
tape. I can just hear the investigators:

"Sounds like she slowed down."

"No she didn't."

"Yes she did."

"Get your stopwatch out and we'll time it."

The second, and more important reason a controller will slow
down when asked is: air traffic controllers really want you to
succeed. No kidding. Their job is to ensure the safe and
expeditious flow of air traffic. The only way that will happen is
if they can get you to clearly understand what they want you to
do. If that means talking a little slower to help you understand,
they will do it. A professional air traffic controller with
integrity, which includes almost all controllers, will strive do
the right thing, whether or not her actions are recorded.

One last thought on the topic and then we'll call it done. It
absolutely does not matter what other pilots are doing on the
frequency. Play your own game. If other pilots are speed-
talking, and the controllers are responding with speed-talking,
that in no way means you have to do the same thing. We are
getting back to that parental quote: "If your friend is stupid
enough to jump off a cliff, it doesn't mean you have to follow."
(The word, stupid, was added this time for extra emphasis. Do

you feel it? I'm talking about the emphasis, not the stupidity.)

Other pilots don't set the standard for aviation safety in your airplane. The only standards are the ones written in the Aeronautical Information Manual or the ICAO Air Traffic Management Manual. As a pilot in command, you will do your best and safest job on the radio if you follow the standards in the applicable manual and disregard the lunacy you hear other pilots create on the radio.

It takes a certain amount of bravery to not follow the crowd and to cut your own path. You can do it. I know you can.

Makes sense? Good. End of topic.

Take Action

Using an aircraft radio, a portable aviation receiver, or a source on the internet, listen to the radio exchanges between air traffic control and pilots. As you listen, keep this question topmost in your mind:

Who is easier to understand, people who speak quickly, or people who speak at a relaxed, conversational pace?

The following exercise will probably make you laugh, which is okay. The humor in it helps prove a point.

Find someone with whom you would feel comfortable acting a bit silly. Explain you would like to try an experiment to improve your radio skills. Tell this person something along the lines of: "For the next minute or so, I would like for us to have a conversation on any topic you pick. Our only rule is, we each have to speak at a rate that is at least double our normal rate. Each person needs to speak as soon as the other person stops talking."

When your mad minute is over; and after both of you stop laughing, evaluate your conversation. Did either of you stumble on your words? Were you able to focus on and understand what the other person was saying at all times? Did your conversation feel natural and easy, or did it take more effort than your typical conversation? Relate the conversation you just had to a conversation on the aircraft radio. Does speed talking on the radio seem more efficient and less error-prone than talking at a conversational rate?

Chapter 3: It's Not English, It's ATC English

We have covered the basics of using the aircraft radio microphone--how you say it. Now, it's time to get into what you say. In this chapter, we are going to look at the structure of air traffic control language. It sounds pretty boring, doesn't it? It could be, but it won't be, if I have anything to say about it. Which I do.

Do you speak a language other than English? If you only know how to speak English, and you are in flight training, guess what, you are about to learn a second language. I'm not kidding.

When you talk to air traffic control, you have to use a very specific language. It's called standard phraseology. There are precise words and phrases that you must use when communicating with ATC. The speech requirements are so exact, you can think of pilot-to-controller communication as a language separate and apart from English.

Think I'm kidding about this? Try this experiment. The next time a friend asks you for directions to your house, try answering in the language of air traffic control:

"Cleared to my house via Main Street, Old Forty-One, Maple. After the 7-11 intersection, complete the Belmont Arrival. On departure drive heading zero two zero. Contact me on five five five point seven two four one. Standby on your read back. Break, break, Jenny, I'm on the phone. Will you let the dog out?"

My guess is, your friend will either say "Huh?" or hang up on you, thinking she called a wrong number.

Or, try this, if you haven't alienated your friend with your driving directions. Point out a radio tower to your friend and say, "If we wanted to get to the top of that radio tower we'd have to climb and maintain one thousand five hundred."

My point is this: Yes, the language of air traffic control uses English words, but the language is much more formal and scripted than everyday English. So much so, that speaking it is not a natural act. You have to learn the phrasing and language rules as you would for learning any foreign language.

You might ask, why does it have to be this way? The answer is, standard phraseology is the way we avoid confusion. As you and I know, misunderstanding between pilots and controllers can lead to all kinds of bad situations.

Here are some examples. If I were an air traffic controller and I said to you, "Go faster," what does that mean to you as you are flying? It could mean I want you to increase airspeed, but then you would want to know how much to speed up. If you were descending to an assigned altitude, it might mean I needed you to descend more quickly. Or it could mean your rate of descent is just fine, but I need you to increase your airspeed as you descend. Basically, "go faster" is open to interpretation. You have to guess what I want you to do.

If, on the other hand, I say "Increase speed two zero knots"--a standard air traffic controller phrase--you know exactly what I mean. If I say, "Maintain at least one thousand five hundred feet per minute in your rate of descent"--another standard phrase-- you know exactly what I want.

Occasionally, both pilots and air traffic controllers forget to use standard phraseology. The controller says "Do this," in a nonstandard way, and the pilot does something completely different from what the controller intended. Or, a pilot reports "Doing that," and the controller interprets the pilot's nonstandard statement as something completely different. The result can be anything from a non-event, to a violation of the Federal Aviation Regulations, or, to a disaster.

Big Sky Theory

Most of the time, when we use nonstandard phraseology on the radio, there are no consequences, and there is no violation of the regs. We call that "Big Sky Theory." Big Sky Theory is what keeps an airplane from running into another airplane when a pilot accidentally strays off course, or off an altitude assignment. Thanks to a big sky, there is plenty of room for airplanes to wander about, without meeting each other.

You might think I'm crazy when I say this, but when nothing bad happens as a result of using nonstandard language on the radio, we actually put ourselves in a very dangerous situation. You can get a hint about where this is heading by reading the following Aviation Safety Reporting System (ASRS) records. Each of these records represent separate, unrelated incidents.

ASRS record from a pilot who misunderstood a nonstandard reply from ATC:

> We had just landed and were waiting to cross runway 13. The PNF [Pilot Not Flying] queried ground control if we could cross runway 13. The controller responded 'not yet.' I thought the controller responded 'yeah' and taxied forward, across the hold short line. Unsure, I stopped the aircraft prior to runway 13, but the aircraft was past the hold short line at this point. The PNF then radioed for verification of our crossing clearance. The ground controller then responded, 'negative, hold short, well it looks like you've already past the hold short line -- I did not receive clearance from the tower controller until now, you're cleared to cross runway 13.' lessons learned: standard communication phraseology is imperative. The ground controller used nonstandard phraseology ('not yet') and I accepted what I thought to be a clearance to cross an active runway with nonstandard phraseology. Both pilot and controller erred, in my opinion.

ASRS record in which an air traffic controller who misunderstood a pilot's nonstandard check-in on the radio:

> While working a secondary departure sector; I failed to catch an altitude report by a pilot and subsequently the aircraft violated the airspace of

another facility. During the investigation; it was revealed that the pilot had been assigned 170 [Ed.: an altitude of 17,000] but the last instruction the previous controller issued him was 'fly heading 330 degrees.' the pilot's readback was '330.' when the pilot checked in with me; he stated 'aircraft X with you 13 for 33;' I failed to catch the abbreviated altitudes he read me. The aircraft then climbed through my altitudes resulting in an operational deviation. 3 things about this deviation bother me. 1) the pilot's sloppy readback to the first controller '330;' 2) the pilot's sloppy check-in with me '13 for 33;' and 3) why aren't pilots held to a standard of phraseology that would help prevent hearback/readback incidents. Had the pilot checked in with some semblance of standard phraseology and stated the word 'climb' or 'flight levels' it would have caught my attention and clued me in to listen; 'aircraft X with you 13 thousand climbing to flight level 330.'

I fly with aviation professionals: pilots who have been making a living in airplanes for 20 to 30 years, or more. They are extremely safety-conscious people who exhibit a high level of self-discipline. It's odd, then, that many of these aviation professionals don't use standard phraseology on the radio.

For example, I frequently fly with people who say, "Center, Airliner 821, eleven for eighteen." The correct phrasing should be, "Center, Airliner 821, passing one one thousand for flight level one eight zero."

I can only conclude my fellow pilots never learned the ATC language, or, they learned it long ago, and then forgot it. I don't believe my colleagues would intentionally do something to create a misunderstanding with ATC, given their strong character and sense of purpose. I'm sure they don't recognize the potential risk in using nonstandard phrasing.

Risk Assessment

Here's the full story on risk. Most of the time, pilots can get away with nonstandard phrasing because air traffic controllers are intelligent and well-trained. By looking at their radar display, controllers can interpret where and what an airplane is doing on that display. A controller can usually put a nonstandard radio call into context.

For example, a controller takes the handoff of an aircraft from another controller. The controller who takes the handoff can see the airplane's data block on his radar display. The data block shows, among other information, the airplane's current altitude and its assigned altitude. If a pilot checks in and says "Airliner 2819, eleven for eighteen," the data block for that airplane displays:

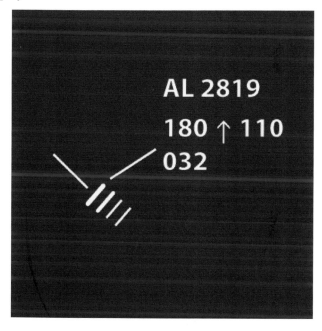

Airliner 2819, assigned Flight Level 180, climbing through 110 (11,000).

The controller puts what he hears on the radio into context

with what he sees on the radar display. In this case, the radar display shows the aircraft assigned Flight Level 180 and the aircraft is climbing through 11,000. If this worked all of the time, there would never be a problem related to nonstandard phraseology used by pilots.

Sometimes, that very same radar datablock can act like a bear trap. Here's how. Let's say a controller looks at the datablock on his radar screen and sees an assigned altitude of Flight Level 180 and the airplane is currently climbing through 6,000. The pilot in the plane represented by that datablock checks on and says, "Airliner 2819, out of six for eight." The pilot, using nonstandard phraseology, says he is climbing to 8,000 feet. The datablock showing 180 predisposes the controller to hearing 18,000. When the pilot says "eight," the controller hears "eighteen." What happens after that is up to luck and the Big Sky Theory.

More often than not a controller's radar helps him put non-standard radio calls into context. It's as though ATC's radar system acts as universal translator. It helps controllers understand all of the ridiculous variations on standard phrasing they hear from pilots.

That's great, right? We pilots can twist the facts into any language we choose, and ATC will figure out what we mean. It's actually one of the worst things that can happen. When a pilot habitually uses nonstandard phraseology, and feels no negative consequence, he is being set up. He learns that nonstandard phraseology is okay, when, sooner or later it's going to get him into trouble.

Do you remember the Columbia space shuttle disaster? A large chunk of foam insulation fell off the shuttle's external tank during launch. The chunk hit the leading edge of the shuttle's wing, puncturing it. Later, during re-entry, the puncture allowed super-heated air to penetrate the wing. This resulted in catastrophic airframe failure, and the breakup of the space shuttle.

It turns out, prior to this disaster, there were over 400 documented cases of insulating foam striking various space shuttles during the launch phase. In every case, the foam did not do enough damage to cause catastrophic failure. Despite the evidence that something was terribly wrong with the shuttle's construction, NASA continued launching shuttles with the foam problem unresolved.

Why? NASA downplayed the significance of all these early warnings. The foam problem was not perceived as significant enough to warrant a change to the shuttle.

I believe the same force is in play when pilots continue to use nonstandard phraseology. When we pilots speak incorrectly, and ATC misinterprets, the Big Sky Theory and good luck usually save the day. I believe this combination--Big Sky Theory and good luck--has blinded us to the risks of using nonstandard phraseology.

Very occasionally, luck runs out; and when it does, look out! Later, I'll give you an extreme example of how misinterpreting a radio transmission can kill a lot of people.

You've heard of that saying, "I'd rather be lucky than good." That statement should not be applied to aviation. Pilots need to be good, not lucky. Stick with standard phrasing. One day, in a crowded block of airspace, standard phrasing may save your pilot's license, or your airplane, or your life.

Standard Numbers

Where will you find standard phrasing? Several places. The Aeronautical Information Manual has it in its pilot/controller glossary. That same glossary also appears in the Air Traffic Controller's Manual, J.O. 7110.65. The ICAO Air Traffic Management Manual (Document 4444) contains radio phrasing for operations outside the U.S. in *Chapter 12 Phraseologies*.

We can't cover every item in those manuals. We'll hit the foot stompers--the important standards that apply to most of the flying you will do. Let's start with numbers.

I was finishing an airline trip by flying from Puerto Vallarta, Mexico to Atlanta, GA in a Boeing 757. The Boeing 757, or Seven Five, as we call it, has two very expensive, high-fidelity VHF communication radios that are usually crystal clear. They transmit very well, and they receive very well. However, it can be difficult to hear transmissions coming through the radio. Not because the radio quality is poor, but because the cockpit is so noisy.

You would think the Seven Five has a quiet cockpit. It is very well insulated against sound. The jet's two engines are more than 50 feet behind the cockpit and are barely audible in flight from the pilot's seat. The atmosphere is very thin in the upper 30-thousands, so wind noise is not a problem. Still, the cockpit is not as quiet as you would think.

The Seven Five's cockpit has tremendous ventilation, in the form of cooling vents for the pilots, defogging vents for the windows, and cooling fans for the electronics. All that air circulation and fan motor operation makes for a lot of noise in the cockpit. The worst offender is the cooling system in the overhead panel that holds all of the aircraft's system controls and circuit breakers. There are a couple of slot vents up there that produce a very loud white noise when all of the cooling fans are operating at full blast.

Most pilots in the Seven Five do not wear noise-canceling headsets, and those that do, usually put one of their noise-canceling ear pads on their head behind the ear so they can hear the other pilot in the cockpit. Captain and first officer do not use an intercom to talk to each other. We simply talk directly to each other across the cockpit.

On some Seven Fives, with very loud cockpit fans, it's sometimes hard to hear our crystal clear radios above the white noise. The only solution is the crank up the volume of the radio, which we are reluctant to do because high radio volume can erode hearing over time, and cause fatigue in the short term.

There I was, flying back from Mexico, in a loud cockpit. Our call sign was Airliner 390. (Sorry. I can't tell you the name of my airline and that's not the actual flight number. The rest of the story is true.) Since it was my leg of the trip to fly, the captain was working the communication radio. He was talking to Monterrey Center, the northernmost enroute control center in Mexico.

Here's where we come to the part about pronouncing numbers on the radio. The AIM says the numbers in an airliner's call signs may be pronounced in combination form. For example, Airliner 390 may be pronounced "Airliner Three-Ninety." The ICAO Air Traffic Management Manual, however, says numbers in all call signs are to be pronounced individually. For example, Airliner 390 should be pronounced, "Airliner three nine zero." Here's where it gets weird.

If a non-U.S. air traffic controller has had a lot of contact with U.S. controllers, the non-U.S. controller may begin to adopt the U.S. habits of pronunciation. I wish it were the other way around, but it isn't.

As I said, Monterrey Center is the northernmost control center in Mexico. That means, its northern boundary touches Houston Center's southern boundary. Monterrey controllers working the sectors that touch Houston Center sectors have to talk to Houston controllers on the landline to coordinate border crossings for northbound and southbound aircraft. That means a controller in Houston might pick up the landline, connect with Monterrey and say, "I've got Airliner Two Twenty-Eight requesting direct Saltillo." The Monterrey controller approves or denies the request, and then something else happens.

As the Monterrey controller hears the U.S. form of handling numbers, the Monterrey controller begins to adopt the form as his own. This process gets reinforced as U.S. pilots check on the frequency as "Airliner Two Twenty-eight," or, "Business Jet Three Seventy-five Foxtrot Kilo."

Getting back to the story. There we were, operating as Airliner 390, with Monterrey Center, when another airplane from our company checks in with Monterrey as Airliner 398. On paper, 390 and 398 look very different. On the radio, with cockpit air vents blowing for all they are worth, "Three Ninety" and "Three Ninety-Eight" are very hard to distinguish. The "Eight" gets muddled by cockpit noise. When a Monterrey controller, with his Mexican accent, says "Airliner Three Ninety-eight," it's nearly indistinguishable from "Airliner Three Ninety."

It was a very stormy day over northern Mexico. The thunder boomers were popping everywhere. We needed approval to deviate off course, change altitudes, and do whatever it took to avoid flying into a storm. So did all of the other pilots on the radio frequency, including Airliner 398. You can guess what's coming next.

For the next 40 minutes, it took multiple radios calls to clear up each misunderstanding when either we (Airliner 390), or Airliner 398, got approval from Monterrey to deviate for the storms: "Airliner Three Ninety___, cleared to deviate left of course. Fly direct Newla when able."

I said, "Uh, Center, was that for Airliner Three Nine Zero, or

Three Nine Eight?"

Monterrey: "Airliner, Three Ninety___, left deviations approved. Direct Newla when able."

Our Boeing 757's radar display showing massive thunderstorms north of Saltillo, Mexico (SLW). The solid line with the 4-point stars shows our original route. The triangle near the bottom of the screen represents our aircraft. The solid line extending straight up from the triangle shows our current course. We are deviating left of our route to avoid the storms.

I said, "I'm sorry, we're still not getting that. Was that for Airliner Three Nine Zero or Airliner Three Nine Eight?" And so on.

To make matters worse, when Monterrey called Airliner 398, the pilot would answer without his call sign.

Monterrey: "Airliner Three Ninety___, Monterrey."

Other pilot: "Go ahead."

How did the controller in Monterrey even know who answered him if the numbnut in Airliner 398 wouldn't use his own call sign? Keep that question in your hip pocket. I'll get to it in the next chapter. For now, know that it is completely wrong to not use the company name in an airline call sign.

As you can see, it's extremely important to say numbers on the aircraft radio as individual numbers. That includes numbers in call signs, altitudes, airspeeds, and headings. Many general aviation aircraft do not have the highest quality radios. Most reciprocating, general aviation aircraft generate loud noise that is barely diminished in the cockpit. Hearing the radio is a real challenge.

Not all numbers, when spoken in doublets, such as "ninety-five," come across the radio clearly in even the most quiet cockpits with high-fidelity radios. This problem is especially true when the radio quality is questionable or when the number is spoken with an unfamiliar accent.

Imagine the type of trouble you could get into if you didn't use standard phraseology for numbers. Let's say you checked in with an air traffic controller and told him you were "Climbing to fourteen thousand," but he heard "Climbing to four thousand," because your transmission was weak and scratchy sounding.

Altitude busts--when a pilot mistakenly flies through an ATC-assigned altitude--happen far too frequently. Why? Altitude busts are almost always the result of a pilot misunderstanding what he hears on the radio.

The single best way to avoid misunderstanding is to speak in a language that both speaker and listener understand clearly. For numbers, that means always, and I mean always, saying numbers individually. The only exception to the rule is the use of zeros in altitudes and in rates of climb or descent. In altitudes and rates, the zeros are counted as hundreds, or thousands. For example:

Climb and maintain one four thousand (14,000).

Maintain one thousand, five hundred (1,500).

Maintain at least two thousand (2,000) feet per
minute in your descent.

Descend and maintain one two thousand, five
hundred (12,500).

Maintain one thousand five (1,500) feet per minute
or better in your climb.

Climb and maintain one zero thousand (10,000).

Descend and maintain flight level two four zero (FL
240).

For headings, airspeeds, altimeter settings, distances, and
time, zeros are pronounced individually. For example:

Turn right, heading two zero zero (200).

Reducing speed to one three zero (130).

We are five zero miles south of the VOR (50).

The current time is one four four eight Zulu
(1448Z).

Altimeter three zero zero zero (30.00).

Numbers in call signs and in radio frequencies are all
pronounced individually:

Cardinal Five Two Three Six Uniform (5236 U).

Contact Ground Control on one two one point nine
(121.9).

In the U.S., the decimal point in frequencies is pronounced "Point." In all other countries using ICAO standards, the decimal point is pronounced "Decimal." For example, in South America, a frequency change would sound like this:

> Contact Curacao Control on one two seven decimal one (127.1).

The decimal point is usually not spoken for altimeter settings:

> Altimeter three zero one two (30.12).

If you really follow the standards to the letter--I mean number--you would pronounce certain numbers differently from everyday language. According to the standards, 3 is pronounced "Tree" for clarity. The number 5 is pronounced "Fife," and, everyone's favorite, 9, is pronounced "Niner."

As you look at those ATC clearances and declarations in the list above, you notice each number is spoken individually. That's clear. There is something else going on in those sentences. Can you spot it?

Let's go to the books and see where this is heading:

Here's a paragraph from the Aeronautical Information Manual (AIM) talking about reading back ATC instructions:

> The readback of the 'numbers' serves as a double check between pilots and controllers and reduces the kinds of communications errors that occur when a number is either 'misheard' or is incorrect (*AIM 4-4-7b*).

It's a good and accurate statement, but it leaves something out. What's missing from the sentence in the AIM? Units, expressed as a noun or verb, such as "Heading" or "Knots." Here's an example that illustrates the problem:

ATC: "Cessna 57 Mike, traffic you're following is two zero knots slower. Turn right heading one one zero."

Pilot: "Cessna 57 Mike, one one zero."

My question to you is this: Is the pilot of Cessna 57 Mike turning to a heading of 110 degrees, or is he slowing to 110 knots to stay behind the preceding aircraft? He is following the AIM's guidance to repeat the numbers. You might say common sense applies here, and the pilot is turning to 110. Let's blur the line a little more.

ATC: "Piper 38 Uniform, turn right heading one one zero to intercept final. You're cleared the visual pproach, Runway One Four. Maintain one two zero knots until a five mile final."

Pilot: "Piper 38 Uniform, one one zero, one two zero. Cleared the visual, One Four."

You might say, "Give me a break! No one talks like that on the radio." I'm here to tell you, I hear readbacks on the radio like this all the time.

Unitize

The solution is simple: Read back numbers and their associated units. Controllers are always required to say the numbers and a unit (*J.O. 7110.65, Chapter 2-4-17*). You should, too.

(The Air Traffic Controller's Manual, JO 7110.65, is available free online as a .pdf document. The manual's document number 7110.65 ends with a letter that indicates the latest update. For example, 7110.65U was the latest update at the time this book was published. As a pilot, you are not required to know the contents of the Air Traffic Controller's Manual, but it will expand your understanding of how ATC operates. I highly recommend it.)

If the controller says "Heading one one zero," read back "Heading," plus the numbers. If the controller says, "Maintain one two zero knots," read back the numbers, plus "knots."

The AIM only says "read back of the numbers." It never says read back the number and the associated units or noun. There are some examples of pilot radio transmissions in the AIM that include numbers and units, but the concept is only emphasized for airspeed.

For airspeed, the AIM reminds you to say the digits of your current airspeed or assigned airspeed, followed by the word, "Knots." The AIM says you don't have to say "knots" if you precede your airspeed transmission with the word "speed." For example, "One two zero knots," or, "Speed, one two zero."

Strangely there is no direction in the AIM about what to say for heading assignments, other than to repeat the numbers and add the word "True" if you are flying a true heading.

This is what I meant when I said the manuals have gaps and inconsistencies. It is no wonder there are gaps and inconsistencies in the way most pilots talk on the radio.

The ABCs of ATC

I'm telling you, learning the language of air traffic control is like going back to kindergarten. What is the first thing your teacher tried to teach you in kindergarten? No, not how to play with modeling clay without eating it. She tried to teach you the alphabet. It's the same with ATC language. You have got to know your alphabet.

Can you rattle off the ATC alphabet without thinking about it? Alpha, bravo, charlie, delta, etc? If not, get thee to Chapter 4 of the Aeronautical Information Manual, and go to paragraph 4-2-7, Phonetic Alphabet. Learn that thing, then practice like your life depends on it, because it may some day. An example follows.

The air traffic controller at Maiquetia, serving Caracas, Venezula, said to us, "Airliner Two One Four, when ready, descend to flight level one two zero. Cleared direct Chreem." The captain looked at me.

"What fix did he say?"

"I'm not sure. I'll ask," I said. Then into the radio, "Maiquetia, Airliner Two One Four, descending to flight level one two zero, and say that fix again."

The controller said, "Airliner Two One Four, you're cleared direct Chreem."

I scanned my map for the Chreem intersection. It wasn't

anywhere along the border of Venezuela or Columbia. I scanned the open area on the map between Curacao and Caracas that represented the Southern Atlantic Ocean. No Chreem intersection. Besides, all intersections are made up of 5 letters. Chreem had 6.

I said, "Maiquetia, Airliner Two One Four. Can you please spell the name of the intersection?"

"Airliner Two One Four, tango oscar romeo india mike. Chreem," the controller replied.

"Airliner Two One Four, got it! Direct Torim. Tango oscar romeo india mike."

"Airliner Two One Four. That is correct."

Phew! It pays to have a clear understanding of where you are supposed to be going. It's important when:

You are flying through a pitch black night; over a featureless ocean; descending towards 12,000-foot high mountains on the coastline; your clearance is to descend to 12,000 feet; and, you are talking to a controller who has an accent different than your own.

In that case, and in many others, knowing the phonetic alphabet may save your butt.

Before we wrap up this overview of the ATC language, I want to put in a pitch for reviewing the pilot/controller glossary of any of the manuals that discuss ATC (AIM, JO 7110.65, ICAO Doc. 4444). Think of the pilot/controller glossary as your guidebook to speaking a foreign language. The vocabulary you need is right in those pages. We'll cover a lot of it in this book, but it really is worth your time to review the glossary and learn the standard phrases.

Take Action

I'm about to tell you about what is on the next page of this book, but don't turn the page! First, read all of the directions below. If you are male, force yourself to read the directions. As a member of your demographic, I know how hard this is for you. If you are female, I know you will do the right thing without any additional coaching from me.

On the next page, there are illustrations of cockpit instruments. Each instrument has a letter labeling it. Below each instrument, there will be an answer key. Here's what I want you to do:

1. Before turning to the next page, get a piece of opaque paper or card stock large enough to cover an entire page of this book.

2. Cover up the next page of this book.

3. Advance to the next page.

4. Carefully slide down the paper covering your book, so it only exposes the first illustration at the top of the page.

5. Look at the instrument and read the letter label out loud, using the standard phonetic alphabet phrase for the letter. For example, if the letter is L, say "Lima."

6. Next say the numbers displayed in the instrument out loud, using the standard pronunciation for numbers. For example, if the instrument shows 2500, say "Two thousand, five hundred."

7. Slide the page down just enough so that the correct answer is exposed below the instrument.

8. Slide the paper down to expose the next label and instrument; and repeat Steps 4 - 8.

There is no sliding scale for performance on this exercise. If your results feel deficient, read AIM sections 4-2-7 and 4-2-8. Then practice until phonetic letters and numbers roll off your tongue without thought.

A

Phonetic Alphabet: "Alpha."
Correct phrase: "Five thousand, eight hundred."

B

Phonetic Alphabet: "Bravo."

Correct Phrase: "Nine zero knots."

C

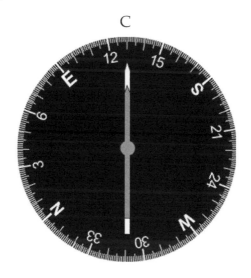

Phonetic Alphabet: "Charlie."

Correct Phrase: "Heading one three zero."

D

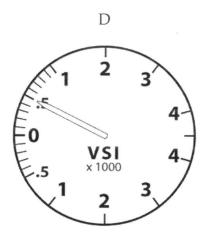

Phonetic Alphabet: "Delta."

Correct Phrase: "Climbing five hundred feet per minute."

E

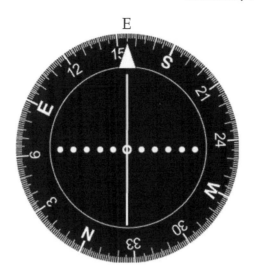

Phonetic Alphabet: "Echo."

Correct Phrase: "One five five degree radial."

F

Phonetic Alphabet: "Foxtrot."

Correct Phrase: "One three thousand, five hundred."

G

Phonetic Alphabet: "Golf."

Correct Phrase: "One two five knots."

H

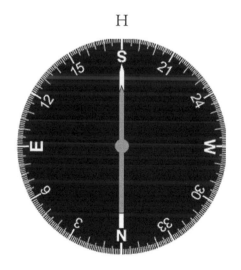

Phonetic Alphabet: "Hotel."

Correct Phrase: "Heading one eight zero."

I

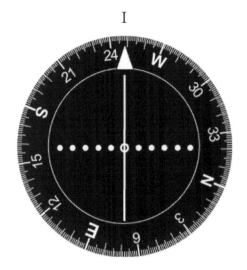

Phonetic Alphabet: "India."

Correct Phrase: "Two four eight degree radial."

J

Phonetic Alphabet: "Juliett."

Correct Phrase: "Flight level two four three."

K

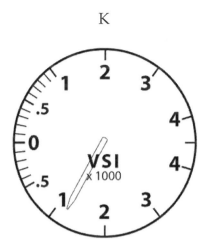

Phonetic Alphabet: "Kilo."

Correct Phrase: "Descending one thousand two hundred feet
per minute."

L

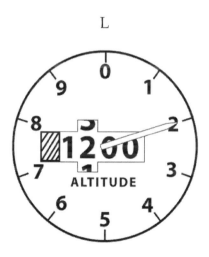

Phonetic Alphabet: "Lima."

Correct Phrase: "One thousand two hundred."

M

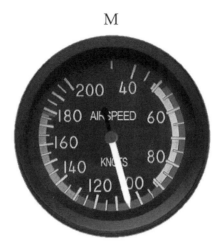

Phonetic Alphabet: "Mike."

Correct Phrase: "One zero five knots."

N

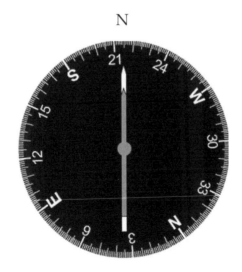

Phonetic Alphabet: "November."

Correct Phrase: "Heading two one five."

Test yourself on the rest of the phonetic alphabet. Slide your card down just enough to reveal one letter at a time, but not the correct pronunciation below the letter.

O

Oscar

P

Papa

Q

Quebec

R

Romeo

S

Sierra

T

Tango

U

Uniform

V

Victor

W

Whiskey

X

X-ray

Y

Yankee

Z

Zulu

Chapter 4: A Callsign by Any Other Name Smells Bad

Your cell phone rings. You look at the screen on your phone and it only shows the incoming phone number, but no name for the caller.

"Hello?"

"Hey, howya doin'?"

You think to yourself, "That's sounds like Steve, but I'm not sure."

"Good," you say. "How are you?"

"You know. Can't complain." Now you aren't sure if it's Steve. It could be Brian.

"That's good. What's up?" you ask.

"Nothing really. I was just wondering if I could come over and pick it up. Is now a good time?"

You wonder what Steven or Brian could be talking about. Steve did mention last week he could use a wheelbarrow to remove pile of dirt from his back yard. You told him you have a wheel barrow he could use if he needed it.

"I'm not doing anything for the next couple of hours," you reply." Come on by."

"Um," says the voice at the other end of the connection, "I'm really kinda busy this morning. Are you going to be around this afternoon?"

"Geez, I'm sorry. I'm going to be out all afternoon running errands," you say. "Tell you what. I'll just leave it outside for you on the side of the house. Come by when you can and pick it up."

"Is that really a good idea?" says Brian-Steve.

"Is what a good idea?" you say.

"Well, I was thinking leaving it outside like that might not be good for it."

"It'll be fine out there, and it's a safe neighborhood. No one will steal it," you say.

"I'm not worried about anyone stealing it," says Steve-Brian. "I'm just worried it's going to melt out in the sun before I can get it. The kids won't like that."

"Oh, I thought you were talking about the wheelbarrow, "you say.

"No man, it's that 10-gallon tub of ice cream you're keeping in the big freezer for me. My kid's birthday party is this afternoon. Wheelbarrow?" says Brian-Steve.

"Is this Brian?" you ask. There's a long pause on the phone.

"Uh, no. Is this Rick?"

"Umm. I think you have the wrong number."

"Sorry." Click.

Have you ever had a phone conversation like that? I'm not talking about wheelbarrows and ice cream. I mean a phone conversation where you assumed you were talking to one person and it turned out to be someone else, or someone you didn't even know. The worst thing that comes of situation like that is a little embarrassment.

In aviation, you have got to know who you are talking to at the other end of the radio. When ATC gives a clearance to an aircraft, the pilot of the aircraft has to be absolutely sure the clearance was intended for him. Put another way, if you aren't sure who the clearance was given to, you must not randomly grab that clearance and use it as your own. This issue is so important, it is one of the few radio transmissions that is covered by a regulation:

**Consolidated Flight Regulations, Sec. 91.123 -
Compliance with ATC clearances and instructions**

(e) Unless otherwise authorized by ATC, no person

operating an aircraft may operate that aircraft according to any clearance or instruction that has been issued to the pilot of another aircraft for radar air traffic control purposes.

The only way to be 100% certain about who is talking to whom on the radio is to use an aircraft call sign in each and every transmission. Here is what the Aeronautical Information Manual has to say on the subject:

Section 2. Radio Communications Phraseology and Techniques

4-2-1. General

b. The single, most important thought in pilot-controller communications is understanding. It is essential, therefore, that pilots acknowledge each radio communication with ATC by using the appropriate aircraft call sign.

The AIM is clear about the requirement to use your call sign in each and every transmission. Almost always, if you fail to include your call sign, air traffic control will ask you to repeat your read back of a clearance with your call sign included. Why? To avoid confusion.

ATC: "Comanche 38 Kilo, traffic twelve o'clock, ten miles, an eastbound Beech Baron one thousand feet below you."

Comanche 38K: "Comanche 38 Kilo, looking for the traffic."

ATC: "Baron 5 Foxtrot Lima, traffic twelve o'clock, niner miles, opposite direction PA-24 at niner thousand."

Baron 5FL: "Baron 5 Foxtrot Lima, looking."

ATC: "And Comanche 38 Kilo, you were requesting direct to where?"

"Uh, direct to Ketle."

ATC: "Comanche 38 Kilo, I have your request."

ATC: "Comanche 38 Kilo, climb and maintain one zero thousand."

?: "Climbing to one zero thousand."

My question to you is this: After this radio exchange, who is climbing to 10,000 feet? If it's Comanche 38K, who is already flying above Baron 5FL, everything is okay. That pilot is climbing away from the converging traffic below him. If Baron 5FL took the call, the Baron is now climbing towards a potential collision with the Comanche above.

What is in play here? The communication between the air traffic controller and the pilot of Comanche 38K turned into a phone conversation. When we talk on the telephone, we don't say:

"Mary, this is Bill. How are you?"

"Bill, this is Mary. I'm fine. How are you?"

"Mary, this is Bill. I'm good. Listen, I was calling to ask you . . ."

The reason we are able to drop our "call signs" on the telephone is because, unless we are on a conference call, we know who is at the other end. Of course, knowing who is on the other end of the phone conversation is very important, as we saw at the beginning of this chapter:

"Is this Brian?"

"Uh, no. Is this Rick?"

"Umm. I think you have the wrong number."

Even in a conference call of 3 or 4 people, we can generally get away with not identifying ourselves each time we talk, because the high fidelity of a phone call, plus the limited number of people on the call, means we can usually get away with recognizing who is talking by voice recognition.

Not so on the aircraft radio. There may be 10, 20, 30, or more people on the same frequency. Most general aviation radios are not high fidelity. For these reasons, voice recognition and phone-style conversation have no place on an aircraft radio. Besides, the AIM and the CFR's are unequivocal about what you are required to include with each radio transmission: Always, always, include your call sign, period.

Knowing you have to use your call sign in every transmission is all well and good, but what is a call sign?

> **Note:** The following section about what makes up a call sign is pretty basic stuff. If you feel confident you absolutely know what a call sign is, skip this section. I don't want to bore you. I'll highlight the next section where it gets interesting again. Go ahead, skip it.

Skippable part.

A call sign is usually your aircraft's registration number. It begins with a prefix, usually "N" in the U.S. and then the numbers and letters after your prefix. For example, November Five Seven Eight Romeo Charlie. Outside of the U.S. you are more likely to have only letters in your call sign. For example, Charlie Echo Romeo India Sierra.

Skip this too.

You may use your aircraft's type, manufacturer's name, or model in place of the prefix. For example, Cessna Five Seven Eight Romeo Charlie, or Skyhawk Five Seven Eight Romeo Charlie are both acceptable. I think it's a good practice to use your make or model instead of the prefix, because it gives the air traffic controller more information about the capability of your airplane: Learjet 421TM flies faster than Piper Cub 8817U by a country mile!

Use the aircraft's type, make, or model in your call sign, or use the prefix, but not both. An air traffic controller told me he knows he's talking to a novice when the pilot says, for example, "Cessna November Five Seven Eight Romeo Charlie."

Interesting stuff resumes here.

The Aeronautical Information Manual, knowing we pilots have more important work to do than saying our full call sign, gives us some relief from that difficult task. In some circumstances, rather than being forced to say our full call sign--oh, it's so much work!--we can use an abbreviated call sign.

An abbreviated call sign, according to the AIM, is the prefix, plus the last three digits or letters of your aircraft's registration. For example, November Five Seven Eight Romeo Charlie, can be abbreviated to *November* Eight Romeo Charlie. What a time-saver! Who said there is inefficiency in government?

The AIM says you can drop the prefix if you use the aircraft's make, model, or type in its place. So, instead of November Eight Romeo Charlie, you can say Cessna Eight Romeo Charlie, or Centurion Eight Romeo Charlie, or Twin Cessna Eight Romeo Charlie. Nowhere in the AIM does it say you can drop the prefix, or your make, model, or type. You have got to use one or the other, every time.

You are going to hear this all of the time on the radio:

ATC: "Falcon Nine Alpha Whiskey, turn right, heading two four zero."

Chucklehead: "Right, two four zero, Nine Alpha Whiskey."

This lamebrain's response is wrong, wrong, six-ways-to-Sunday wrong. When you are given the a-okay by ATC to use your abbreviated call sign, you are still obligated to use your aircraft's pre-fix, or make, or model, plus the last three digits and/or letters of your call sign. (The preceding call sign is fictitious. I'm picking on pilots of business jets because they seem to violate this rule as though the violation is a rule. If you are a biz jet pilot who does it by the book, my apologies for lumping you in with the rest of the chuckleheads, and good on you.)

There are specific circumstances when you may use an abbreviated call sign. First, each and every time you make initial contact with an air traffic controller, you must use your full call sign. After initial contact, follow the controller's lead.

Here's the quote from the AIM:

> ATC specialists may initiate abbreviated call signs
> of other aircraft by using the prefix and the last
> three digits/letters of the aircraft identification after
> communications are established. The pilot may use
> the abbreviated call sign in subsequent contacts
> with the ATC specialist (*AIM 4-2-4 a. 2.*)

If the controller does not abbreviate your call sign, you shouldn't either. I'll explain why.

When you check in on a new frequency, you initially have no idea of who else is on the frequency with you, other than the air traffic controller. There may be no other pilots using the frequency besides yourself, or, there may be 50 other pilots on the same frequency. Only your air traffic controller knows the full inventory of pilots on the frequency.

When sharing the same frequency, each pilot identifies himself with a call sign. Occasionally, there will be two call signs on the same frequency that sound similar.

For example, Cessna 3383 Romeo and Cessna 3183 Romeo. What would happen if both pilots decided to use their abbreviated call sign?

ATC: "Cessna 3383 Romeo, descend and maintain 5,000."

Pilot: "Descend and maintain 5,000. Cessna 83 Romeo."

Of course, the air traffic controller is going to immediately question that response because he can't be certain which of the two Cessna pilots took the clearance. Was it Cessna 3383 Romeo, or Cessna 3183 Romeo? Only the pilot who answered knows for sure, and that is not acceptable.

The point is this. Don't abbreviate your call sign unless the controller does it first. Only the controller knows whether abbreviated call signs are appropriate for the situation. Enough said on that, but, there's more to say on how to use your abbreviated call sign when the controller gives you the green light to do so.

To make this absolutely clear, here are some examples with more fictitious call signs and their abbreviated equivalents:

Cessna 921 Alpha Charlie = Cessna 1 Alpha Charlie

Beechjet 754 Lima Hotel = Beechjet 4 Lima Hotel

Lancair 6026 Juliett = Lancair 26 Juliett

November 283 India Foxtrot = November 3 India Foxtrot

You will notice when ATC abbreviates a call sign, the controller does not exclude the aircraft's prefix or make or model or type. You shouldn't either. Hey, it's written in black and white in the AIM. Don't shoot the messenger.

I don't care what you hear other nitwits do on the radio, use your call sign correctly. Use it fully until ATC begins using the abbreviated form. If ATC abbreviates, then you may do so. Use the abbreviation the way the AIM says it should be used.

Start to Finish

You might have noticed, in some of the examples for call sign use, some radio calls began with the call sign and some ended with the call sign. It raises the question: Should pilots use their call sign at the beginning or at the end of a radio transmission?

A while back, someone in the standards department at my airline said we should strive to precede every acknowledgement to ATC with our flight call sign.

ATC: "Airliner 353, descend and maintain 5,000."

Pilot: "Airliner 353, descending to 5,000."

Most pilots acknowledge ATC directives by reading back the directive, and then stating the call sign.

ATC: "Airliner 353, turn right, heading 240."

Pilot: "Heading 240, Airliner 353."

The standards guy said beginning each read back with the

call sign is good radio discipline. I agree. He also said the practice lets ATC immediately know which flight got the message. His concern was, busy controllers listen to the read back to make sure the vector or altitude change was correctly received, but may stop listening before verifying the clearance went to the correct flight.

My opinion? Six of one, half a dozen of the other. Either the controller hears the entire read back or he doesn't. Hearing the call sign and hearing the read back of the clearance are equally important.

An air traffic controller I know also believes it's better to begin every read back with your call sign. The controller says some pilots with lousy mic-keying habits tend to chop off the first syllable of their transmissions: "__ted 398, passing 9,000 for 6,000."

That controller would rather have part of the call sign chopped off than the meat of the read back chopped off. I'll raise the B.S. flag on that. Truncating a call sign can have serious consequences, especially when there are 2 aircraft on the frequency with similar sounding call signs. A wise controller would ask for a repeat of the read back if any part of the transmission was missing.

Let's go to the source to see what the AIM says is a best practice:

4-2-3. Contact Procedures

c. Subsequent Contacts and Responses to Callup from a Ground Facility

Acknowledge with your aircraft identification, either at the beginning or at the end of your transmission, and one of the words "Wilco," "Roger," "Affirmative," "Negative," or other appropriate remarks;

EXAMPLE-
"United Two Twenty-'Two on one two three point four"
or *"one two three point four, United Two Twenty-Two."*

I still believe preceding each read back with your call sign is the way to go. It may challenge your short term memory to mentally hang on to ATC's clearance while you rattle off your call sign, but flying is challenging. The AIM says it doesn't matter whether you precede or follow your read back of the numbers with your call sign, as long as you include your call sign, and you use your call sign accurately.

We have laid the foundation for basic radio work. We have focused on good microphone technique, on using standard phraseology, and on the correct use of an aircraft call sign. It's time to flip on the master avionics switch, tune in a frequency, pump up the radio volume, and start talking on the radio.

Take Action

I challenge you to use your call sign and your abbreviated call sign the way it is desctibed in the AIM section 4-2-4, even when almost every other goofus out there uses his callsign incorrectly. Be a rebel!

Here's your Rebel's Checklist:

1. Include your callsign in every radio transmission.

2. Include either your aircraft's prefix or its make, model, or type in every transmission of your call sign--even when using your abbreviated call signs.

3. Do not abbreviate your call sign until the controller has first done so.

4. If you have been using your abbreviated call sign with one controller, revert to using your full call sign when switching frequencies to a new controller.

Bonus Action:

Answer this: You have been using your abbreviated call sign, Cessna 30 Delta, while talking to a controller. That controller says, "Cessna 30 Delta, change to my frequency, 127.4" When you contact the same controller on the new frequency, should you check in as Cessna 30 Delta, or should you check in using your full call sign, Cessna 9130 Delta? (The correct answer is on the next page.)

Bonus Question Answer:

Either form is correct. Using your full call sign is always acceptable. You may also choose to use your abbreviated call sign on the new frequency.

The AIM says you should revert to using your full call sign when checking in with a new controller. In this situation, you are only changing frequencies, not changing controllers. The controller has the full inventory of call signs he is working with on both of his frequencies. If he used your abbreviated call sign when giving you the frequency change, that means he knows there is no one on the new frequency who is using a call sign that sounds similar to yours. You are free to use the abbreviated call sign when you check in on the new frequency.

Chapter 5: Grab the Microphone and Speak

Coming up, we'll talk more about the nitty gritty behind radio work. Right now, I think it's time to speak and be heard. Let's squeeze off a few radio calls and see where it gets us. Turn on the master avionics switch. Tune your Number 1 Comm radio to 123.05 and make some calls to UNICOM. I'm not asking you to actually do this in an airplane. Do try to visualize the action, though. Work with me here.

> **Caution:** Numerous acronyms ahead (NAA). You know the old saying. If it can't be expressed as an acronym, it has no place in aviation.

Today, we are flying from Atlanta Town and Country Airport (KATC), a fictitious uncontrolled airfield near Atlanta, Georgia. Atlanta Town and Country has 2 runways. One runway is 36/18. The other runway is 9/27. The runways intersect at midfield. (See the sectional map, next page.)

Airport elevation is 950 feet above mean sea level (MSL). The traffic pattern for all runways is a left-hand pattern. The traffic pattern altitude is 1000 feet above field elevation (AFE), or 1,950 feet MSL on the altimeter. (I did some higher math to figure that out.) The only instrument approach for the airfield is a VOR/DME approach to Runway 18. The approach uses the Town and Country VOR and DME transmitter, located near the center of the airport.

In Comm Radio Number 2, you dial in the frequency for KATC's Automated Weather Observing System System (AWOS) and hear the following:

> "Atlanta Town and Country Automated Weather Observation, 1755 Zulu weather. Ceiling unlimited. Visibility 7 miles. Wind 190 at 10 knots. Temperature 27. Dewpoint 18. Altimeter 30.01. AO2831, check density altitude."

KATC is a fictitious uncontrolled airport west of Atlanta

Although AWOS reported 7 miles visibility, the visibility appears to be a million miles. It's a great day to fly. Other pilots must think so too. You can see aircraft landing and departing on Runway 18, but as you watch, one airplane takes off from Runway 27.

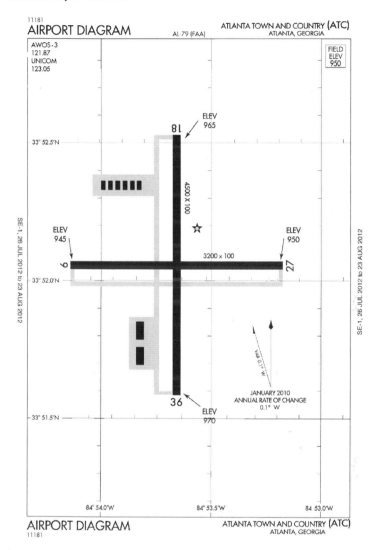

KATC has a north-south and an east-west runway.

Selecting the transmit button for Comm Radio 1, you press the push-to-talk switch and make your first radio call to UNICOM. "Town and Country Airport Information, Cessna 9130 Delta on the north ramp. I have the automated weather. Request an airport advisory."

The reply comes: "Aircraft calling Town and Country Airport, Town and Country is landing and departing Runway 18. Runway 27 is also in use for departures only. Current winds are 190 at 10. There is currently one airplane in the traffic pattern."

After calling "Clear prop!" you crank your airplane's engine. Before taxiing, you make your first radio call to other pilots on the frequency.

"Town and Country Traffic, Cessna 9130 Delta, taxiing from the southwest ramp to Runway 18, Town and Country." Let's look at this radio call and see what's important in it.

First, when making a radio call to UNICOM, you always begin every radio call with the airport's name. Although the full name for KATC is Atlanta Town and Country Airport, pilots use the shorthand name Town and Country. The shorthand name is usually not printed anywhere, so you wouldn't be criticized for using the formal, full name of the airport. If you know how other pilots refer to the airport, use the familiar name for clarity. You add the word "traffic" to indicate you are calling all other airplanes (traffic) on the UNICOM frequency for the airport.

Next, when making radio calls to UNICOM, or any general-use frequency not moderated by an air traffic controller, always, always, always use your full call sign. Never abbreviate your call sign because you will have no idea who is on frequency with you. You also cannot anticipate who might be joining the frequency after you. The best way to distinguish your call sign from another similar sounding call sign on the frequency is to use your full call sign.

After your call sign, state your position. In this case, your position is on the southwest ramp of the airport. With your position called out, state your intentions: "Taxiing to Runway 18."

Finish off every radio call with the name of the airport again. With a limited number of frequencies allocated for UNICOM use, two or more airports in the general area may share the same UNICOM frequency. If that is the case, it's important for pilots listening in on the frequency to be able to distinguish traffic movement at the airport they are using. Many announcements from pilots at two different airports makes it easy to get confused about who is operating where. By tagging the beginning and the end of each radio call with your airport's name, you improve the odds that your airplane's location will be noted at the correct airport.

The practice of saying the airport call sign at the beginning and end of each transmission is spelled out clearly in the AIM:

> **4-1-9. Traffic Advisory Practices at Airports Without Operating Control Towers**
>
> **g.** Self-Announce Position and/or Intentions
>
> **6.** To help identify one airport from another, the airport name should be spoken at the beginning and end of each self-announce transmission.

You gun your airplane's engine. . . I meant to say, you gently advance the throttle and begin to taxi. To reach Runway 18 from the southwest ramp, you follow the taxiway that parallels Runway 18. You continue on the parallel taxiway to the point where it crosses Runways 9 and 27. (See the illustration, next page.)

Approaching this intersection you clear the traffic pattern visually. You are looking to see if any aircraft are taking off of, or landing on Runway 27 or Runway 9. Although the airport advisory suggested most aircraft are landing and departing on Runway 18, some aircraft may depart Runway 27. Remember, this is an uncontrolled airfield, so nothing is really stopping pilots from using any runway at the airport, except common sense. As your mother used to say, "Look both ways before you cross the street." Similarly, look both ways before you cross the runway.

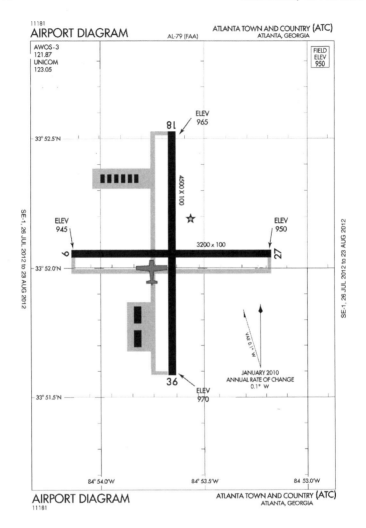

Holding short of Runway 9/27.

Your mom would have done well to also advise you to listen before you cross the street. This advice is especially true at airports with intersecting runways. Almost every aircraft has one or more blind spots that prevent a pilot from scanning every section of the sky. A high-wing airplane, such as a Cessna 172, has some huge blind spots when looking upwards. That's why it pays to also clear the traffic pattern with your ears.

You are listening for radio calls from pilots who intend to use the runway you are about to cross. For example, this might be a clue: "Town and Country Traffic, Piper 634 Golf Echo, base leg, Runway 27, Town and Country." When you have cleared the pattern visually and by ear, before crossing any runway, make a radio call:

"Town and Country Traffic, Cessna 9130 Delta, crossing Runway 27, Town and Country."

I want to point out that announcing your intentions to cross a runway on the radio is a technique. It's not required by the AIM. I like to do it for safety.

Even if the wind is howling from the south at 35 knots and a pilot would be crazy to use Runway 27, I recommend making the radio call anyways. It's an added measure of safety that alerts the numbskull who chooses to ignore the runway best aligned with the wind in favor of landing in a 35-knot crosswind. Chances are if that genius chooses Runway 27, he might also not have the sense to announce his position and intentions on the radio. Maybe you will wake him up with your radio call announcing your intention to cross Runway 27.

What's the Point of Listening?

After safely crossing Runway 27, you continue down the parallel taxiway. You reach the hold short area for Runway 18 and turn into the wind for your engine run-up. As you run through your pre-departure checks, you listen to the radio for the calls from other pilots:

"Town and Country Traffic, Cessna 705 Uniform Whiskey, downwind, Runway 18, Town and Country."

"Town and Country Traffic, R.V. 227 Tango X-ray, final, Runway 18, full stop, Town and Country."

"Town and Country Traffic, Mooney 2034 Oscar, 10 miles southeast of the airport at 3,500. Landing Town and Country."

All the radio calls you hear help you build a mental picture of what is going on in and around the airport traffic pattern. That mental picture helps you build a plan of action for your impending takeoff.

You might say to yourself, "I've got an R.V. aircraft on final. He will land soon, so I'll let him go by before considering my takeoff. But I'll have to give him time to roll down the runway and exit before I can take off. By that time, the Cessna on downwind may be on base leg or even turning on to final approach. If I line up and wait on the runway after the R.V. lands, I'll be able to release brakes and depart before becoming a factor for the landing Cessna. That Mooney is 10 miles from the airport, so I have to consider where he will be after I lift off. I want to stay in the traffic pattern for a couple of touch and goes, so the Mooney might be a factor for those."

Listening to the radio is a great way to build situational awareness, or SA. With good SA, you can build a plan. Planning ahead is part of good airmanship. It beats the heck out of launching into the air with no plan and reacting moment to moment. It may make the difference between staying mentally ahead of a changing situation, or falling behind.

Listening in order to plan is important in an uncontrolled airport traffic pattern. It is part and parcel of working with air traffic control, as we'll see in the coming chapters. Practice listening now. It will pay off later.

Your engine checks out during the run up. Your pre-departure checklist is complete. You have a good idea of where you fit into the current picture in the traffic pattern. It's time to depart.

The R.V. aircraft shoots by in a landing attitude. You throttle up and announce, "Town and Country Traffic, Cessna 9130 Delta, entering Runway 18, Town and Country." Immediately after, you hear, "Town and Country Traffic, Cessna 705 Uniform Whiskey, base leg, Runway 18, full stop, Town and Country."

You see the R.V. aircraft beginning to exit the runway at the far end. Perfect! This is working out just as you planned. You make the radio call, "Town and Country Traffic, Cessna 9130 Delta, taking off Runway 18, remaining in the pattern, Town and Country."

You advance power and make your takeoff roll. As your main wheels lift off the runway, you hear, "Town and Country Traffic, Cessna 705 Uniform Whiskey, turning final, Runway 18, full stop, Town and Country." That's good. The Cessna behind you should be no factor for your traffic pattern work. What about that Mooney?

As you turn your airplane towards crosswind, you hear, "Town and Country Traffic, Mooney 2034 Oscar, 3 miles east of the field, entering downwind for Runway 18, touch and go, Town and Country."

Air-to-Air Communication

Uh oh. There's the Mooney. He's at your 10 o'clock position and about 4 miles away as you fly your crosswind leg. There's a chance you and the pilot of the Mooney are going to meet at the midfield downwind entry point for Runway 18. (See illustration.)

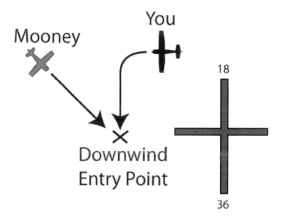

The Mooney might be conflict with your aircraft at the downwind entry point.

What now? Maybe you can sort it out by talking to the pilot of the Mooney. Is that the right thing to do?

Let's put this situation on hold and go to the "Book of Common Wisdom," the Aeronautical Information Manual. The

AIM has no procedure or methodology for pilots coordinating their movements with other pilots. Here is all the AIM has to say about radio procedures on UNICOM:

h. UNICOM Communications Procedures

In communicating with a UNICOM station, the following practices will help reduce frequency congestion, facilitate a better understanding of pilot intentions, help identify the location of aircraft in the traffic pattern, and enhance safety of flight:

(a) Select the correct UNICOM frequency.

(b) State the identification of the UNICOM station you are calling in each transmission.

(c) Speak slowly and distinctly.

(d) Report approximately 10 miles from the airport, reporting altitude, and state your aircraft type, aircraft identification, location relative to the airport, state whether landing or overflight, and request wind information and runway in use.

(e) Report on downwind, base, and final approach.

(f) Report leaving the runway.

For outbound traffic, the AIM has a table that says to report before taxiing, and before taxiing on to the runway (*AIM Table 4-1-1, next page*).

	Facility at Airport	Frequency Use	Communication/Broadcast Procedures		
			Outbound	Inbound	Practice Instrument Approaches
1	UNICOM (No Tower or FSS)	Communicate with UNICOM station on published CTAF frequency. If unable to contact UNICOM station, use self-announce procedures on CTAF.	Before taxiing and before taxiing on the runway for departure.	10 miles out. Entering downwind, base, and final. Leaving the runway.	
2	No Tower, FSS or UNICOM	Self-announce on MULTICOM frequency 122.9.	Before taxiing and before taxiing on the runway for departure.	10 miles out. Entering downwind, base and final. Leaving the runway.	Departing final approach fix (name) or on final approach segment inbound.
3	No Tower in operation, FSS open	Communicate with FSS on CTAF frequency.	Before taxiing and before taxiing on the runway for departure.	10 miles out. Entering downwind, base and final. Leaving the runway.	Approach completed/terminated.
4	FSS Closed (No Tower)	Self-announce on CTAF.	Before taxiing and before taxiing on the runway for departure.	10 miles out. Entering downwind, base and final. Leaving the runway.	
5	Tower or FSS not in operation	Self-announce on CTAF.	Before taxiing and before taxiing on the runway for departure.	10 miles out. Entering downwind, base and final. Leaving the runway.	

Abridged version of AIM Table 4-4-1. UNICOM frequencies were omitted from this version.

There is an inconsistency here. Although it's not mentioned in the table in the AIM, look further down section h. UNICOM Communications Procedures. You will see additional information about departing aircraft. In that section, the AIM says you should also report departing on the runway in use and your intentions after takeoff, such as remaining in the pattern, or your direction of departure, if exiting the traffic pattern. These additional calls are not mentioned in Table 4-1-1, but they are mentioned in the text. It's enough to give you indigestion, if you are are stickler for details.

Does any of this guidance prevent you from talking to other pilots in the airport pattern? Not exactly, but the AIM sort of gives hints that pilot-to-pilot communication is not recommended. For example, the AIM refers to radio work in an uncontrolled pattern as "Self-Announce Phraseology." You won't find any instance of pilot-to-pilot phraseology. Then there is this in the section on Common Traffic Advisory Frequency (CTAF):

4-1-9. Traffic Advisory Practices at Airports Without Operating Control Towers

g. Self-Announce Position and/or Intentions
General.
Self-announce is a procedure whereby pilots broadcast their position or intended flight activity or ground operation on the designated CTAF. This procedure is used primarily at airports which do not have an FSS on the airport. The self-announce procedure should also be used if a pilot is unable to communicate with the FSS on the designated CTAF. Pilots stating, "Traffic in the area, please advise" is not a recognized Self-Announce Position and/or Intention phrase and should not be used under any condition.

That last sentence says, don't ask other pilots in the traffic pattern to give you information about activity in the pattern. In other words, self-announce procedures are exactly what they mean. They have nothing to do with talking pilot-to-pilot in the traffic pattern.

Is there a specific regulation or procedure that prohibits one pilot from coordinating with another pilot? Paragraph **4-1-9 g. 1.** is all there is. It's certainly not okay to tell the pilot of the Mooney aircraft what to do: "Hey Mooney 2034 Oscar. Make a right 360 and then enter downwind. That will let me pass you on downwind before you enter the pattern." You aren't a certified air traffic controller, so you should not direct other pilots. Even if you happen to be a certified air traffic controller, your credentials give you no authority to control the movement of other aircraft when you are flying.

What you may say: "Town and Country Traffic, Cessna 9130 Delta is departing the traffic pattern to the east. I'll re-enter downwind for Runway 18 behind the Mooney east of the airfield. Town and Country." This radio call, while targeting the pilot of the Mooney, conforms to self-announce procedures. It follows the standard for reporting departing the traffic pattern and for announcing your intention to enter downwind for the active runway. In short, it follows the AIM's standards and it enhances safety.

You depart the traffic pattern by extending your crosswind leg to the east and by climbing 500 above traffic pattern altitude. Once east of the downwind leg, you are clear of the traffic pattern. Now it's time to turn left and aim your aircraft towards the midfield downwind entry point for Runway 18. As you do this, you hear, "Town and Country Traffic, Mooney 2034 Oscar, entering downwind, Runway 18, touch and go, Town and Country."

Great! You have good spacing behind the Mooney. You begin your descent to traffic pattern altitude as you approach the downwind entry point at midfield. (See the illustration of better spacing below.)

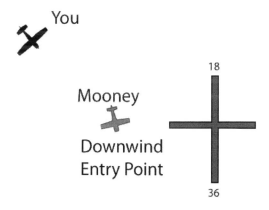

You now have good spacing behind the Mooney.

You make the radio call: "Town and Country Traffic, Cessna 9130 Delta, entering downwind, Runway 18, touch and go, Town and Country." Immediately after you release your radio's push-to-talk switch, you hear, "Town and Country Traffic, Mooney 2034 Oscar, base leg, Runway 18, touch and go, Town and Country."

You pull the carb heat lever out to prevent carburetor icing. Then, you reduce power and begin to slow so you can lower your flaps. Turning base leg, you are at a good altitude and airspeed to continue. You also hear, "Town and Country Traffic, Mooney 2034 Oscar, final, Runway 18, touch and go, Town and Country." Perfect.

Rolling out on base leg, you can see the Mooney down low, approaching the end of Runway 18. You call on the radio, "Town and Country Traffic, Cessna 9130 Delta, base leg, Runway 18, touch and go, Town and Country."

Your next call is, "Town and Country Traffic, Cessna 9130 Delta, final, Runway 18, touch and go, Town and Country." Ahead, you can see thE Mooney has already completed a touch and go and is beginning to turn towards the crosswind leg of the traffic pattern.

After your own touch and go, you decide to exit the traffic pattern for some air work away from the airport. As you climb out, you make a 45-degree heading change to the southeast and announce, "Town and Country Traffic, Cessna 9103 Delta, departing to the southeast, Town and Country." You are out of there. Everybody who is working in, or monitoring the movement in the airport traffic pattern now knows you are about to become a dot on the horizon.

(Trivia: Turning your airplane into a dot on the horizon generated the fighter pilot expression "We're dots," which means, "We're out of here. See you later.")

The AIM advises staying tuned to the UNICOM frequency until you are at least 10 miles away from the airport. Staying on the frequency will allow you to listen up for any airplanes inbound to the airport who might cross your path.

From here, it's on to your air work. You might practice some stalls and falls; or, you might decide to sight-see around the local area. Whatever you decide, it's probably a good idea to contact ATC for VFR flight following as you do your air work.

Let's cover how to do that in the next chapter. I'll see you there when you turn the page.

Take Action

Using a ruler and a pencil, draw a representation of a runway in the center of a sheet of paper. It doesn't have to be detailed. A simple rectangle will work. Leave enough room on the paper to insert a a line drawing of an airport traffic pattern around the runway.

Draw the rectangular airport pattern around the runway. It doesn't matter if the pattern represents a right-hand or left-hand traffic flow around the runway. For guidance, look at the example below.

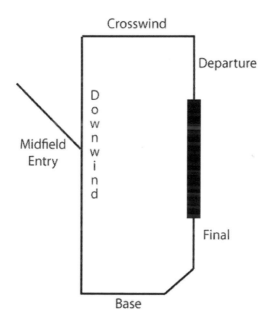

Components of a Traffic Pattern.

Take your pencil and place the point at the takeoff position of the runway. Out loud, say the radio call you would make before beginning your takeoff roll at an uncontrolled airport.

Begin moving the point of your pencil down the runway and then around the lines representing the airport traffic pattern.

As your pencil point reaches a place in the sketch of the airport traffic pattern where you would make a position report, make that report out loud. If you have any questions about what should be said at each reporting point, review this chapter, or check the AIM *Section 4-1-9* for guidance.

Continue making circuits around the pattern with your pencil point, calling out each radio call when the pencil reaches the appropriate point. Keep doing this, adding variations for each flight situation, for example, touch-and-goes, low-approaches, etc. If you can envision a place where you would make a 360-turn for spacing behind other traffic, simulate that with your pencil and make the appropriate radio calls.

Repeat this exercise until you can make any radio call at any point in the airport pattern, almost without thinking about it.

Chapter 6: Is the Cost of Speaking to ATC Tax Deductible?

You've departed the traffic pattern at Atlanta Town and Country Airport. It's a beautiful day for sight-seeing. You consider contacting ATC for flight following, but then you think, "What's the point?"

The route you have in mind is not going to pass through--or even near--any controlled airspace, so there really is no point in contacting Air Traffic Control. After all, there is absolutely no requirement to use flight following, or what the government calls Basic Radio Service for VFR Aircraft. (Sorry, no acronym for that one.)

So why, oh why, would you want to invite the FAA into your cockpit when you are perfectly legal to aviate through uncontrolled airspace without the help of the feds?

The second you link up with air traffic control, even when V.F. and R, you inherit a couple of obligations. ATC gives you a transponder code to squawk; and, you must report altitude changes to the controller. You also have to listen to the controller. You don't necessarily have to take direction from him, because all his radio calls to you are advisory only. But you do have to listen, so no turning down the VHF volume in order to better hear music on your iPod.

That's the cost of linking up with air traffic control on a Visual Flight Rules jaunt. What do you get in return? You get traffic advisories and safety alerts. Yes, there are some other bennies, but the big deal is having ATC call out potential traffic conflicts and low altitude alerts.

Which brings us to the loaded part of the question: How good and how reliable are you at picking out fast-moving aircraft overtaking you from your four-o'clock to eight-o'clock position? How good are you at spotting traffic climbing to and crossing your flight path from underneath your aircraft? If you fly a high-winged aircraft, how good are you at seeing aircraft above the wing as you make a prolonged turn? If you fly a low-winged aircraft, how good are you at seeing traffic below the wing as you make a prolonged turn? How good are you at seeing air traffic coming toward you from the other side of a puffy cloud?

When you link up with ATC, you have someone else on your team who has a bird's eye view of the area around your airplane. With radar, ATC does not have any of the blind spots you have from your airplane. While radar's coverage is not perfect--it can't see through mountains and it can't see beyond a certain distance--radar can cover a lot more sky than your Mark 1 eyeball.

Here's another way ATC has the upper hand when it comes to spotting air traffic: While you have to divide your time between maintaining aircraft control, navigating, and spotting air traffic, a controller's primary job is to watch for traffic. Sure, an air traffic controller has other tasks besides watching for traffic, but keeping airplanes separated is a controller's primary job.

A controller has other assets to help handle competing tasks when traffic gets heavy. An air traffic controller has an automated system that helps him with traffic handoffs to the next sector. He has other controllers just a call away on the landline to help him coordinate aircraft movement from sector to sector.

In sectors with very heavy traffic, an air traffic controller may have an assistant controller, called a D-side, to help him with his workload.

In your airplane, it's just you, you and you to handle everything. Wouldn't it be nice to get a little help with even one task--looking out for traffic? Bear in mind, ATC helps, but does not relieve you of the obligation to look for traffic. Don't expect to connect with ATC and then give up all responsibility for clearing for traffic. ATC has got your back, but you should not shut down your traffic scan. Let's go to the book:

AIM 4-1-15. Radar Traffic Information Service
This is a service provided by radar ATC facilities.
Pilots receiving this service are advised of any radar

target observed on the radar display which may be in such proximity to the position of their aircraft or its intended route of flight that it warrants their attention. This service is not intended to relieve the pilot of the responsibility for continual vigilance to see and avoid other aircraft.

I Need Help!

There is another advantage to having ATC connected to your flight. If you have a problem with your aircraft that requires assistance from someone on the ground, you will already be talking to someone who can provide immediate help.

For example, let's say you were tooling around the countryside, V.F.R., taking in the sights from 3,500 feet. Suddenly, your aircraft's one and only powerplant goes into "automatic rough." Your home airport is a lot further away than you would care to fly at this point, because you aren't sure how much longer your engine is going to last. You need on the ground, right now!

Fortunately, you were already connected to ATC when this happened. All you need to do at this point is say, "November 468 Sierra Golf is declaring an emergency for engine trouble. I need a heading to the nearest airport with 2,500 feet or more of usable runway."

Within seconds the controller you were speaking to will find a suitable airport and give you a heading to fly toward it. He'll also clear all other conflicting air traffic out of the way. He'll contact whoever is in control of the arrival airport and prepare them for your arrival, including setting up rescue and fire fighting services if you request them. If you need help troubleshooting your engine, he has access to checklists for your aircraft as well as phone connections to your aircraft's manufacturer. He might even be able to put you in touch with another controller in his building who flies your category of aircraft. Many air traffic controllers are pilots as well.

Let's back up to the beginning of this scenario. Your engine starts running rough. Shortly after this happens, you smell smoke that has an oily odor. It's time to get on the ground as soon as possible. This time, you are on your own, not in contact with ATC. You sure would appreciate assistance from someone on the ground. While dealing with your malfunctioning engine, you have to put out a navigation chart and try to find a frequency for the nearest ATC agency. Or, you have to dial up 121.5 and work the radio to get in touch-with ATC. Either way, the process of getting in touch with ATC is going to eat up time and part of your attention.

Once you get in touch with ATC, you are going to have to state your situation and your location. You will be given a transponder code and probably told to hit the ident feature on your transponder. There goes more precious seconds while the engine gets rougher and the smell of smoke intensifies. Once ATC positively identifies your aircraft, only then can you get the help you need.

I know what you are thinking. ATC cannot fly your airplane for you. You can probably handle your emergency without ATC's help. I'm sure that's true. Look again at the laundry list of help you can get from ATC if you go that route:

- Navigation to a suitable airport.

- Moving other traffic out of your way.

- Keeping you clear of obstacles as you deal with your emergency.

- Coordination with the arrival airport for your emergency.

- Preparation and deployment of rescue and fire fighting service, as needed.

- Assistance with checklists.

- Access to experts at the company that built your aircraft.

- A team member with a clear, calm head who can help you assess your situation.

Know what this all costs you? Absolutely nothing. Who wouldn't want this free assistance?

Ignoring ATC would be like paying for a membership at a commercial gym and then never going to the gym. You would never do that, would you? You don't have to answer that.

Anxious Moments

Here's the number one reason pilots give to me when explaining why they don't contact ATC for basic radar service (drum roll, please): Anxiety.

If you are anxious about talking to a representative of the federal government, join the crowd. The club of pilots who are worried about talking to ATC is broad and deep. Truth be told, I can't think of anyone, off the top of my head, who really enjoys having to talk to ATC. It's just something we do because, in some cases we have to, and in other cases, because it's our best option.

Let's spend a few minutes talking about where this anxiety comes from. My goal is to relieve you of most of your anxiety about talking to ATC. Think I can do it? Let's find out.

Talking to ATC is a big hairy issue for some pilots. The anxiety some of us feel about talking to the feds leaps at us from two directions. First, no one wants to expose himself as a dumb bunny on the aircraft radio. Second, no one wants to expose himself to the wrath of the government if a mistake is made in the airplane.

The first reason is fairly easy to understand. Fighter pilots have an expression that covers it: "I'd rather die than look stupid." There is another quote that works here:

> *"Better to remain silent and be thought a fool than to speak out and remove all doubt."* Abraham Lincoln.

Let's face it, aviation radio frequencies are a public forum. When you speak, everyone else on the frequency can hear your mastery, or lack of mastery, of the ATC language. If you haven't got your act together on the radio, the experience can seem like getting up on stage in front of a huge crowd and singing karaoke with a voice that is way off-key. Or it can be like the amateur comedian who gets up on stage, on Open Mic Night, and forgets his material. There's only one word that describes either example: Ugh! Okay, maybe there's more than one word, but that one pretty much sums it up.

When people focus on the chance they might flop when speaking to ATC, they decide to fly under the radar--literally-- and never contact ATC. You have heard that expression, "Nothing ventured, nothing gained"? If you have anxiety about flopping on the radio, you might adhere to "Nothing risked, nothing lost."

Since I brought it up, let's look at people who voluntarily sing karaoke, even though they cannot sing well. Or, look at the person who stands up in front of an unappreciative audience and forgets the punchline. What's going on here? There's one of two possibilities.

Either the bad singer or bad comedian is drunk or self-deluding. Or, it could be, that person wants something bad enough that it's worth going through a little trial by fire to reach a goal. We are back to, "Nothing ventured, nothing gained." For some people, it's worth going through some growing pains to grow.

Take a look at what it takes to learn to fly. You don't get your pilots license without cost. It costs a lot of money, time, and effort to learn how to fly. It isn't an easy skill to learn, but with perseverance, you eventually become a pilot. "Something ventured, something gained."

It's the same exercise for learning how to talk to ATC on the radio. It takes time and effort, and maybe exposing yourself in ways that show you don't have the language down cold. In other words, you risk looking incompetent in front of your peers.

Fine. Great. All well and good. You understand it takes practice to learn how to talk on the radio with a certain level of competence. Then there is the big bad air traffic controller, judging you; measuring your worth and finding you wanting.

Let me let you in on the big secret. When you falter on the radio, no one cares, except you. Seriously. The rest of us on the frequency are not judging you, and here's why. We've all been there. We all had to start from the beginning just like you. We know what it is like to struggle on the radio.

How does an air traffic controller look at your unskilled radio call? Let me explain it with an illustration. ATC has to deal with air traffic, whether the controller is talking to the pilot on his radar screen or not. A controller is obligated to maintain safe separation between aircraft the controller is talking to. He also has to keep aircraft under his jurisdiction from running into aircraft he is not talking to. If you spend any time working with ATC, you are bound to hear a radio call from the controller that sounds like this:

"Piper 7729 Victor, traffic is twelve o'clock opposite direction, type and altitude unknown."

When Piper 7729 Victor says, "Traffic not in sight," ATC will say, "Piper 7729 Victor, for traffic avoidance, suggest turning right, heading zero one zero."

Then, "Piper 7729 Victor, your traffic has changed course. Traffic is now at your 11 o'clock, southeast bound. Turn left, heading 340." This game of avoiding traffic that is completely unpredictable will continue until the traffic passes by your position. Then, ATC says, for example, "Piper 7729 Victor, traffic passing by your 3 o'clock position now. No factor. Resume own navigation on course."

You know that old video game called Frogger? It's the one where the object is to move a cartoon frog across multiple lanes of car traffic without getting hit. That game is pretty good representation of what ATC goes through when the airspace is congested and a pilot wanders through without talking to anyone on the radio.

Put bluntly, pilots who do not contact ATC are a pain in the butt for everyone. Air traffic control is forced to deal with your airplane, even if you aren't speaking to ATC. I guarantee you an air traffic controller would rather hear your less-than-perfect radio calls than not hear from you at all.

Here's another less-known fact about air traffic controllers. Try to keep this between you and me. Air traffic controllers are just people. They are hard-working people who take their role of keeping you safe very seriously. In that regard, they will do what needs to be done to work with you, no matter how inexperienced you may be.

Most controllers recognize an inexperienced pilot, or one who has little experience with ATC, by the quality of the pilot's radio transmissions. If a controller hears a pilot struggling on the radio, the controller is not going to give that pilot a hard time. To the contrary. The controller is going to slow down the pace of his own transmissions and actually do what it takes to accommodate the inexperienced pilot.

I didn't make this up. I've interviewed air traffic controllers and asked them specifically how they handle pilots who falter or sound nervous on the radio. To a person, they all said the same thing. When they hear a pilot on the radio who sounds inexperienced, they slow down and give that pilot a little more time and little more room to absorb and execute ATC instructions. Isn't that great? Controllers don't have to do this, but all the ones I know have said they try to accommodate inexperienced pilots.

A Student of the Radio

There is a standard practice for how ATC is supposed to handle student pilots. ATC assumes a student pilot will be inexperienced in radio communication. It's spelled out in the AIM and the Air Traffic Controllers Manual. Here's the quote from the AIM:

> **4-2-4 c.** Student Pilots Radio Identification.
>
> **2.** This special identification [student pilot] will alert FAA ATC personnel and enable them to provide student pilots with such extra assistance and consideration as they may need. It is recommended that student pilots identify themselves as such, on initial contact with each clearance delivery prior to taxiing, ground control, tower, approach and departure control frequency, or FSS contact.

If you are a student pilot, you can help yourself by

identifying yourself as a student pilot when you contact ATC. For example, "Cleveland Approach, November 3506 Hotel, student pilot, VFR at 4,500." The air traffic controller will slow down her delivery, keep her clearances short, and give you extra time to respond.

If you are certified pilot, you should not identify yourself as a student pilot in order to receive special handling. You won't have to, as I just explained. Controllers know how to adjust.

Believe me when I say the number of inexperienced pilots flying worldwide far outnumber the experienced pilots. To be an experienced pilot, you have to fly a lot. The only people who can afford to do this are pilots who fly professionally, and pilots who are wealthy enough to afford to fly several times per week. That means ATC spends a lot of time working with inexperienced pilots just like you.

Experienced or not, very few pilots make perfect radio calls. Even pros, the men and women who fly 3 or 4 days per week, can be just plain awful on the radios, as I explained in an earlier chapter. The pros may not stumble and stutter very much on the radio, but their phraseology is rarely 100% correct. Your less-than-ideal radio work is nothing special, and raises no particular concern with ATC or the rest of the flying world.

This is where we are so far:

- Nothing ventured, nothing gained. This means, you won't improve on the radio unless you practice.

- An air traffic controller would much rather communicate with you than have to move everyone else out of your path because you are not communicating.

- When you speak on the radio, no one is judging you. We all have had our struggles with radio work. Welcome to the club.

- ATC will take you as you are. If you struggle a bit on the radio, a controller will modify his communication to meet you at your experience level. It's part of the controller's training to do this.

Hopefully I've pointed you in the right direction to help you overcome your anxiety about talking to ATC on the radio. I still haven't addressed that other bugaboo--the one that says, if you make a mistake, ATC is going to hammer you with big time penalties.

A Big Bonk on the Head

Air traffic control is not the FAA's hired muscle. Controllers are not enforcers, waiting to pounce on you for the slightest error. An air traffic controller would prefer to spend her time controlling traffic, not trying to trap you as you commit an error. With this in mind, an air traffic controller focuses on three jobs. Here they are, as spelled out in the Air Traffic Controller Manual:

> **2-1-1. ATC SERVICE**
> The primary purpose of the ATC system is to prevent a collision between aircraft operating in the system and to organize and expedite the flow of traffic, and to provide support for National Security and Homeland Defense (J.O. 7110.65).

Notice the title of the very first paragraph in the manual: "ATC Service." Air traffic control is a service. Controllers work in service to you. I didn't reproduce the full text of this opening paragraph, but you can look at it for yourself. You will notice that nowhere in the description of an air traffic controller's job does it say a controller is a law enforcement officer.

This is not to say a controller has no obligation to do anything when a pilot deviates from a clearance. There is a section in J.O. 7110.65 for what a controller is expected to do when a pilot deviates from a clearance:

2-1-26. PILOT DEVIATION NOTIFICATION
When it appears that the actions of a pilot
constitute a pilot deviation, notify the pilot,
workload permitting.

PHRASEOLOGY -
(Identification) POSSIBLE PILOT DEVIATION
ADVISE YOU CONTACT (facility) AT (telephone
number).

REFERENCE -
FAAO 8020.11, Aircraft Accident and Incident
Notification, Investigation, and Reporting, Para 84,
Pilot Deviations.

Let me tell you this, based upon personal experience and the
stories from other pilots. Air traffic controllers will bend over
backward to help you out if you make an error. I believe this is
because they take their commitment to serve pilots very
seriously. They really do want to help you get from A to B with
as little hassle as possible.

Every air traffic controller I've ever talked to hates doing
paperwork on his or her break. If you commit a deviation from
a clearance, a controller would rather help you correct back to
course or altitude than face the paperwork that is required to
document a deviation.

This is not to say if you commit a willful violation, such as
reckless flying, you can expect an air traffic controller to turn
the other way and pretend it didn't happen. If you purposely
flaunt the rules and fly recklessly, you probably deserve to have
your rear end handed to you. Or, if you demonstrate that you
are way out of your league, and shouldn't have been given a
pilot's certificate in the first place, you probably should be
scheduled for additional training.

Air traffic control centers also have an automated system that
records and reports altitude deviations that cause traffic
conflicts. I'll have more to say about how this system works in a
later chapter. For now, it's enough to say, when the system
catches your altitude deviation, it doesn't matter whether your
air traffic controller is willing to work with your error. The
automation has the last word.

If you are doing everything in your power to conduct a safe flight and ATC catches you in the middle of making an error, ATC is almost always going to work with you to get you safely on your way, end of story. I cannot guarantee this will be the case 100% of the time, but so far, in 34 years of flying and speaking with others who have flown at least that long, air traffic controllers would rather support you than report you.

Rather than thinking of air traffic controllers as an offensive line, trying to crush you, think of them as your defensive team, there to keep you from getting sacked. When thunderstorms are building and air traffic is filling the airspace around you, ATC will do everything it can to lighten your load and keep you safe.

ATC, as your defensive team, isn't a bunch of idealistic crap. I'm not trying to blow sunshine up your shorts. It's the absolute truth that I can back up with example after example.

I will admit one thing. Some controllers, on some days, behave like a-holes. Why? Controllers are people, just like you and me. Load any of us up with too much work, with insufficient resources, over long work days, under the watchful eye of a strict supervisor, and we are likely to get a little irritable. I'm fairly certain if I had to work the sector of Chicago Center that feeds aircraft into Chicago Approach's arrival corridors between 5 and 6 pm in the middle of a stormy day, I might get a little short-tempered. I don't know how those controllers manage to stay cool, and do the great job they do, day after day.

It's not as though some air traffic controllers have the market cornered on being cranky. I've heard more than one pilot act like a 2-year old on the radio simply because the controller didn't have the airspace to let the pilot climb 2,000 feet to escape some light turbulence.

Just because one pilot or one air traffic controller has heartburn doesn't mean all pilots or air traffic controllers need anger management training. It also doesn't mean you should shy away from communicating with ATC. One bad controller having a lousy day is not enough reason to avoid the entire ATC system.

A short story to wrap this up. One day I was sitting on a bench at Dekalb-Peachtree Airport (KPDK) in Atlanta. I was recording PDK Tower radio transmissions for my bi-weekly podcast at ATCcommunication.com. A man, who was at the airport fence watching airplanes, noticed my recording equipment, and approached me. He asked me what I was doing. I explained I was recording radio calls for a website that teaches pilots how to talk on the radio.

The man said, "Yeah. I could probably use that. I have a Cessna 210 that I've been flying for 15 years. I tend to stick to uncontrolled airspace so I don't have to talk to ATC."

I said, "I get it. You like the freedom of flying around without having to talk to ATC."

He said, "No, that's not it. I just never learned how to talk to ATC. I could never fly into a place like this." He gestured towards the runways. "Things move too fast for me here. I could never keep up."

I didn't tell him this, but that is exactly the flow of reasoning that prevents most pilots from taking advantage of everything ATC has to offer. I hope my pitch for putting your anxiety on a shelf helped a little bit. I also hope I've helped you realize that air traffic controllers are on your team. They aren't hired assassins for the FAA. Their focus is on helping you fly safely.

That's my whole pitch on the subject. I'm tuckered out. You know what would help? A little cross-country flight with flight following. (You knew I was going to say that.) Tell you what. Tune your number 1 comm radio to 127.3 and I'll meet you on the next page for your initial contact with Atlanta Center.

Take Action

Visit your local air traffic control facility by taking advantage of Operation Raincheck. Operation Raincheck is a familiarization program, instituted by the FAA, which allows anyone to observe and learn from air traffic controllers on the job.

By phoning the administration office of almost any ATC facility, you may schedule a visit to an airport tower, approach control room, or enroute control center. Your visit will include a guided tour, and in many cases, an opportunity to plug into a working air traffic controller's station. You will be able to listen and watch as he controls traffic. Some facilities have a radar simulator that you may use to try your hand at controlling computer-generated air traffic!

The best part of the orientation is having the chance to speak face-to-face with air traffic controllers. You will discover they are friendly people who are proud of their work. They can answer your questions and help you feel comfortable about talking to ATC.

Operation Raincheck is 100% free. If you have any anxiety at all about talking to ATC, a visit to your friendly neighborhood controller will free you of that anxiety for good.

Chapter 7: Following Your Flight

"Atlanta Center, Cessna 9130 Delta, one five miles northeast of the Town and Country VOR at three thousand five hundred, VFR for sight-seeing around the west side of Atlanta, request flight following."

Wait, wait, wait a second! Hold on there partner. When was the last time you made a phone call to someone and said something like this, the second you heard that person answer:

"Hi this is Jeff and I know it's kind of early I really need that 10-gallon tub of ice cream you were holding in your large freezer for me, so I was wondering if I could come over right now to pick it up because I figure I can be there in 20 minutes, grab it from you and be on my way in time for my kid's birthday party at 11:00."

You know what I would say to you if you called me and said that? I would say, "Huh?" That's simply too much information to give anyone in one shot. It may even be rude to blurt out your request before saying hello and asking whether the other person has time to talk.

Here is a better way to make initial contact with ATC:

1. ATC's call sign.

2. My call sign.

3. Where I am.

4. What I'm doing or what I need (in a very short statement).

Some pilots use this memory aid for the format used during initial contact:

You, me, where, what.

[You:] "Atlanta Center, [Me:] Cessna 9130 Delta, [Where:]15 miles northwest of the Town and Country VOR. [What:] VFR."

Let's define what we mean by initial contact. Then we can go over each of these items in a bit more detail.

According to the AIM, initial contact is your first radio call to a new controller or flight service specialist. This seems simple, but actually it's not. It turns out, there are two types of initial contact. There is initial radio contact while in radar contact. There is initial radio contact prior to radar contact.

If your aircraft is in radar contact, the first air traffic controller you speak to will say, "Cessna 9130 Delta, radar contact." From that point on, you are operating in a radar environment. Your aircraft's callsign and other data associated with your flight are now displaying next to the radar signature of your aircraft on ATC's radar display. (See the illustration of a radar signature and data block below.)

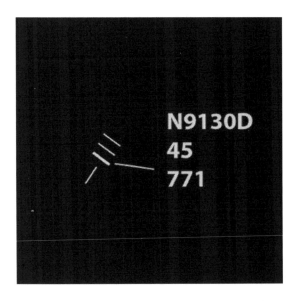

Radar datablock shows (from top to bottom)your call sign; your altitude (4,500); ATC computer I.D.

Let's regress a step further. I promise we'll be moving

forward again in a moment. In areas where radar is present, your aircraft will display on the radar screen of the air traffic controller as a primary target if you have no code set in your transponder. A primary target is a blip on a radar display that has no data associated with it. The controller sees this blip simply as a reflection of radar energy bouncing off your airplane. When a controller looks at a primary target on his display, he can watch the target's direction of movement. He can even get a general idea of the target's speed by watching it track across his screen.

If your transponder is squawking 1200 (the code for VFR), the controller's display will modify the target to show it as a VFR aircraft. If you set your transponder so it squawks Mode C (altitude data) on your transponder, the controller will also see your altitude on his display. (See the illustration of a VFR radar target.)

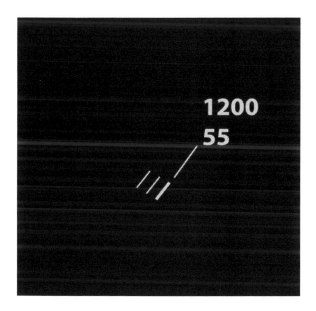

Radar datablock for a VFR aircraft with Mode C showing 5,500.

Other than these basic bits of information, an air traffic controller looking at your VFR target knows nothing about who you are, what you are, or where you are going. Until you tell him where you are, he has no way of knowing which of the VFR targets on his screen is you. This is why it's critical that your initial contact with ATC, prior to radar contact, must include your position.

Once you are told by a controller that you are "radar contact," initial contact with subsequent controllers will not require a position report. Each controller in the ATC system hands your aircraft's radar target off to the next controller. When in radar contact, your position is continually updated so each subsequent controller knows where you are. The positive handoff from controller to controller ensures the next controller is expecting you. This is why initial radio contact while in radar contact does not require you to check in with your position over the ground. Hang on to that for a minute. I'll come back to it as we go over the 4 items of any radio check in. Let's begin with how to specify who you are contacting upon initial checkin.

You

Who you are contacting is pilot-simple, but it's critical. You begin by saying the name of the facility, plus the type of facility controlling the airspace in which you are flying or taxiing. Examples:

Flight Operation	ATC Name	ATC Type
Taxiing:	Ann Arbor	Ground
Runway Operations:	Ann Arbor	Tower
Departure Control:	Detroit	Departure
Enroute Traffic Control:	Cleveland	Center
Approach Control:	Milwaukee	Approach

You will have to find the name of the first facility you contact in the listings on the chart that covers the airspace you are using. For example, if you want to get in touch with the approach control facility handling aircraft around the Denton, Texas airport, the Dallas-Fort Worth terminal area chart would tell you to contact Dallas-Fort Worth Approach. The chart is wrong! The correct name of the approach control facility is Regional Approach. There's a confidence builder for you. The controller you contact at Regional Approach will not hammer you for calling him Dallas-Fort Worth Approach. He hears it all the time.

The chart notation for Dallas-Fort Worth Approach is one of only a few exceptions where the charts get the name wrong. If you want to ensure absolute accuracy when identifying an ATC facility by name, look at the listing for your intended destination, or for an airport you will be overflying, in the Airport Facility Directory (A/FD). For example, the Denton Airport is located within the radar coverage of what the sectional chart calls Dallas-Fort Worth Approach. However, the A/FD correctly lists the approach control facility that serves Denton's as Regional Approach. By the way, access to a digital version of the A/FD is available online for free at:

http://avn.faa.gov/index.asp?xml=aeronav/applications/d_afd

All of the extra work to find the name of an ATC facility is not necessary once you are in radar contact. When a controller hands you off to the next controller, he will tell you the name of the facility you will be contacting. For example, he might say "Cessna 9130 Delta, contact Seattle Center on one three three point eight."

You might think calling an ATC facility by its name is ridiculously simple and does not warrant as much attention as I have given it. It's worth emphasizing because some pilots have found a way to screw it up.

For example, a pilot contacts an airport control tower without stating the control tower's name. The tower controller clears the pilot to enter the traffic pattern. As the pilot enters the airport pattern the tower controller cannot see the aircraft even though the sky is perfectly clear. It becomes apparent the pilot is talking to the wrong tower. I'm not kidding. This type of error has been taken to the limit. Pilots have landed at airport B while talking to the tower at airport A. This is why it is critical to include the name of the ATC facility in your first radio call to that facility.

Me

Let's return to our list of items that need to be covered in your initial radio call to ATC. Item 2, "Who you are," is fundamental. It's your call sign. We have already beat this subject to death, so I won't elaborate.

Where

"Where you are," Item 3, needs to be answered two ways:

- Your position over the ground (if not already in radar contact).

- Your altitude.

Stating your position over the ground can be expressed in more than one way. Usually, if the airspace in which you are operating is not crowded, giving ATC your position as miles and general direction from a navaid, such as a VOR, will work just fine. For example, "Pig Slop 221 Papa Charlie, two zero miles northwest of the Pig Sty VOR."

If the airspace is very crowded, ATC might ask you to be more precise in your position report. He may ask you to give your position as a specific radial and DME from a VORTAC or VOR/DME. For example, "Mud Slinger 362 Bravo Sierra is on the Campaign VOR three two five degree radial for two six DME."

If you don't have DME, or if you are out of range of a VORTAC, ATC may simply tell you to "ident." This means press the ident button on your transponder. Pressing the ident button on your transponder will send a signal to the controller's radar display. The ident signal highlights your aircraft on the controller's radar display. It helps the controller distinguish your aircraft's symbol from all of the other symbols on his radar display.

Your position over the ground may need to be expressed a little differently if your initial contact is with a controller who does not have access to radar, such as a tower controller at some airports. If you are calling an air traffic control tower at an airport, the general rule is to report your position relative to the airport. For example, "Rusty Bucket 5934 Hotel is one zero miles southwest of the airport."

Some airports have charted landmarks for position reporting. You may find these on your sectional navigation chart. They are indicated by a magenta flag next to the landmark on the chart. (See the example chart.)

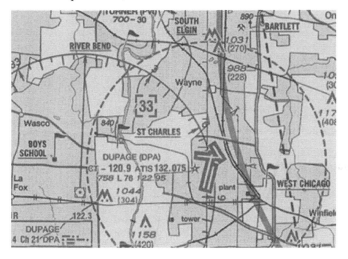

Charted landmark examples: River Bend; Boys School; etc.

These landmarks are usually large, geographic or man-made features, such as racetracks, fuel tank clusters, bridges, toxic waste dumps, or very distinctive and large buildings. (I'm just kidding about toxic waste dumps.) An example of a position report over a charted landmark might be, "Cesspool 538 Victor X-ray, over the sewage plant."

Stating your altitude in your position report is straightforward. Simply say your current altitude if you are level. If climbing or descending, you say the altitude you are passing and the altitude to which you are climbing or descending. For example, "Shaky Crate 406 Oscar Quebec, passing two thousand, one hundred for five thousand, five hundred."

You give your altitude to each succeeding air traffic controller for confirmation. Each controller can confirm your altimeter matches the altitude readout shown on his radar display. In many airplanes, the transponder either converts the airplane's altitude from analog information to digital information; or, it transmits altitude from its own internal altimeter. The transponder passes along its digital interpretation of your altitude using its Mode C feature. Electronics being what they are--garbage in, garbage out--it's possible your Mode C might transmit an altitude that does not exactly match your altimeter. Your altitude statement to the air traffic controller assures him that you are both looking at the same altitude readout.

What

The final item in our list of things to say to ATC on initial contact is a statement that helps the controller understand what you are doing or what you need. For example, you might say "VFR" or "Emergency." This is where pilots can overload an air traffic controller by relaying too much information.

For example, instead of simply stating you are "VFR," it might be tempting to say, "VFR on Victor Two Thirty-Four enroute to Augusta." Or, "In the clear but encountering moderate chop." This may be too much data for an air traffic controller to absorb during initial contact.

Make your request in a followup transmission, after you and the controller have said your hellos. In many cases, the controller will tell you when he is ready for your request. It might sound like this:

"Cessna 9130 Delta, squawk two seven zero four and say your request." Or this:

"Cessna 9130 Delta, squawk two seven zero four. Say your aircraft type and your destination."

Make initial contact and then let the controller ask his questions. The controller might be very busy or he might have plenty of time to talk to you. Let him lead the conversation in the manner which fits his circumstances.

Try to look at this from an air traffic controller's perspective.

When you make initial contact with ATC, it's similar to showing up at the front door of a friend's house with no prior notice. Before you contact him, a controller may be generally aware of your presence because your airplane is displaying on his radar screen as a VFR aircraft. Prior to your first call to him, he has no idea who you are. Your first radio call should be a simple introduction.

You're Terminated

Let's say you have made initial contact with ATC. You are under radar contact as you get handed off from controller to controller. Eventually, you approach your destination airport, which is not served by radar. The air traffic controller will say "Radar service terminated." You are now, at least temporarily, disconnected from ATC's system. The next controller you contact, in this case a tower controller, will need the whole format for initial contact in a non-radar environment: You, me, where, what.

"Radar service terminated" is a different animal from "radar contact lost." Don't confuse the two. "Radar service terminated" means exactly what it sounds like. "Radar contact lost" means you are still in radio contact with ATC and still receiving service. You aren't being covered by radar but ATC is tracking your progress. When radar contact is lost with your aircraft, ATC will ask you to compensate by making position reports at specific places along your route of flight. The controller may also ask you for your estimated time of arrival (ETA) for the next reporting point: "Cessna 9130 Delta, say your estimate for Spartanburg." If you don't have GPS to spoon-feed the estimate to you, you will have to do a speed-distance-time calculation to come up with an ETA. Good luck, we are all counting on you.

Keeping it Real with 3

Whether you are making initial contact with ATC, or making a follow-up radio call, every radio transmission should contain 3 or less bits of information in it, not counting your call sign. The 3-or-less rule, while not written anywhere, is just common sense. Air traffic controllers know this. They will try their best to hold their clearances and advisories to the 3-or-less rule. Here are some examples of exchanges on the radio where both parties transmit 3 bits of information or less:

You: "Cessna 9130 Delta,

1. one five miles northeast of the Town and Country VOR."

Controller: "Cessna 9130 Delta, Atlanta Center.

1. Squawk two six zero five

2. and say your altitude

3. and request."

You: "Cessna 9130 Delta,

1. squawking two six zero five.

2. I'm at three thousand five hundred,

3. request flight following."

Controller: "Cessna 9130 Delta,

1. radar contact 17 miles northeast of Town and Country.

2. Say your destination."

You: "Cessna 9130 Delta,

1. I'll be sight-seeing around the west side of Atlanta."

Controller: "Cessna 9130 Delta,

1. maintain VFR

2. and advise me of any altitude changes."

Do As You Please, But Keep Me Advised

Here we are, flying along in flight, VFR under radar contact with Atlanta Center. We should fly a straight-line course and not climb or descend, right? Heck no! Do whatever you feel like doing as long as you operate under the rules for VFR flight and all of the other rules of CFR Part 91. You would need to heed those rules whether you were in radar contact or not, so really, nothing changes during VFR flight following.

Turn left. Turn right. Practice stalls, steep turns and figure eights. Your only obligation to ATC is to advise the controller when you make an altitude change. You could even fly aerobatics if your airplane could tolerate aerobatics, as long as you tell the controller the altitudes you expect to work between as you loop and roll.

Pilot: "Pitts 557 Tango Whiskey will be practicing aerobatics in this general area between three thousand and six thousand."

ATC: "Pitts 557 Tango Whiskey, roger. Maintain VFR," is all a center controller will likely say.

Working under flight following while VFR is just another layer of security. It does not restrict your movement in any way.

By now, if you are as sharp as I think you are, you might be asking, "Why do I need to advise the controller of altitude changes? He has a readout of my altitude on his radar display." Good question. Here's the answer:

An air traffic controller can see your altitude on his display. He knows what you are doing right now, but he can't tell what you will be doing with your altitude in the future. He's not a mind reader.

Let's say you were cruising at 3,500 feet. The controller is also working with an IFR flight at 4,000, heading your way. The controller will say to the pilot flying IFR, "Traffic is a Cessna 172, twelve o'clock and five miles, opposite direction, VFR at 3,500." Before the controller can point out the IFR traffic headed your way at 4,000, you decide to climb to 5,500 to find smoother air. If you don't say anything before climbing, all hell is going to break loose on the radio as the controller scrambles to prevent a collision between you and the other aircraft:

Controller: "Learjet 88 Charlie, turn right immediately,

heading two four zero!"

Pilot: "Two four zero, Learjet 88 Charlie."

Controller: "Cessna 9130 Delta, turn right immediately, heading zero five zero!"

For goodness sake, answer the radio and turn immediately. Then expect some followup from ATC, reminding you to advise the controller of any altitude changes. That's why it's important to keep the controller in the loop if you decide to change altitude.

I've Got My Priorities Straight

Normally, if you keep ATC advised of your altitude changes, you won't hear very much from ATC. ATC will point out traffic to you if it might pass near your location. Generally, if traffic will pass well above you, well below you, or off to one side, you may not hear anything from ATC about the traffic. How often you receive traffic callouts from ATC will depend on how crowded the skies are around you and how busy the controller finds himself.

If an air traffic controller is loaded up, he will likely not have time to point out every airplane that passes your general vicinity. He might not even have time to help you get eyes on an airplane that passes fairly close to your position. When he's really busy, control and separation of IFR traffic may take his attention away from VFR aircraft.

Here's how the Air Traffic Controllers Manual puts it:

2-1-4. OPERATIONAL PRIORITY
Provide air traffic control service to aircraft on a
"first come, first served" basis as circumstances
permit.

There is nothing in that statement that says a controller
should give priority to IFR aircraft. Then there's this:

7-6-11. TERMINATION OF SERVICE
Basic radar services [for VFR aircraft] should be
provided to the extent possible, <u>workload
permitting</u>.

Ed. Note: I inserted the underline for emphasis. It's not in the
original text.

Sometimes, a controller will not intentionally ignore you. His
eyes may be pulled away by the need to pay attention to a lot of
IFR targets on his screen. Controllers call the visual scan
required to notice and mentally process everything that is
happening on a radar display "the flick." The expression comes
from the flicking motion of a controller's eyes as his focus
moves from target to target to target. Most of the time, your
VFR flight will be part of a controller's flick. Sometimes it won't.
That's why the AIM says flight following does not relieve a
pilot of the obligation to continually scan for traffic.

Back to Our Flight, Already in Progress

Today is a good day for sightseeing. The skies are not
crowded and the air traffic controller is not very busy. From
time to time, he calls out traffic to you:

"Cessna 9130 Delta, traffic is a King Air, at your one o'clock
and eight miles, west bound, at 5,000."

You check one o'clock in your windscreen and see a dark dot
traveling east to west. Your reply is, "Cessna 9130 Delta, traffic
in sight."

A little while later, you hear, "Cessna 9130 Delta, traffic ten to eleven o'clock and six miles, squawking VFR. Mode C indicates 3,500 unverified." This type of radio call indicates the air traffic controller has a VFR aircraft displaying on his screen, but he is not talking to the pilot of that aircraft. That's why the altitude readout on his screen is unverified.

You check 10 to 11 o'clock and see nothing. You answer, "Cessna 9130 Delta, searching."

Less than a minute later, you hear, "Cessna 9130 Delta, previously reported traffic now your eleven o'clock and 4 miles, opposite direction. Mode C still indicates 3,500 unverified." You don't see anything, so you say, "Cessna 9130 Delta, still searching."

It's a Good Suggestion

"Cessna 9130 Delta, for traffic avoidance, suggest a right turn, heading of three zero zero." You are VFR, so the controller can only make suggestions. You can either follow his suggestion and turn, or you may decide to change altitude. The controller told you the other airplane's altitude, but advised you the readout he saw on his screen was unverified. The airplane coming at you may be above or below the altitude showing on the controller's radar display.

Following the controller's recommendation is usually a good idea, unless you have a very compelling reason to do something other than what the controller suggests. Examples of reasons to not follow a controller's recommendation:

- Following his directions might cause you to fly into clouds while under VFR. In that case an altitude change or turn in another direction might accomplish your goal of avoiding traffic without violating visual flight rules.

- If the controller suggests a climb which would place your aircraft above its maximum operating altitude, you should not climb.

- If the controller suggests a climb and that climb will put you at an altitude where supplementary oxygen is required when you don't have oxygen, you should not climb.

- The controller will never suggest a descent to an altitude that puts you in conflict with terrain, but if his suggestion compromises your comfort level, don't go there.

When suggesting a move to avoid traffic, an air traffic controller will almost always recommend a heading to fly. If you can't think of a reason to turn, don't waste a lot of time debating the issue. Turn and avoid the traffic. If you cannot follow the controller's direction, let him know what you are going to do instead.

As the traffic passes by, the controller will tell you where to spot the traffic--above, below, or to your left or right, along with, "Traffic no factor." At that point, secure your ship from general quarters and continue on your merry way. It's as simple as that.

An air traffic controller might also give you a suggested heading to avoid certain types of airspace. For example, even though you are allowed to enter an active military operating area (MOA) while VFR, it's a lousy idea to do so. A MOA, when active, usually has high-performance military aircraft operating throughout the airspace. When I say "throughout," I really mean throughout. An F-16 operating in the MOA can be cruising just under Mach 1 at 500 feet above the ground and in just a few seconds, zoom to well over 10,000.

With military aircraft zorching around a MOA seeing and avoiding traffic inside the MOA might not be possible. That's why ATC will strongly discourage you from going in there. The controller will give you a heading to avoid the MOA and suggest alternate routing around it.

I've actually heard a VFR pilot argue with a controller about cutting through an active MOA. The pilot wanted to cut through to save flying distance. The controller ultimately talked him out of it. You might think, "That's an example of a good reason to avoid talking to ATC." In truth, ATC may have saved the life of that pilot and the life of a military pilot flying in the MOA.

Don't think ATC discriminates against pilots who fly VFR. I have heard an air traffic controller really stomp on a military pilot who strayed outside the boundaries of MOA. It sounded like this:

ATC: "Gunslinger 21, work south immediately! You need to stay inside your working area." I couldn't hear the fighter pilot's reply because the pilot was transmitting on a UHF radio. (Most ATC enroute controllers transmit simultaneously on a VHF channel for civilian traffic, and a corresponding UHF channel for military traffic.)

I can surmise what the fighter pilot said in reply because this is how the air traffic controller answered: "You were out of the area a few seconds ago. Don't try to tell me you weren't out of your area. If you bust the boundary again, I'm sending you home. Do we understand each other?"

A controller can also help you avoid flying accidentally into Temporary Flight Restriction (TFR) areas, active warning areas, restricted airspace, or prohibited airspace. If your flight path looks like it will take you into one of these areas, ATC will give you a heading to avoid the airspace. Again, this is a good thing. Flying under VFR does not give you the right to enter TFRs, active warning areas, restricted areas, or prohibited areas. You are expected to avoid these areas on your own, but ATC will help you out if you need a vector to avoid airspace.

Don't Even Go There

By the way, if you ever accidentally approach or blunder into airspace you are not supposed to be in, you are going to hear about it on the emergency frequency 121.5. The military unit responsible for guarding that airspace will make a broadcast announcing the impending violation. You will hear the military controller give a report on your position, heading, approximate speed, and altitude, if your transponder's Mode C is operating. You will then hear instructions to fly an avoidance heading immediately. If you ever hear a radio call like this on 121.5, and you believe they are talking about you, follow the avoidance heading like your life depended on it.

If the warning on the radio is about you, and you fail to avoid the airspace you've been warned about, you may be intercepted by fighter aircraft. If you blunder into a prohibited area, you might be intercepted by a surface-to-air missile. If the prohibited airspace surrounds a high-value asset, such as a presidential residence or other important government building, I'm betting on missiles.

This brings up 2 important points. Even if you are reluctant to fly VFR under ATC's watch, I'd strongly recommend overcoming your reluctance before flying near restricted and prohibited airspace. Get ATC on your team before you start navigating your way around, say, the White House or the Pentagon. If, despite my urging, you decide to go it alone, be sure to keep one of your radios tuned to 121.5. If you hear something along the lines of: "This is the United States Air Force on Guard. Aircraft 7 northwest of the DCA VOR heading one one zero, approximate speed one hundred and ten knots, altitude unknown. You are approaching a prohibited area. Turn to a heading of three one zero immediately and contact Potomac Approach on one two seven point three," get the hell out of there! Even if you aren't sure they are talking about you, GET THE HELL OUT OF THERE!

Avoiding Cumulo-granite

ATC can also make other safety calls when working with you under flight following. The controller can point out terrain and obstacles on the ground that your flight path might cross. If either terrain or obstacles become a factor, the controller will issue a safety alert. A safety alert contains a warning about possible danger ahead. ATC usually adds a suggested heading and/or altitude change to avoid the danger. It's a good idea to follow that suggestion, especially if you do not have the terrain or obstacle in sight.

Handoff

As you continue VFR, clear of obstacles, restricted airspace, and conflicting traffic, you may reach the boundary of an air traffic controller's sector. Several miles before the radar target for your aircraft reaches the boundary of the controller's area of responsibility, the symbol and data block for your aircraft will begin to flash on his display. (This change is initiated automatically by ATC's computer system.) The letter H, meaning handoff, along with the next sector's I.D. number will appear in your aircraft's radar data block. Your aircraft's radar target will also appear as a flashing symbol on the radar display of the air traffic controller in the adjacent sector into which your airplane is heading. (See the example of a radar datablock for handoff below.)

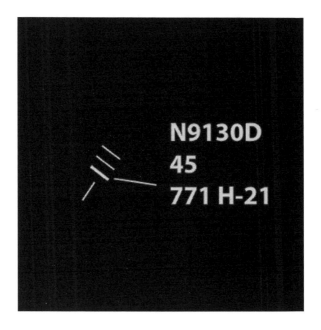

Aircraft N9130D, at 4,500 feet MSL, with computer I.D. 771, is being handed off to the controller working Sector 21 of an air route traffic control center (ARTCC).

The controller in the next sector will take his display cursor and click on your aircraft's flashing symbol. The letter H will change to a O, meaning the handoff was accepted by the next controller. The controller you are currently talking to will see the change in symbology and know the next controller is ready to accept your aircraft. Your current controller will then say to you, "Cessna 9130 Delta, for further flight following, contact

Atlanta Center on one three three point zero. Have a good day."

"Cessna 9130 Delta, one three three point zero. Good day."
You tune 133.0 into Comm Radio 1 and flip the new frequency
to the active window of the radio. You key the transmit button,
remembering this radio call is an initial radio contact while in
radar contact.

You say, "Atlanta Center, Cessna 9130 Delta, three thousand
five hundred, VFR."

The controller answers, "Cessna 9130 Delta, Atlanta Center,
three thousand five hundred. Call me with any altitude
changes."

"Cessna 9130 Delta."

From this point, nothing about your VFR flight changes. Do
what you want. You may even fly back to the previous sector's
airspace. In that case, your flight will get handed back to the
first controller you talked to.

Don't be surprised if you return to the first controller's sector
and find you are talking to a different person. All ATC agencies
give their controllers periodic breaks from their controlling
positions. The duration of on-duty and rest periods depend on
the facility, the type of controlling duty, and the time of day.

There will inevitably be times when, as you move from one
enroute sector to the next, your current controller will give you
an incorrect frequency for the next sector, or you will
misunderstand the frequency. When you switch to the new,
incorrect frequency, you will either fail to make contact with the
next sector's controller or you will make contact with the wrong
sector's controller. Don't worry, it happens.

When you do end up on the wrong frequency, simply return
to your original frequency and ask your former controller for
clarification. The controller will restate the new frequency. You
will make the switch, and you are on your way like nothing
happened.

Sometimes, when you switch frequencies to a new controller,
the controller might not answer you right away. Give it 30
seconds or so, and then try again. The controller on the new
frequency was probably offline to take care of coordination
with a controller in another sector. Most controllers try to keep
one ear open to the radio as they work another task on the side,

such as talking on the landline. Sometimes, they are so involved in a side task, they might miss your radio call when you check in.

As I said, just give the controller a chance to come back on line. If, after a while, the controller does not say, "Aircraft calling center, say again," make another attempt to check in. The second attempt usually works. This is all just part of doing business with ATC, so don't get frustrated and lose your cool on the radio. Patience on the radio always produces the best results.

There are also cases where an air traffic controller might be working 2 different sectors on 2 different radio frequencies. The controller transmits simultaneously on both frequencies, but you can only hear other pilots on your frequency. You cannot hear the radio calls from pilots on the other frequency. When you attempt to check in with the controller, he may also be listening to a pilot who is transmitting on the controller's other frequency. For this reason, he may ignore your radio call and it won't be immediately apparent why he did that. He may also say "Two aircraft calling at once. Piper 275 Charlie Bravo, was that you checking in at 7,000?" When he says that, give it a few seconds for the other pilot to complete his check in, even though you can't hear him. When that transaction is complete, you may hear, "Other aircraft calling Center, say again." That's your cue to check in.

Time to Head Back to the Corral

Let's say, today all your radio check-ins went smoothly. Now, you are ready to return to the home drome. You may retain VFR flight following all the way to the airport if you desire. Even though you can fly where you want without intervention from ATC, a little help from ATC is always available, if you need it.

For example. Let's say you would like to fly the most direct route back to the Atlanta Town and Country Airport. You decide the best way to do this is to tune in the Town and Country VORTAC, located at the center of the airport. When you tune in the VORTAC, you see an orange "Off" flag pop into view next to the course needle on your VOR indicator. You also see the DME indicator shows nothing but dashes in the indicator window. The VORTAC is a low altitude navaid, and you have probably flown out of range of its signal. ATC can help.

You: "Cessna 9130 Delta requests a heading direct to the Town and Country VORTAC."

Controller: "Cessna 9130 Delta, fly heading one five zero. When able, proceed direct Town and Country," Atlanta Center says.

That heading should work very well. It not only gives you a heading to fly, it is usually a wind-corrected course.

If the air traffic controller has data on the winds aloft, he will plug that into his radar's computer system and give you a wind-corrected heading to fly. Sometimes ATC will input forecast winds aloft into the system. If the forecast winds are old or not available, he may ask you or a nearby aircraft to "Say your heading." He will compare your reported heading to the actual track your radar target is making over the ground and calculate the drift angle, or crab, for that heading.

For example, if you tell the controller you are flying 180 degrees, and the controller sees your track over the ground is 190 degrees, he knows there is a wind component from the right that pushes your aircraft on a track 10 degrees to the right of your heading. He will use this information to build a wind-corrected heading for your desired course. If your current heading is nowhere near what you will need to fly direct to a point, the controller might ask another pilot for his heading if that pilot's heading is more aligned with the course you will need to fly.

Note in his instructions, the controller said, "When able, fly direct Town and Country." That means, when you have a reliable navigation signal from the VORTAC, feel free to abandon his suggested heading and fly whatever you need to proceed direct to the VORTAC.

Let's reverse the situation. Let's say ATC gave you a heading to proceed direct to the Town and Country VORTAC. You see there is a rain shower between you and the airport, which you shouldn't fly through. Under VFR, you may do whatever is necessary to maintain VFR, including deviating as necessary. Since you are not tied to assigned headings by ATC under VFR, you would simply advise the controller of your intentions. This arrangement is also in force in all controlled airspace when you are flying VFR. Even in closely-controlled Class B airspace, you are required to deviate from the controller's instructions as necessary to maintain VFR. Always advise the controller of your deviations.

That said, many controllers think in terms of positive control, meaning they call the shots on where airplanes fly. When you tell the controller what you plan to do, the controller may say, "Approved as requested." This means, "Everything you asked for is okay with me." This type of coordination is important. Your plan to deviate may keep your airplane VFR, but it may put you in conflict with another airplane. ATC might follow up with alternate directions to keep you VFR and avoid other airplanes. Keep ATC in the information loop, no matter the circumstances.

You Deviant

Let's clarify the subject of deviations for airspace in which your airplane is under positive control. If you were operating in Class D airspace, under positive control by an airport's tower controller, you must get approval to deviate from the controller's last instructions. For example, let's say Tower told you, "Make left closed traffic." You decide, for whatever reason, you would like to fly a right-hand traffic pattern. You must request approval to fly your pattern to the right because your last clearance was for a left-hand pattern.

You say, "Cessna 9130 Delta, requests right traffic."

Tower answers, "Cessna 9130 Delta, approved as requested." (It is more likely the controller will say, "Right closed traffic approved," but "approved as requested" means the same thing in this context.)

Usually, when you make a specific request, an air traffic controller will approve your request with specific instructions: "Cessna 9130 Delta, right traffic approved." Occasionally, when your request has multiple parts, and the radio is very busy, the controller might simply summarize by saying, "Approved as requested," rather than repeat your multi-part request. Either way, the operative word is "Approved." Make sure you get it before deviating from an ATC clearance in positively controlled airspace.

Almost There

Right now, you are not enroute to Class D airspace. You are approaching an uncontrolled airport. It's time to start thinking about your arrival. While maintaining flight following with Atlanta Center, you can dial in the UNICOM for Atlanta Town and County Airport on Comm Radio 2 and call for an updated airport advisory.

Ten miles from the airport traffic pattern, you can say to Atlanta Center, "Cessna 9130 Delta would like to terminate flight following." The reply will be, "Cessna 9130 Delta, radar service terminated. Squawk one two zero zero and frequency change approved." You may acknowledge this call with your call sign only. There's no need to repeat the squawk since squawking VFR is pilot simple. All that remains is to switch over to the UNICOM frequency for KATC into Comm Radio 1. You may then make your self-announce radio calls in the airport traffic pattern, just as you did earlier.

That's all there is to VFR flight following with ATC. Getting in touch with ATC for traffic advisories is a simple process. It won't cramp your flying style, and it enhances safety. You can use ATC's radar to your advantage when you need course guidance. Any course changes given by ATC are suggestions you may follow at your own discretion. Air traffic control can also be a life-saving resource when you find yourself in the middle of an emergency or when you are disoriented. You may terminate VFR flight following at any time with one simple radio call. There's really no reason not to contact ATC when traveling VFR; and there are many advantages to giving them a call.

News flash: The Georgia Department of Transportation has just approved the funds to expand the Atlanta Town and Country Airport. (It was an easy decision for the politicians because the airport doesn't actually exist.)

The expansion of the airport will include the construction of an air traffic control tower; lengthening Runway 18/36 so it is suitable for use by business jets, and the installation of an instrument landing systems (ILS) for Runways 18 and 36. Additionally, there are plans to add taxiways to the airport and install lighted taxiway signs.

All this construction will take about a year, so do me a favor. Please put this book away for a year and come back when the airport additions are finished. If you can't afford to wait a year, I've got another idea. Let's run through some other topics in the next chapter, and maybe the airport will be finished by then. (I'm betting it will be done, because guess who controls the passage of time in this book.)

Take Action

Try these exercises that cover initial contact with ATC. For all of these exercises, your callsign will be Cessna 9130 Delta. Write your answers on a piece of paper. The correct answers are on the last page of this chapter.

You are 25 miles northwest of the Knoxville VORTAC at 5,500, heading 170-degrees. You are enroute to Clemson, South Carolina and you would like to pick up VFR flight following with Memphis Center. What would you say in your initial radio call to Memphis Center?

You are 10 miles south of the Lebanon Airport in New Hampshire at 2,500, VFR. You would like to overfly the airport (commonly called "the transition"), enroute to the north. What would be your initial radio call to Lebanon Tower?

You have been practicing stalls in uncontrolled airspace 30 miles east of the airport at Scotts Bluff, Nebraska. As you level off at 3,500, you smell oily smoke in the cockpit and see dark gray smoke streaming out of the engine compartment your aircraft. The engine also sounds like it is running rough. After you run through the appropriate checklist to address the problem, nothing changes. The engine is still running rough and the smoke is still coming out of the engine compartment. Although you had not been in contact with ATC, you decide you should contact ATC now and declare an emergency. Your intent is to get assistance and priority handling from ATC as you make your way back to Scotts Bluff. What would be your initial radio call to Denver Center, the facility covering your area?

You have been talking to Oakland Center while under VFR following. Your position is 30 miles southeast of the Modesto VORTAC at 5,500. You are enroute to Fresno. The controller at Oakland Center says, "Cessna 9130 Delta, for further flight following, contact Oakland Center on 125.35." You acknowledge this frequency change and tune in the new frequency. What would you say to the new controller when you check in on the radio?

You are flying VFR over Brownsville, Texas at 8,500, heading south. You have been talking to Houston Center for flight following. Houston Center has also coordinated with Monterrey Center to expect your arrival into Mexico. As you approach the Mexican border, Houston Center says, "Cessna 9130 Delta, radar service terminated. For further flight following, contact Monterrey Center on 128.4." You acknowledge this radio call and note your present position is on the Matamoros VOR-DME 005-degree radial for 15 DME. What would you say to make initial contact with Monterrey Center?

Answers:

"Memphis Center, Cessna 9130 Delta, two five miles northwest of Knoxville at five thousand five hundred, VFR."

"Lebanon Tower, Cessna 9130 Delta, ten south of the airport at two thousand five hundred for the transition (or, for overflight)."

"Denver Center, Cessna 9130 Delta, three zero miles east of Scotts Bluff at three thousand five hundred, declaring an emergency."

"Oakland Center, Cessna 9130 Delta, five thousand five hundred."

"Monterrey Center, Cessna 9130 Delta, one five miles north of Matamoros at 8,500, VFR."

Explanation:

Answers 1, 2 and 3 all use the standard format for initial contact of You, Me, Where, What. Answer 3 seems incomplete, considering the complexity of your emergency. Do remember, when making initial contact, you want to keep your radio call relevant, but brief. You can get into the particulars of your emergency after initial contact.

For Answer 4, you do not need to include What. You have been handed off from one controller to the next controller. The new controller already knows the What because of the handoff process.

In Answer 5, you are making initial contact with the next controller because the last controller informed you, "Radar service terminated." You are starting over with ATC in Mexico. Even though the controller at Monterrey Center is expecting you, he must verify basic information about your flight through the process of initial contact on the radio. Even though this question involved a border crossing between 2 countries, you would be obligated to make initial contact with the next controller whenever radar service is terminated, no matter where you are flying.

Chapter 8: Switchology

Have you ever been flipped off?

I have. It happens many times a day on the aircraft radio. Here's how it typically happens. A pilot tunes a new radio frequency into the standby window of his radio. With the new frequency set in standby, the pilot hits the radio's transfer switch, flipping the frequency from the standby window to the active window.

So far, so good.

As soon as the new frequency moves into the active window, the pilot immediately presses his microphone switch and starts talking: "Blah blah blah."

Here's the problem with flipping and talking. If some other pilot was already talking on the new frequency when our pilot flips and immediately starts talking, he is going to jam the radio. Here's what that will sound like:

"L.A. Cent-skreeeeeeeeeeeeeeeeeeeeeeeeeeeeeeeeeeeeeee-sand."

Here's the next thing you will hear on the radio. In the most acid, sarcastic tone of voice you can imagine:

"Blaaaaahkt."

The radio call, "Blocked," means one pilot transmitted on top of another pilot's transmission, canceling out both transmissions. In case you are keeping score, that means 2 pilots tried to talk, 1 air traffic controller tried to listen, and, at the bottom of the eighth inning, with no hits, no runs, and one error, the score is all tied up at zero to zero. Nobody heard anything except a bunch of noise on the radio.

There was a phrase I learned when I was growing up. Maybe you have heard this too. "Stop, look, and listen before you cross the street." The point of this lesson to children is, don't step out into traffic because they might get hit by a passing car they did not notice.

The same thing can be said when you flip to a new frequency on the radio. Stop, look and listen for radio traffic before you step into the frequency. If you don't, your ill-timed radio call might just get hit by other radio traffic.

Stop

And think about what you are about to do. Think about what you want to say before you say it, and consider if now is a good time to say it.

Look

And make sure the radio frequency you want is in the active window. (More on this a little later.)

Listen

For other pilots talking on the radio so you won't cut them off with your own transmission. This takes some skill. You have to know something about air traffic control to understand when a conversation is over between a pilot and an air traffic controller.

Even if you don't know all of the ins and outs of the ATC language, you can follow a simple rule to recognize when it's okay to jump on the radio. When another pilot is talking to ATC, listen for the transmission that confirms the information that is passed from one person to the other. Examples:

Example 1:

Pilot: "Astra 347 Lima Mike, at 7,000."

ATC's confirmation: "Astra 347 Lima Mike, Washington Center. 7,000."

It's okay to make your radio call here.

Example 2:

ATC: "Piper 502 Echo Kilo, turn right, heading one seven zero."

Pilot's confirmation: "Piper 502 Echo Kilo, right, heading one seven zero."

It's okay to make your radio call here.

Example 3:

Pilot: "Baltimore Ground, Twin Cessna 2240 Tango, ready to taxi with information Alpha."

ATC: "Twin Cessna 2240 Tango, Runway 15 Left via taxiways Double-Alpha, Sierra, and Juliett."

Pilot's confirmation: "Runway 15 Left, Double-Alpha, Sierra, Juliett, Twin Cessna 2240 Tango."

It's okay to make your radio call here.

Simple enough? Not so fast. It can get more complicated, and even a little frustrating. Here's what I mean.

Pilot in another airplane: "Peachtree Ground, Falcon 4892 Romeo, taxi from the north ramp with information Golf."

There is no answer from Peachtree Ground Control. Should you jump in here with your own radio call? Etiquette says no. Give Ground Control time to answer the other pilot. But, while you are waiting, this happens:

Pilot in a different airplane: "Peachtree Ground, Cessna 352 Uniform Hotel, clear of runway Two Zero Right. Taxi to the northwest ramp."

Ground Control: "Cessna 352 Uniform Hotel, Peachtree Ground. Taxi to the north ramp via Alpha and Bravo. Cross Runway 9."

Pilot confirmation: "Cessna 352 Uniform Hotel, Alpha, Bravo and cleared to cross Runway 9." Should you jump in with your radio call now?

First Pilot: "And Peachtree Ground, Falcon 4892 Romeo, taxi from the north ramp with Golf." I guess not.

Ground Control: "Falcon 4892 Romeo, Runway Two Zero Left via Hotel and Alpha."

First Pilot's confirmation: "Runway 20 Left. Hotel. Alpha. Falcon 4892 Romeo." Okay, now Studley. Make your radio *now*, before someone else jumps in.

This type of confusion happens all of the time, especially at busy airports. Many pilots don't have the patience to wait for a controller to reply to another pilot. Radio transmissions hate a vacuum. If the radio frequency is open for more than a second or two, someone is going to fill the vacuum with a transmission, even it is ill-timed or inappropriate. The trick is to be patient and not fall into the trap other pilots fall into.

The Party Line

There has to be a better way to organize communication on the radio. Fortunately or unfortunately, depending on how you look at it, with texting common among cell phone users, radio communication between ATC and pilots should be growing obsolete. Progress moves slowly in aviation, so we will be stuck with voice communication by radio for awhile. With the radio being a party line where anyone can key a microphone and speak at any time, blocked radio transmissions and overlapping conversations are going to continue until voice communication with ATC is replaced by texting.

By the way, ATC is progressing towards giving airplane directions by text. Some airliners that are outfitted for ocean crossings have equipment that allows pilots to communicate with ATC by text. The texting procedure replaces the use of high frequency (HF) radios to communicate with air traffic control.

HF radios can transmit and receive over the very long distances encountered when airliners fly across oceans. HF transmissions are usually accompanied by a lot of static and poor sound quality, making communication difficult at times. Texting with ATC bypasses the limitations of HF. Texting does have its own limitation, however. It takes much longer to type a sentence than it does to say the same sentence. In time-critical situations, where a quick exchange of information between a pilot and ATC is essential, texting is too slow. Texting does sidestep the problem of one pilot stepping on the radio call of another pilot.

On Guard

Even if you work out all of the kinks in your radio technique so you don't step on other pilots' radio calls, it's still possible to talk on the wrong radio at the wrong time. Listen to this radio exchange to see what I mean:

Pilot: "Fremont traffic, Cessna 4827 Echo, entering downwind, Runway 17, touch-and-go, Fremont."

Some Wise Guy on 121.5: "You're on Guard, dude."

Pilot: "Fremont traffic, Cessna 4827 Echo, left base, Runway 17, touch-and-go, Fremont."

Some Other Concerned Pilot on 121.5: "You're transmitting on Guard!"

Pilot: "Fremont traffic, Cessna 4827 Echo, final, Runway 17, touch-and-go, Fremont."

Denver Center Controller on 121.5: "Cessna 27 Echo, if you read this transmission, be advised you are transmitting on 121.5. Check your switches."

I hear transmissions like this every once in a while on transcontinental flights.

Pilots flying aircraft with more than one voice transceiver generally use the secondary communication radio to monitor the emergency frequency, 121.5. The reason is, due to the high (terrorist) threat level associated with aircraft, pilots must listen for warnings from ground-based defense agencies, although that's not the reason the AIM wants you to monitor Guard. Here's why the AIM says you should monitor Guard:

6–2–5. Emergency Locator Transmitter (ELT)

d. Inflight Monitoring and Reporting
Pilots are encouraged to monitor 121.5 MHz and/or
243.0 MHz while inflight to assist in identifying
possible emergency ELT transmissions.

ELTs are slowly being replaced in cockpits by Emergency
Position Indicating Radio Beacon units (EPIRB). An EPIRB is an
emergency radio beacon that transmits on the 406 Mhz distress
frequency. The transmission is picked up by a satellite called
COSPAS-SARSAT that is dedicated to geo-locating the source of
a distress signal. EPIRBs do not transmit on a frequency that
can be received by standard aviation radios. Since there are
many ELTs still in use, the recommendation to monitor 121.5
remains in the AIM.

Additionally, the AIM says you should maintain a listening
watch on 121.5, if able, in case your aircraft is intercepted by
fighter aircraft. This is the frequency that will be used to
communicate if your airplane is intercepted. We won't go into
the reasons why you might be intercepted. If an F-16 shows up
on your left wing, it might be a good idea to have a
communication channel open to talk to the pilot of that F-16.

The problem with managing two radio frequencies at the
same time is, it's easy to mess up the radio control switches and
transmit on the wrong radio. How might that happen?

Let's say you have been talking on Radio Number 1 to some
agency--Approach, Center, UNICOM, etc. As you are flying
along in flight, you decide to give a flight service station (FSS) a
call to get a weather update.

You want to keep monitoring Radio 1, so you smartly decide
to continue listening to Radio 1, but use Radio 2 to talk to FSS.

You tune the local FSS frequency into the "Standby" window
of Radio Number 2, and hit the flip-flop switch to move the FSS
frequency into the radio's "Active" window. The Guard
frequency, 121.5, in Radio 2 moves to the "Standby" window.

You check the "listen" button for Radio 1 is on so you can
continue to monitor Radio 1 for calls to your flight. Finally, you
rotate the transmit dial on the Comm Control Panel to "Comm
2." You're ready to call FSS on Radio 2, and listen to Radio 1 in

case anyone calls you.

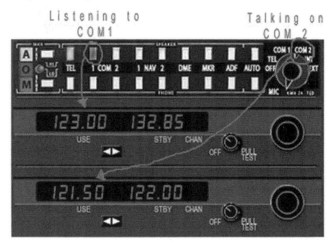

Here is the formula for unintentionally transmitting on Guard: Speaker switch set to Radio 1 (123.00) and Transmit Selector set to Radio 2 (121.5).

When you finish your conversation with the FSS specialist, you smartly hit the flip-flop switch in Radio 2, moving 121.5 back into the "Active" window. Just then, you hear: "Fremont traffic, Cardinal 217 Sierra Foxtrot, departing Runway 17, straight out." Time to get with the program and make your next call: "Fremont Traffic, Cessna 4827 Echo is 15 miles west of the airport, inbound for touch-and-go." There's no reply, but that's okay. You didn't expect any.

You're transmitting on Guard . . . dude. I'll refer you back to the reminder, "Stop, look, and listen before transmitting." Pay particular attention to "look." Make sure you have the communication radios tuned, and the communication panel switches set so you end up talking and listening on the correct frequencies for your situation. As a technique, I talk to myself as I review the radio switch positions:

1.   I want to talk on Radio 1.

2.   I want to listen to Radio 1 and Radio 2.

3. I have the transmit dial set to Radio 1.

4. I have the headphone listen buttons for Radio 1 and
    Radio 2 pushed in.

Talk yourself through your radio setup each time you
prepare the radios before flight and each time you change the
radio setup in flight. This technique takes a degree of self-
discipline to follow every time, but it will keep you out of
trouble.

Guess what. While we have been flapping our jaws about
radio technique, the contractors have finished construction of
the airport expansion at Atlanta Town and Country Airport.
Yes, I know it has not been a full year since you finished the last
chapter of this book. It just seems that way.

Grab the keys to the family aerospace wagon and prepare to
launch aircraft from the new and improved airport everyone
calls Town and Country. I'll see you there. By the way, I know
I've been sandbagging a lot of flying time in your airplane. I'll
make it up to you somehow before this book closes.

Take Action

Your goal in this exercise is to develop a feel for timing your
radio calls on a busy frequency so they don't interfere with
other conversations.

Find a very busy airport and tune in your handheld radio to
the airport's ground control frequency. If you don't have a
handheld radio, you can access live ATC transmissions on some
websites on the internet. For example, at the time of publishing
this book, there is a dedicated website that accesses ATC
frequencies for the Atlanta Hartsfield-Jackson International
Airport. If you pick online access, be sure to choose a website
that has the option to play only the ground control frequency,
as opposed to one that scans several frequencies at once.

Listen to the ground frequency and try to find gaps in the
conversation between the ground controller and pilots on that
frequency. Concentrate on when you would key the
microphone to make your initial call to the ground controller.

Chapter 9: An Exercise For Pilots Who Suffer Brain Lock Whenever They Press the Push-to-Talk Switch

When a pilot becomes task saturated, his/her mental bucket is full. Once that mental bucket fills up, the bucket will not hold even one extra drop of input. This may explain why task-saturated pilots tune out, or fail to understand radio calls from air traffic control.

When first learning to fly, student pilots can easily become task-saturated by basic aircraft maneuvers. In the early stages of training, before a student pilot begins to develop a bit of muscle memory, aircraft control requires total concentration.

Most instructor pilots realize a student pilot, focused solely on aircraft control, is task-saturated. At that point, as a survival mechanism, the student pilot's brain will filter all other stimuli not directly related to aircraft control. Students will not hear the radio, and they may not hear directions from the instructor. This is a completely natural mechanism. Prodding the student will not help, and may even add to task-saturation.

There are two takeaways from this:

In the early stages of training, instructor pilots should not be expect students to hear and digest every radio call that comes in.

If you are a student pilot, don't sweat missing or misunderstanding ATC during the early stages of training. Basic aircraft control will require less and less mental strain as your training progresses. As your brain spends less time planning and processing your next move on the controls, it will become more receptive to stimuli not directly related to aircraft control. Over time, your ability to see more, and to hear more will improve as you fly.

Fortunately, I have a strategy for you, if you have difficulty flying and talking at the same time. This method works for student pilots or certified pilots who have not come to grips with the fast-paced world of ATC communication. The method targets radio communication in an airport traffic pattern.

Most pilots get their first exposure to fast-paced, dynamic communication in an airport traffic pattern. If an airport pattern is busy with many aircraft, ATC is likely to fire off clearances at a high rate. A controller might also have to improvise a bit to keep aircraft in a busy pattern separated and flowing smoothly. When a tower controller is really cranking out the instructions over the radio, there is a threshold for what an inexperienced pilot can handle.

I'm am going to teach you how to nudge that threshold a little further past what you are able to handle right now. If you can handle very little right now, the method I am going to suggest will help you cope with clearances delivered in a moderately busy airport pattern. If you can already handle a moderate pace, this method will amp up your radio skill so you can comprehend a controller who is firing off instructions like there is no tomorrow.

I wish I could say this method is entirely my idea. It isn't. It's adapted from a technique we used in the U.S. Air Force when teaching new pilots how to fly. Please read through the instructions below, all the way to the end, before setting up this exercise.

What you will need to prepare:

1. A fairly large, unobstructed area to walk around in. As a minimum, find a space at least 3 meters wide by 4 meters long (approximately 10 feet by 14 feet). Again, this should be empty, open floor space. If you cannot find an indoor space that meets these requirements, use an empty area of backyard or a driveway.

2. A roll of opaque tape, such as masking tape. The tape will be stuck to the floor of your walking area. If you prefer not to stick tape on the floor, you may use card stock, paper plates, or anything else that's unbreakable to mark spots on the floor. If you use an outdoor concrete surface for your walkable area, you may mark the pavement with a chalk stick instead of tape.

3. Seven pieces of card stock or 7 large index cards.

4. A felt marking pen, preferably black.

The Setup:

You are going to lay out a bird's eye view of an airport traffic pattern within the boundaries of your walking area. You will use the tape, or another marking device, to mark key spots within the traffic pattern.

To begin, mark your runway on one long side of the walking area. Set the runway up so it parallels the long side and covers about 1 meter, centered on the midpoint of the long side. You will mark the takeoff position of the runway, and the departure end of the runway. (See the illustration of the example.)

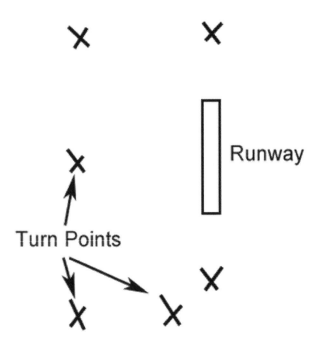

1. Next, mark the point off the extended runway centerline where you would begin a turn to crosswind.

2. Mark the turning point where you would turn from crosswind to downwind.

3. Mark the point at midfield on the downwind leg.

4. Mark the point where you would turn from downwind to base leg.

5. Mark the point where you would turn from base leg to final approach.

6. Mark the point where you would roll your airplane out of a turn onto final approach.

With all of your points marked, it's time to create a list of ATC clearances you might receive at each point in the pattern. Begin by labeling each of your index cards with the following titles:

1. Takeoff

2. Turn to Crosswind

3. Turn to Downwind

4. Midfield Downwind

5. Turn to Base

6. Turn to Final

7. Final Approach

You will be writing almost every possible ATC clearance for each position in the traffic pattern on the cards, so plan your paper size and writing size accordingly. I suggest looking at the list below to help you plan your layout. For this exercise, we'll use Runway 28 as an example. You should substitute the runway label for the runway you use most often at your home airport. I'll also use the abbreviated aircraft call sign Cessna 30 Delta. You should substitute an aircraft call sign you use most often. If you don't feel like writing your aircraft call sign 50 times, leave it off of the card, and remember to speak it during the exercise. This will make more sense as you read through the rest of the instructions.

Where you see brackets [ ] in the lists below, insert whatever information you would like. For example, if the brackets contain [aircraft type] you might insert "PA-28." For aircraft position in bracket, you may insert, for example, "at your one o'clock, slightly low," or "on a 2 mile final." Use your imagination.

Here's what to write for each card, by airport position:

1. Takeoff
Cessna 30 Delta, Runway 28, line up and wait.

Cessna 30 Delta, continue holding in position, traffic crossing downfield.

Cessna 30 Delta, back taxi on Runway 28. Line up and wait.* (Outside of the U.S., substitute the phrase "back track" for "back taxi.")

Cessna 30 Delta, Runway 28, cleared for takeoff.

Cessna 30 Delta, make left/right (closed) traffic. Runway 28, cleared for takeoff.

Cessna 30 Delta, report a left/right downwind. Runway 28, cleared for takeoff.

Cessna 30 Delta, depart straight out, Runway 28, cleared for takeoff.

Cessna 30 Delta, fly runway heading, (or, fly heading [degrees]). Runway 28, cleared for takeoff.

Cessna 30 Delta, left/right turn out approved. Runway 28, cleared for takeoff.

2.   Turn to Crosswind

(There may be no ATC clearance at this position if a departure clearance was given with the takeoff clearance.)

Cessna 30 Delta, continue on the takeoff leg. I'll call your turn to crosswind.

Cessna 30 Delta, start your turn to crosswind _____ miles off the departure end.

Cessna 30 Delta, continue on the departure leg. I'll call your turn.

Cessna 30 Delta, left/right turnout approved.

Cessna 30 Delta, cleared to depart to the [direction of flight, such as southwest].

Cessna 30 Delta, traffic is a [aircraft type] at your _____ o'clock. Report him in sight.

Cessna 30 Delta, report a midfield (left/right) downwind.

3. Turn to Downwind

(There may be no ATC clearance at this position if a departure clearance was given with the takeoff clearance.)

Cessna 30 Delta, traffic is a [aircraft type] at your _____ o'clock, entering the downwind. Report him in sight.

Cessna 30 Delta, report turning base. (Or, "report base.")

4. Midfield Downwind

Cessna 30 Delta, cleared touch-and-go.

Cessna 30 Delta, cleared stop-and-go.

Cessna 30 Delta, cleared low approach.

Cessna 30 Delta, cleared for the option.

Cessna 30 Delta, make a left/right 360. (Possible addition: Report re-entering the downwind.)

Cessna 30 Delta, begin slowing. You're following a [aircraft type], [aircraft position.] Report the traffic in sight.

Cessna 30 Delta, continue on the downwind. I'll call your base. (Tower might add an advisory on traffic you are are following with aircraft type and position.)

Cessna 30 Delta, number 2 (or number 3.) Traffic you're following is a [aircraft type] [aircraft position.] Report that traffic in sight.

Cessna 30 Delta, number 2 following a [aircraft type] [aircraft position]. Runway 28, cleared to land.

Cessna 30 Delta, report base.

Cessna 30 Delta, Runway 28, cleared to land.

Cessna 30 Delta, make short approach. Runway 28, cleared to land. Traffic is a [aircraft type] [aircraft position.]

5. Turning Base

(If not cleared for any of these options on downwind, you may receive these clearances on base leg.)

Cessna 30 Delta, cleared touch-and-go.

Cessna 30 Delta, cleared stop-and-go.

Cessna 30 Delta, cleared low approach.

Cessna 30 Delta, cleared for the option.

Cessna 30 Delta, cleared to land.

6. Turning Final

(If not cleared for any of these options on base, you may receive these clearances as you turn toward final approach.)

Cessna 30 Delta, cleared touch-and-go.

Cessna 30 Delta, cleared stop-and-go.

Cessna 30 Delta, cleared low approach.

Cessna 30 Delta, cleared for the option.

Cessna 30 Delta, cleared to land.

Cessna 30 Delta, continue. Traffic is [aircraft type] [traffic position].

7. Final Approach

(If no landing clearance was given prior to final approach, you will receive clearance at this point. Otherwise, unless told to go around, you will not receive further clearance from tower.)

Cessna 30 Delta, cleared touch-and-go.

Cessna 30 Delta, cleared stop-and-go.

Cessna 30 Delta, cleared low approach.

Cessna 30 Delta, cleared for the option.

Cessna 30 Delta, cleared to land.

Cessna 30 Delta, are you able to land and hold short of Runway _____?

Cessna 30 Delta, cleared to land, Runway 28. Hold
short of Runway _____.

Cessna 30 Delta, go around. (A reason to go around
will be given. After a go-around is initiated, any of
the post-takeoff clearances may be given.)

Next:

Stack the index cards in the order the same order I have listed
above. The top card in the stack should be Takeoff Position,
followed by Turn to Crosswind, followed by Turn to
Downwind, etc.

The exercise:

1. Stand at the marked takeoff position in your airport
    pattern.

2. Pick an ATC clearance on the top index card in your
    stack.

3. Say the ATC clearance out loud. (Speaking out loud is
    an absolute requirement. I'll explain why later. If you
    are in an area where others might hear you and you
    would be embarrassed to speak out loud, pick another
    area.)

4. Say the appropriate response, as a pilot, to the ATC
    clearance. As you do this, visualize what the view
    would be like out of the windscreen of your airplane if
    you were actually flying over this position at your
    home airport. (This visualization process is critical.
    Don't skip it.)

5. Then, open your eyes and walk to the next marked
    position in the pattern, but don't stop at the mark.

6. Keep walking as you move the top index card to the

bottom of the stack. At the next mark, say your next clearance and response, as you did in Step 2 above. If a clearance was already given at a previous point that negates the need for a clearance at the current point, move to the next marker. For example, if ATC clears you to land at the midfield downwind point, you would not receive a clearance to land at any subsequent point.

7. Keep circulating around the pattern, without stopping, until you have exhausted all of the ATC clearances on each index card.

Repeat this exercise once or twice a day, continuing until you can say each ATC clearance and response without looking at the lists on the cards.

Here's why this works. We all understand, when it comes to flying, muscle memory is extremely important. It's what flight instructors call "developing a feel for the airplane," or, "flying by feel." The process differs slightly from rote memory learning. In this method, you learn by repetition, and by visualizing yourself in the same physical and mental space you would be if you were actually flying. The act of pacing around the simulated airport pattern, plus the visualization at each point, builds a connection between physical location and the phraseology used at each location. It's developing a feel for radio work. Additionally, by maintaining your walking pace--without stopping to think at each point in the pattern--forces you to think, speak and move simultaneously. This is a difficult skill that emulates what is required of a pilot flying around an airport traffic pattern.

That's as far as I want delve into theory. There might be other explanations why this method works. I just know, it works.

You goal is to build automatic responses in your brain that spit out the appropriate responses to ATC clearances. This frees you up to concentrate on aircraft control. Bear in mind, it's important to not only respond verbally to a clearance, but also to know what that clearance means. Clearances mean nothing, if you cannot apply them in your airplane.

Fear not. Beginning in the very next chapter, we are going to beat the daylights out of ATC clearances in an airport traffic pattern. I'll emphasize how to apply clearances in your airplane. When all is said, in this exercise; and done, in the next chapter, you are going to be the ace of your base. . . on the radios, at least.

Take Action:

Do follow through by practicing this exercise at least 3 times per week. Initially, the exercise will be very difficult if you have limited or no experience in a controlled airport traffic pattern. I promise, as you repeat this exercise, it will become easier. It also translates nicely to the airplane. Your traffic pattern radio calls will improve as a result of this exercise.

Take your new skill into the air. After you feel you have a good grip on making radio calls to Tower in a controlled pattern, test yourself by flying around a controlled airport pattern for an hour. Be sure to try various landing options, such as low approaches, touch-and-goes, stop-and-goes, etc. If the airport procedures permit, try flying right-hand and left-hand closed traffic circuits.

Chapter 10: Getting Control of a Controlled Airport

Here we are, once again, at good old KATC on the western end of the Greater Atlanta Metropolitan Area. Since the Georgia Department of Transportation signed on the dotted line for the airport's expansion project, quite a bit has changed. Here's a tour of the changes.

Atlanta Town and Country Airport has a brand new control tower, operated by a team of air traffic controllers who work in shifts from 0700 to 2200 local time. Prior to, and after those hours, KATC uses a Common Traffic Advisory Frequency (CTAF) manned by a junior employee at a remote flight service station.

I say, "junior employee" because the person at the flight service station obviously doesn't have enough seniority to work during daylight hours. We'll talk more about that poor shmoe and CTAF in a little while. Right now, let's talk a little bit more about the new features at Town and Country. It pays to know this stuff if you plan to fly in and out of here.

Within the Town and Country control tower, there are two controlling positions:

A ground controller, who is responsible for the movement of all aircraft and other vehicles on the surfaces of the airport.

A local controller, who you and I call Tower. Tower is responsible for all aircraft operating on the airport runways and in the airport traffic area, also known as Class D airspace. We'll talk in detail about Tower later.

Ground

Let's begin with a closer look at the ground controller's

position. The ground controller only controls traffic on movement areas of the airport. Movement areas include most taxiways and all runways. At most airports, the ground controller handles control of aircraft on all taxiways and also authorizes aircraft to cross runways. There are exceptions. At some airports, the ground controller may hand an airplane off to the tower controller for runway crossings.

At some busy airports, Ground may control the movement of aircraft in on some aprons. Exceptions are listed in an airport's NOTAMs, and in the Airport Facility Directory, published by the FAA. Special instructions for airport apron areas may also be included in the airport ATIS. For example: "All aircraft contact ground control on 121.9 prior to taxi." The ground controller has no control over the movement of vehicles operating in non-movement areas.

"Non-movement area" is a ridiculous name that only a government agency would invent. A non-movement area is an area where vehicles are authorized to travel without clearance from the ground controller. Imagine that. Vehicles can actually move around in non-movement areas! At KATC all taxiways are movement areas. All parking aprons at KATC, usually called "ramps," are non-movement areas. You are free to taxi all around the parking areas without talking to anyone. You can even pop a wheelie or spin a donut on the parking apron if you are so inclined, and the ground controller couldn't care less. Just don't cross the yellow line from a parking area onto a taxiway without approval from the ground controller. (I'm just kidding. Don't drive recklessly on the ramp.) There are even exceptions to this rule. At airports where a taxiway is blocked from the view of the controllers in the airport tower, that taxiway may be considered a non-movement area. These exceptions will be listed in the Airport Facility Directory. (See the example for Dekalb-Peachtree Airport, next page.)

In addition to controlling ground movement, the ground controller at KATC also handles the duties of clearance delivery. Clearance delivery is exactly what it sounds like. The ground controller can deliver pre-departure route clearances to pilots who plan to depart the airport on an IFR flight plan. Pilots flying VFR do not require a pre-departure route clearance from ATC. However, as you'll see, the workload of the ground controller increases with clearance delivery duties. Clearance delivery also consumes time on the radio. All of that may impact your operation as a pilot flying VFR.

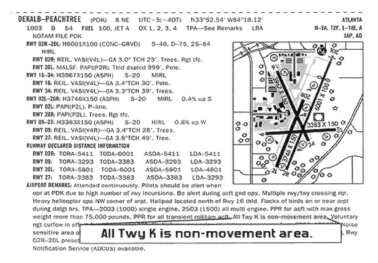

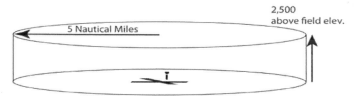

All Twy K is non-movement area.

From the Airport Facility Directory. The listing for Dekalb-Peachtree Airport.

Local

At Town and Country Tower, the local controller handles all aircraft and ground vehicles on the airport's runways. Tower also controls the airspace over and around the airport up to 2,500 above airport elevation, out to a 5-mile radius, measured from the geographical center of the airport. (See the Class D Airspace illustration.)

2,500 above field elev.

5 Nautical Miles

Class D Airspace
tower controlled airport

KATC's airport elevation is 950 feet above mean sea level (MSL). KATC Local controls surface to 3,450 feet on your altimeter (950 feet

+ 2,500 feet).

Atlanta Town and Country Airport's tower has a few interesting features you should know about. There is a radar-repeating display hanging from its ceiling. The repeater, called a Bright Display, shows airborne traffic picked up a remote ATC radar site. In this case, the remote radar belongs to Atlanta Approach Control.

The Bright Display in Town and Country Tower cannot be used to directly control air traffic. Instead, the local controller uses it to monitor the location of airplanes around his airport. The bright display helps him build situational awareness of aircraft he cannot see through the tower's windows.

The local controller also has a light gun hanging from the ceiling near his controller's position in the tower. The light gun puts out a high-intensity light beam through filters that can change the color of the light. If either the local controller or ground controller loses all radio communication with an airplane in his area of responsibility, either controller could grab the light gun and use it to direct the no-radio (NORDO) airplane with light signals.

Nicely Equipped

The tower has an extensive array of landlines, controlled by a central switchboard. Either controller can get in contact with any of the surrounding ATC facilities including the Atlanta TRACON, Atlanta Center, neighboring airport towers, airport fire and rescue service, plus a laundry list of governmental agencies that concern themselves with aviation.

The other significant piece of equipment in the tower is the system that prints out flight strips for arriving and departing aircraft operating under IFR. Both the local controller and the ground controller use these strips to verify an IFR aircraft's route of flight, and the progress of that aircraft from the ground, to airborne, to handoff to enroute radar control.

At KATC, controllers in the airport tower now have access to an automated weather observation system that is an upgrade from the AWOS system previously used at the airport. At least once per hour, the ground controller will take the information from the airport's weather monitoring station and create a message for the Airport Terminal Information System (ATIS). The ATIS is a broadcast of a computer-generated voice that relays the current weather, runways in use, and pertinent Notices to Airmen regarding the airport. Pilots can listen to ATIS by tuning a comm radio to the discrete frequency used by ATIS. Essentially, ATIS replaces the airport advisory service pilots used to get on the old UNICOM frequency for KATC.

Other Good Stuff

The airport is served by Atlanta Approach Control. Atlanta Approach Control is known as a TRACON, pronounced "traykon." TRACON stands for Terminal Radar Approach Control. Atlanta Approach has several radar sites around the metropolitan area. They do not have a dedicated approach control position for Atlanta Town and Country. An approach controller covering the west side of Atlanta will direct airplanes to intercept the instrument approaches at the airport.

The airport's improvement project goes beyond upgrades to its ATC service. KATC's north-south runway, Runway 18/36 has been lengthened to 6,600 feet.

This makes the runway long enough for use by business jets and large turboprop aircraft. After the runway was lengthened, the contractors added 2 instrument landing systems (ILS), one serving Runway 18 and one serving Runway 36. The VOR approach to Runway 18 is still present and unchanged.

If you are not instrument rated, it's hard to get excited about the new ILS setup at the airport. Even if you are a V. F. and R.-only pilot, it helps to know a little bit about the ILS approaches. Traffic flowing into the airport off these approaches may affect how you operate your airplane in the airport traffic pattern. We'll cover the impact of instrument approaches on ATC and VFR pilots later.

The new taxiway layout may be something that is nearer and dearer to your heart. While the airport still has the same taxiways that parallel the runways, contractors have added quite a few shorter taxiways that connect the parallel taxiways to the runways. (See the airport diagram, next page.)

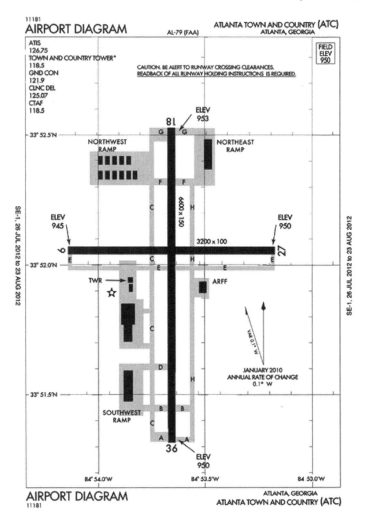

The new and improved Atlanta Town and Country Airport.

Additionally, the old taxiways and the new taxiways have lighted signs that identify each taxiway. The old version of the airport had unlabeled taxiways because the taxiway layout was so simple. The newer layout, and the addition of an airport tower required that the taxiways be labeled and identified by signs. This allows the ground controller to route ground traffic using taxiway identifiers.

The Latest, Greatest ATIS

Now that you have been thoroughly briefed on all the improvements to the Atlanta Town and Country Airport, it's time to fire up the mighty engine of your flying machine and check out the new airport for yourself. But wait! Before you do that, tune in the new ATIS frequency, 126.75, into one of your communication radios and have a listen. No sense in burning costly AVGAS just to listen to a radio. Here's the ATIS:

> "Atlanta Town and Country Airport information Charlie, one seven five three Zulu weather. Few at three thousand, five thousand scattered, twenty-five thousand broken. Visibility seven. Temperature two seven. Dewpoint one nine. Wind two zero zero at 8 knots. Altimeter two nine nine eight. Landing and departing Runway One Eight. Runway two seven. Departing aircraft expect Runway One Eight. Notices to Airmen: The last one hundred and fifty feet of Runway Two Seven is closed. Taxiway Echo is closed between Taxiway Delta and the Northwest Ramp. Use caution for birds in the vicinity of the airport. All IFR departing aircraft, contact Ground Control on 121.9 for your clearance prior to departure. All VFR departing aircraft contact Ground Control on 121.9 for taxi. All arriving VFR aircraft contact Town and Country Tower on 118.5 ten miles from the airport. Read back all runway hold short clearances. Advise the controller on initial contact you have received information Charlie. Atlanta Town and Country Airport information Charlie, one seven five three Zu . . ."

The ATIS plays in a continuous loop. Once you have heard what you need to hear, detune ATIS, lest it drive thee crazy.

I won't run through all of the information on ATIS with you. Your master-of-all-he-surveys flight instructor should have covered this with you already. Let's hit the highlights.

The ATIS indicates it's a beautiful day for VFR flight: few clouds at 3,000; scattered clouds at 5,000. Unless you are flying something with "turbo" in the name, you don't really care about the broken layer of clouds at 25,000. The visibility is reported to be 7 miles, but that's because the visibility-measuring instrument only provides information up to a maximum of 7 statute miles. (There's a technical name for this instrument, but I'm too lazy to look it up.) Your good old eyeball tells you today's vis is at least 15 miles. The winds, 200 at 8 knots, favor Runway 18, so there's no sense getting all spooled up about the closed portion of Runway 27. The lawyers want you to know there are birds in the vicinity of the airport, so it's your own fault if you hit one.

The last message in the ATIS is a biggie: "Read back all hold short clearances." Technically, you are not required to read back any portion of a taxi clearance, except the part that includes a hold short statement. You are also expected to repeat your assigned runway when the controller gives it to you. However, it's a good idea to repeat all taxi instructions so the ground controller can hear and quality-check your understanding of her instructions.

Finally, ATIS tells us we should "advise the controller on initial contact you have received information Charlie." We'll say, "With information Charlie" to the ground controller when we call for taxi instructions. Normally, ATIS gets updated every hour. When there is a significant change in the weather that will impact airport operations, ATIS will be updated to reflect the change, regardless of the time elapsed since the last update.

Here is More Information than You Need About ATIS (Skip this part.)

Each time ATIS changes, a new letter identifier will be attached to the message. For ATIS issued from a tower operating part-time, the first ATIS will begin with an identifier of A and progress through the alphabet throughout the day. After ATIS message Z is issued, the identifier for the next message will begin at A again and continue forward. For a tower that runs 24 hours per day, the ATIS identifiers will continuously cycle through the alphabet, each hour, around the clock. If weather conditions change significantly before the next hourly update of ATIS, Tower will issue a Special ATIS that reports the weather change. The Special ATIS will use the next letter identifier in the sequence.

(Skip this too.)

Some very busy airports, which have special information that is segregated by arrival and departure procedures, will have an arrival ATIS broadcast on one frequency and a departure ATIS broadcast on another frequency. Each ATIS cycles identifiers through 1/2 of the alphabet, with approach ATIS taking A through M, and departure ATIS taking N through Z.

Important Information Resumes Here

Regardless of the ATIS type and identifier, occasionally, you will hear a pilot check in with Ground Control and say, "With the numbers," or, "We have the numbers." This is a bogus statement that does not substitute for actually stating the current ATIS identifying letter. That's not my opinion. It's stated in the AIM:

4-1-13. Automatic Terminal Information Service (ATIS)
h. While it is a good operating practice for pilots to make use of the ATIS broadcast where it is available, some pilots use the phrase "have numbers" in communications with the control tower. Use of this phrase means that the pilot has received wind, runway, and altimeter information ONLY and the tower does not have to repeat this information. It does not indicate receipt of the ATIS broadcast and should never be used for this purpose.

When a ground controller hears "With the numbers," he will usually respond with, "The current ATIS is Tango. Advise when you have it." The phrase "With the numbers" is a valid statement described in the AIM. It means you have the current weather information, whether it's broadcast by AWOS/ASOS or Flight Service. It does not mean you have all of the airport information, such as runways in use, included in ATIS.

More Collectables from the Cow Pen Floor

While we are on the subject, here is another bovine scat response to an ATC instruction: "Numbskull 926 Romeo Mike, we'll do all that." When I hear a pilot answer "We'll do all that," I think one of three circumstances is in play. Either:

The pilot is too lazy to repeat the clearance. The pilot has his thumb fully inserted and didn't actually remember the full clearance well enough to repeat it. The pilot has his thumb partially inserted. He remembered the clearance but cannot figure out how to apply it in his aircraft.

Most air traffic controllers respond to "We'll do all that" one of two ways. Either they repeat the clearance, hoping the pilot will understand it the second time. Or, the controller will watch the offending pilot like a bunny rabbit watching an eagle overhead. The controller will make absolutely sure the pilot follows the clearance. The lack of a read back indicates the pilot bears watching.

Let's Motor, Or Not

Okay partner, put some juice into the engine and let's prepare to taxi. I'll even be a good guy and dial in 121.9 for you. You can make the call to Ground Control when you are ready.

Hey, hey . . . hey! Put that oxygen mask down! This isn't that stressful, is it? Okay, maybe it is. It's a brand new airport with a lot of new taxiways. Let's do a little mental prep work before calling ground. That should reduce the stress level a bit.

In the airline business, we conduct a preflight briefing between the pilot designated to fly the leg, and the supporting pilot. You did know captains and co-pilots alternate flying duties, right? Generally we alternate every other leg, where the captain flies a leg, then the copilot flies a leg, then the captain flies, and so on. Whoever is flying the leg briefs the other pilot on certain elements of the taxi, takeoff, and departure. One of the items we cover is the anticipated taxi route or routes to the runway.

Obviously, if the airport layout is simple, one runway and one parallel taxiway, the taxi route to the runway is obvious.

But if we are at an airport with a complicated layout, one that has multiple runways and taxiways, then whoever is flying will have a more complicated taxi route to brief. Here's where anticipation plays a major role. A good pilot will brief the most likely taxi route to the runway, but also brief one or more alternate taxi routes.

Here's why we do this. First, when the ground controller rattles off taxi instructions, they'll be easier to understand if we have already rehearsed the possibilities out loud. Second, by anticipating various taxi routes, we can plan ahead and determine where we could get ourselves into trouble if we don't pay careful attention. When taxiing at a busy, complicated airport like O'Hare, New York Kennedy, or even Daytona Beach, there is the possibility of getting mixed up on taxi instructions and turning the wrong way. Or, worst case, we might accidentally cross a runway without authorization. By anticipating possible taxi routes, we reduce the possibility of error.

There is a third reason we brief the taxi routes. At busy airports with many taxiways that cross many runways, there are intersections the FAA has designated "hot spots." These are indicated on airport diagrams with a magenta circle. (See the airport diagram for Daytona Beach International, next page.)

A classic hot spot setup is the intersection of a runway and a heavily traveled taxiway. Planes exiting the runway at the hot spot could go beak to beak with airplanes taxiing past that intersection. A hot spot is also a point where disorientation may cause a pilot to accidentally taxi onto the intersecting runway without authorization. Always brief the hot spots along your anticipated taxi route.

If you are flying solo, or if you are flying with a non-pilot who would rather nap than participate in the flight, you will have to brief yourself on the anticipated taxi route. There is no shame in talking it through, out loud. If that is not your preference, at least talk it through in your head. For example,

"Self."

"Yes?"

"I'm going to walk you through this taxi route."

"Go ahead, you handsome devil. I'm listening." (Admittedly,

this technique works better if you have Multiple Personality Disorder.)

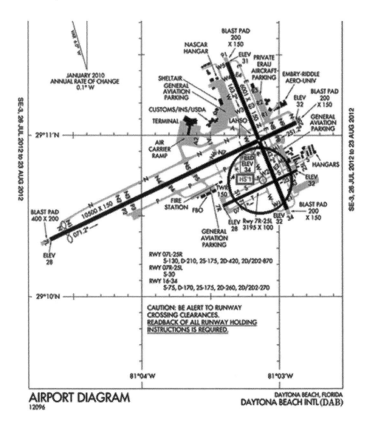

Hotspot HS 1 at Daytona Beach International.

Let's run through the possible taxi routes for Atlanta Town and Country Airport. I'll be your co-pilot, Bubba. You'll be my captain, Skippy. Even though this is going to be your leg to fly, I'll do the demo of the briefing for the taxi portion of our trip.

Okay Skippy, ready for my briefing? Good. Here goes. Please follow along by looking at the airport diagram for KATC.

We are parked at the Seventy-Five Cents Air FBO on the southwest corner of the airport. This parking area is a non-movement area. We don't have to call Town and Country

Ground while taxiing around on the parking ramp, but we do have to make contact with Ground before crossing the hold short line at either Taxiways Alpha, Bravo or Echo. Let's plan on exiting at Taxiway Bravo, since it's a straight shot out of parking to Charlie rather than using Taxiway Delta. I'm anticipating Ground will give us left on Charlie, and then we'll be told to hold short of Runway 27.

After crossing Runway 27, we'll continue north on Charlie to Golf and hold short of Runway 18 at the end. Ground could ask if we can take an intersection takeoff by entering the runway at Taxiway Foxtrot, so we'll be ready for that too. (See the airport diagram, next page.)

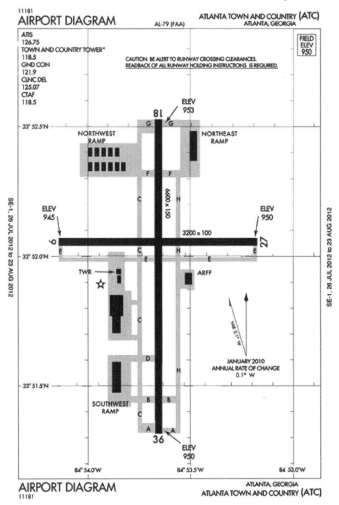

AIRPORT DIAGRAM

*Our anticipated taxi clearance: Exit the Southwest
Ramp at Taxiway Bravo. Then left on Taxiway Charlie
to hold short of Runway 27. After clearance to cross
Runway 27, we'll continue on Charlie either to
Taxiway Golf, or to Taxiway Foxtrot for an intersection
takeoff on Runway 18 from Foxtrot.*

Oh, and by the way, today we are going to stay in the airport
traffic pattern for 3 touch-and-goes or low approaches. We will

pass that information along to Ground on initial contact.
Ground will relay that information to the tower controller. Any
questions or comments, Skippy? Okay, good. That's all I've got.
I'm ready to taxi when you are.

Let's Motor, Really

"Town and Country Ground, Cessna 9130 Delta, on the
Southwest Ramp, holding short of Bravo. Taxi with Information
Charlie. We'll be staying in the pattern." Note the typical
format: You, me, where, what.

The ground controller says, "Cessna 9130 Delta, Town and
Country Ground, Runway 18, taxi via Bravo, left Charlie. Hold
short of Runway 27."

"Cessna 9130 Delta," you reply, "Runway 18, via Bravo, left
Charlie. Hold short of Runway 27." Note what's going on here.
For taxi instructions, all you have to do is repeat the assigned
runway and the hold short instructions. As a technique, I
recommend repeating exactly what the ground controller says
to you. That's called parroting. Advisory messages should be
left out of your parroted radio call. I'll clarify this in the next set
of radio transmissions.

You pull up to the holding line for Runway 27 on Taxiway
Charlie and come to a stop. Looking right, you see an airplane,
in the distance, taxi onto Runway 27 and stop. You don't hear
the airplane being directed to do this because the pilot of that
plane is talking to Tower on another frequency.

The tower controller is standing close enough to the ground
controller to smell what he had for lunch. They can coordinate
movement of airplanes on the airport surface simply by talking
to each other. The tower controller will turn to the ground
controller in this example and say, "I've got that Piper holding
in position on 27. You can cross traffic on 27."

Your only indication of this transaction will be when you
hear, "Cessna 9130 Delta, traffic holding in position. Cross
Runway 27 and continue Charlie and Golf." When Ground
says, "Traffic holding in position," that is an advisory call to
give you assurance the airplane you see on Runway 27 will not
be a conflict for you. You should not repeat advisory

information.

Your reply will be, "Cessna 9130 Delta, crossing Runway 27. Continuing Charlie and Golf." Again, you parrot the ground controller's radio call, omitting advisory information.

Approaching Taxiway Foxtrot on Taxiway Charlie, Ground says to you, "Cessna 9130 Delta, contact Tower on one one eight point five when ready." This means, contact the tower controller after you have completed your engine run up, all pre-departure checklists are completed, and you are ready for takeoff. The ground controller could say, "Monitor tower." This means, switch to the tower controller's frequency, but wait for the controller to call you.

Don't Say "Takeoff"

When you are ready to depart the airport, how do you request a takeoff clearance? Here is what the Airman's Information Manual has to say about requesting a takeoff clearance:

4-3-1 4. Communications
a. Pilots of departing aircraft should communicate with the control tower on the appropriate ground control/clearance delivery frequency prior to starting engines to receive engine start time, taxi and/or clearance information. Unless otherwise advised by the tower, remain on that frequency during taxiing and runup, then change to local control frequency when ready to request takeoff clearance.
NOTE-
Pilots are encouraged to monitor the local tower frequency as soon as practical consistent with other ATC requirements.

There is one gotcha in this passage: "request takeoff clearance." Think of the word "takeoff" as you would think of a loaded gun. Don't pick it up and handle it unless you absolutely intend to shoot. Saying the word "takeoff" means you intend to enter the runway and shove the power up to depart. If you have no intention of doing that at the moment, then don't say "takeoff."

There is a sad story you may have heard about two Boeing 747 aircraft that collided with each other on the runway at Tenerife, Canary Islands. The collision had many causes. The ultimate trigger for the accident happened when the tower controller mistakenly used the word "takeoff" when he had no intention of clearing any airplane for takeoff.

The Tenerife controller was giving one pilot a route clearance and said, "Climb to and maintain flight level 90 . . . right turn after takeoff proceed with heading 040 until intercepting the 325 radial from Las Palmas VOR." This statement on the radio was only a description of the route the pilot was supposed to fly, not a clearance for takeoff. The pilot, unfortunately, heard the word, "takeoff" in the route description and interpreted that to mean he was cleared for takeoff. The controller should not have said the word "takeoff" in his route clearance. The pilot heard the word "takeoff" and reacted by advancing his airplane's throttles to takeoff power.

The pilot began his takeoff roll without being cleared to do so. The co-pilot questioned the captain's decision to begin the takeoff roll. The captain dismissed the co-pilot's comments and continued the takeoff. He ran his 747 into another 747 that was taxiing on the runway. The flight crew making the unauthorized takeoff did not see the other 747 until the last second due to fog. By then, it was too late to stop. I have a complete recreation of the radio calls surrounding this accident at http://ATCcommunication.com/being-dead-wrong-on-the-aircraft-radio. It will give you a chill up your spine.

As a result of this accident, the following was added to the Air Traffic Controller Manual:

4-3-1. DEPARTURE TERMINOLOGY
Avoid using the term "takeoff" except to actually clear an aircraft for takeoff or to cancel a takeoff clearance. Use such terms as "depart," "departure," or "fly" in clearances when necessary.

It's a shame a similar statement isn't included in the AIM reminding pilots to use the same terminology. I believe it's a critical to safety.

At Town and Country, the ground controller tells you when to switch frequencies. At some airports, Ground will not tell you to switch to Tower. It will be left up to you to switch to Tower at the appropriate time. In that case, knowing when to switch from Ground to Tower is fairly simple. Follow the AIM:

1. Monitor the local ground frequency while taxiing to the runway.

2. Stay on the local ground frequency while performing your engine run-up and pre-takeoff checklist.

3. Switch to the local tower frequency and say either

4. "Tower, (your call sign), ready at Runway XX." Or, "Tower, (your call sign), holding short of Runway XX."

Here we are on Taxiway Golf, holding short of Runway 18. I'll just sit here and drum my fingers on top of the glareshield while you run though your run up and pre-departure checks. Don't mind me.

All done? Good. Switch to 118.5 and tell Tower you are ready. Remember to not use the word "takeoff."

"Town and Country Tower, Cessna 9130 Delta. Ready at Runway One Eight."

Tower replies, "Cessna 9130 Delta, Tower and Country Tower. Runway One Eight, line up and wait. Traffic will be crossing downfield."

That part about traffic crossing downfield is an advisory only. It means there will be traffic crossing Runway 18 as you line up and wait. You do not repeat advisory information. Your correct reply: "Cessna 9130 Delta, Runway One Eight, line up and wait."

Into position on the runway we go. Sure enough, there is a business jet crossing your runway about two-thirds of the way down the runway. Tower wasn't lying. Not that he would. The

business jet is clearing the runway. Here comes your next
clearance. Pay close attention because Tower is going to tell you
what he wants you to do after lift off from the runway.

"Cessna 9130 Delta, make left traffic. Runway One Eight,
cleared for takeoff."

Parrot that: "Cessna 9130 Delta, make left traffic. Runway
One Eight, cleared for takeoff."

Turn Left. No--Your Other Left!

And . . . we're off, on a game of fun and flying skill! Tower
cleared you to fly around the airport traffic pattern with left
turns. When you have the speed, the altitude, and the flaps
where you want them, make your left turn to crosswind.

If you will recall earlier, before this airport installed a control
tower, the published traffic pattern called for left turns. With a
tower in place and operating, the controller has the option to
spin you to the left or to the right, based on other traffic around
the airport. So, wait for it. . .

Tower: "Super Cub 823 Papa Victor, Town and Country
Tower. Fly runway heading. Runway Two Seven, cleared for
takeoff."

Aqui tu tienes. That's Spanish for "Here you have it." Tower
just launched a Super Cub off Runway 27. An airplane climbing
off of Runway 27 has a chance to fly up into the airspace that
crosses the downwind leg for a right-hand traffic pattern to
Runway 18. By telling you to fly a left-hand pattern, you will
have no chance of crossing paths with the Super Cub departing
off Runway 27. (See the diagram, next page, to visualize the
flight paths of the Super Cub and you.)

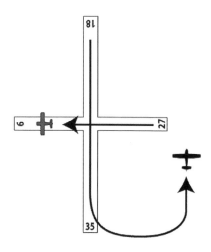

*The Super Cub departs to the west. You fly your pattern
to the east, avoiding the Super Cub.*

Don't expect to hear anything from Tower until you reach
downwind leg or base leg. Do some of that pilot stuff and enjoy.

Here we are on downwind, at midfield. Tower says, "Cessna
30 Delta, Runway One Eight, cleared touch-and-go."

There are three important points to consider in this call from
Tower. First, Tower abbreviated your call sign, which means
you can abbreviate your call sign in all subsequent radio calls to
tower.

Second, Tower cleared you for a touch-and-go, which means
exactly what it says. However, if you booger up your approach
and place yourself in a position from which a touch-and-go
would be unsafe, you always have the option to go around.

Let me repeat that. You never need authorization from Tower
to perform a go-around for safety. Make your go-around for
safety and tell Tower you are going around after you have the
situation under control. In fact, even if you don't make a go-
around radio call to Tower, the controller will figure it out when
he sees your airplane on the go.

Third, to answer Tower, simply parrot his instructions:
"Cessna 30 Delta, Runway One Eight, cleared touch and go."

Badda bing, badda boom. You think I'm imitating a mobster on a famous TV series? I'm not. That's the sound the airframe makes as you execute your first touch and go. Did I get that wrong? Was your landing a greaser? Sorry.

Close Your Traffic

As you climb away from the runway after your touch and go, you hear Tower say, "Cessna 30 Delta, make closed traffic." Interpretation, please.

When Tower says, "Make closed traffic," that's authorization to make circuits around the airport traffic pattern until he says otherwise. You still need clearance to land, to make a touch-and-go, to go low approach, etc. You need no further clearance from Tower to keep circulating around the pattern in between each pass at the runway.

Notice Tower did not specify which direction to turn. If Tower had a preference, the controller would have said, "Make left closed traffic," or, "Make left traffic," or, "Report a left downwind." In this case, Tower couldn't give a hoot which way you turn, so let's try a right-hand traffic pattern just for some variation.

As you roll into your crosswind turn, you hear, "Town and Country Tower, King Air 772 Kilo Foxtrot, over Bowle."

Tower replies "King Air 772 Kilo Foxtrot, Town and Country Tower, the wind is one nine zero at one zero. Runway One Eight, cleared to land."

The question that might come to mind is, "What's Bowle?" Bowle is the name of one of the fixes for the ILS approach to Runway 18. It is a point over the ground, identified as 7.5 DME on the localizer for Runway 18. It appears on the instrument approach diagram for the ILS Runway 18. When the pilot of the King Air made the radio call over Bowle, his aircraft was 6.3 miles on a straight-in final approach to Runway 18. (See the approach plate for the ILS RWY 18.)

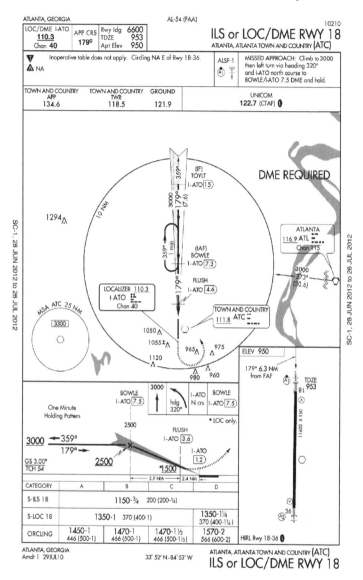

Bowle is the fix at the center of the circle in this diagram.
If you look at the side view of the approach, you will see
there is 3.9 nautical miles (nm) between Bowle and
Flush. Flush is 2.4 nm from the end of the runway. (2.4
+ 3.9 = 6.3 nm from Bowle to the runway threshold.)

Tower has cleared the King Air to land, but the controller has not said anything to you. That means the King Air has been given priority over you to land. One of two things are true. Either the tower controller believes the King Air is flying fast enough to arrive over Runway 18 before you do, or. . .

"Cessna 30 Delta," says Tower. "Continue on the downwind. I'll call your base. Your traffic is a King Air at your one o'clock and five miles on a straight-in to Runway One Eight." In this case, Tower is concerned you and the King Air might cross the finish line at the end of Runway 18 in a neck-and-neck tie. (More likely, a broken-neck tie.) Tower believes, rightly so, it's much easier for you to fly an extra mile or two on the downwind leg than to require the King Air to do a low-altitude 360-degree turn and re-enter final. It's simply easier to have you drop in behind the King Air than to have the King Air drop in behind you.

First, acknowledge the radio call, and then we'll talk about your strategy. "Cessna 30 Delta will continue on the downwind. Looking for the traffic."

Good job. Here's what to do. First and obviously, maintain your downwind heading. Second, slow to your base leg airspeed. There's no sense in going fast and flying more miles than you need to on downwind. Tower is asking you for extra time to fit the King Air in front of you. Tower does not need you to cover extra flying distance. True, you will fly a longer distance on downwind as a result of Tower's instructions, but you don't have to--nor should you try to--fly out of the airport traffic area by flying fast.

Second, and perhaps not as obviously, don't descend. If you start down hill on downwind, as you normally would, to strive to be on glidepath by the time you turn onto a 1/2 to 3/4 mile final for the runway, you will be way too low on final approach when flying from an extended downwind. Does that make sense?

If you fly away from the runway on downwind an extra mile or two, you will not arrive on a 3/4 mile final after your base leg. You will be much further from the runway. If you descend as you would when aiming for a 3/4-mile final, you will be down in the weeds when you roll out on a 2-mile final. Enough said from me. If you need more pointers, talk to your all-knowing one, a.k.a. flight instructor.

While we have been shooting the breeze on traffic pattern geometry, the King Air has zoomed by your 2 o'clock position, and you see it down low. Tower says, "Cessna 30 Delta, traffic is on a 2-mile final. Turn your base now. Runway One Eight, cleared touch-and-go."

You: "Cessna 30 Delta, turning base. Cleared touch-and-go, Runway One Eight. Traffic in sight."

After you answer Tower, you hear, "Town and Country Tower, Bonanza 6251 Golf, ten west with information Charlie. Inbound for landing."

Tower: "Bonanza 6251 Golf, Town and Country Tower. Report entering a midfield right downwind for Runway One Eight."

Other Pilot: "Bonanza 6251 Golf, we'll report a midfield right downwind for Runway One Eight."

You complete a masterful touch-and-go and begin your climbout. Tower says absolutely nothing to you. Your previous instructions from Tower were, "Make closed traffic." With no further amendment, the clearance "Make closed traffic" still stands.

Some pilots mistakenly believe "Make closed traffic only applies to the first circuit around the pattern, unless Tower says, "Make closed traffic until further advised." This notion is completely incorrect. Here's the definition of the term from the AIM:

> CLOSED TRAFFIC- Successive operations involving takeoffs and landings or low approaches where the aircraft does not exit the traffic pattern.

That statement in the definition—successive operations—means you are authorized to keep flying circuits around the traffic pattern without requiring renewed approval for each circuit.

I talked this over with a control tower supervisor at an airport in my area. He said some tower controllers have gotten into the habit of saying, "Make closed traffic until further advised" in response to pilots who keep pestering them for renewed approval for each circuit around the pattern. Adding

"Until further advised" is not specified in the Air Traffic Controller Manual for this type of operation. It's a non-standard phrase used in response to pilots who do not understand the meaning of "Make closed traffic."

Back to our flight. This time, let's circle the wagon to the right. We may do that because Tower never said we are restricted to a left-hand pattern. You turn crosswind and hear Tower say, "Bonanza 6251 Golf, say your position."

Other Pilot: "Bonanza 6251 Golf is three miles west of the field," comes the reply from the pilot of the Bonanza.

"Bonanza 6251 Golf," says Tower. "You're in sight. Make a left 360 and then enter downwind. Your traffic is a Cessna 172 at your one to two o'clock, turning onto the downwind." He's talking about us.

Other Pilot: "Bonanza 6251 Golf. A left 360. Traffic not in sight." To you, Tower says, "Cessna 30 Delta. Your traffic is a Beech Bonanza at your ten o'clock as you roll out of your turn. Report him in sight."

You check 10 o'clock and plainly see the Bonanza as the pilot rolls his aircraft into a left turn. You call, "Cessna 30 Delta, traffic in sight."

"Cessna 30 Delta, roger," says Tower. "You're cleared touch-and-go, Runway One Eight." You are about to answer this radio call, when you decide you've had enough of the traffic pattern. So you say, "Cessna 30 Delta, cleared touch-and-go, Runway 18. We will depart the pattern to the southeast after this touch-and-go."

"Cessna 30 Delta, roger," is all Tower says. That's not approval. It simply means he got the message.

You pass the midfield point on your downwind leg and look to your eight o'clock. The Bonanza is about 3/4 of the way around its 360-degree turn. You can see that airplane is going to enter the downwind well behind you. Then Tower says to you, "Cessna 30 Delta, make short approach. Keep your base leg in tight."

Acknowledge that call with your call sign. Then, I'll explain why Tower made this nonstandard radio call to you and what it means in context.

"Cessna 30 Delta," you reply.

"Keep your base in tight" is a nonstandard phrase used by many tower controllers. Here's why. Nonstandard phrasing, which is authorized by the FAA under certain conditions, allows a controller to control aircraft more precisely. It comes into play most often in an airport traffic pattern.

On any given day in an airport pattern, there will be a huge variety of aircraft using the same runway. Different airplanes mean different operating speeds in the pattern. Some airplanes use up more real estate to lose altitude and airspeed for landing than others. For example, the distance needed for a Boeing 777 to slow and descend from traffic pattern altitude to a landing is going to be a lot different than that required for a light sport aircraft to slow and descend.

Imagine you have a light sport aircraft leading a Boeing 777 to a runway. The Triple-7 is only 3 miles behind the light sport as it enters its final approach. Can you also imagine the front-page story in the newspaper the next morning? The first sentence might read, "The pilot of a Boeing 777 reported hearing a faint bumping sound coming from the nose of his airplane moments before he landed the big jet."

Nonstandard Words from Tower

When you are buzzing around an airport traffic pattern, the tower controller will direct your aircraft using any of the following FAA-approved phrases:

PHRASEOLOGY-

CLEARED FOR TAKEOFF.

CLEARED FOR TAKEOFF OR HOLD
SHORT / HOLD IN POSITION / TAXI OFF THE
RUNWAY (traffic).

EXTEND DOWNWIND.

MAKE SHORT APPROACH.

NUMBER (landing sequence number), FOLLOW (description and location of traffic), or if traffic is utilizing another runway, TRAFFIC (description and location) LANDING RUNWAY (number of runway being used).

CIRCLE THE AIRPORT.

MAKE LEFT / RIGHT THREE-SIXTY / TWO SEVENTY.

GO AROUND (additional instructions as necessary).

CLEARED TO LAND.

CLEARED:TOUCH-AND-GO, or STOP-AND-GO, or LOW APPROACH.

CLEARED FOR THE OPTION, or OPTION APPROVED,or UNABLE OPTION, (alternate instructions).

Or UNABLE (type of option), OTHER OPTIONS APPROVED.

This list of phrases is straight out of the Air Traffic Controller's Manual (J.O. 7110.65). If these are the approved phrases, why do you and I hear controllers say:

O'Hare Tower: "American 723, turn right to two seven zero. Keep it in tight and contact departure."

LaGuardia Tower: "Delta 1586, cleared to land Runway 31. Square your base. Traffic departing Runway 4."

Van Nuys Tower: "Cessna 314 Oscar Papa, fly directly to the numbers."

Greer Tower: "Learjet 521 Kilo Mike, I need you to make that first high-speed. Traffic's on a one-mile final."

San Francisco Tower: "United 340, your traffic is joining final for 28 Left ahead of you. Don't pass him. You're cleared to land 28 Right."

Don't pass him. Keep it in tight. Fly directly to the numbers.
Where is any of that written? The answer: Nowhere. In the very
first section of the Air Traffic Controller's Manual, there's this:

> NOTE-
> Controllers may, after first using the prescribed
> phraseology for a specific procedure, rephrase the
> message to ensure the content is understood. Good
> judgment shall be exercised when using
> nonstandard phraseology.
> (1-2-5 g. ANNOTATIONS.)

Controllers may, and should, resort to nonstandard phrasing,
when standard phrasing does not cover the current situation.
You are required to comply with tower instructions, as long as
those instructions are safe, and as long as you and your
airplane have the performance to comply.

Don't do what I did one night, landing at Albuquerque
International in a T-37. The controller said, "I need you to make
the next right turn off the runway. Traffic's a Boeing 737 on a 1-
mile final."

I was still trucking down the runway at over 100 knots with
the next right turn about 200 feet ahead. I tried to comply by
stomping the brakes. The brakes locked--no anti-skid on the T-
37--and the right main tire immediately blew. Rather than
trying to comply with an ATC clearance that was not safe for
my airplane, I should have said my call sign and "Unable," as I
continued slowing on the runway at a normal rate.

If you don't know what the tower controller means when she
says, "Fly directly to the numbers," or any other nonstandard
phrase, ask her to clarify. Do your best, and always fly safely.

Then, after landing, if you are still confused about what just
happened, use the telephone to call the tower supervisor. If you
feel a nonstandard instruction may have compromised flight
safety, fill out an Aviation Reporting System NASA report using
the online form at this link:

http://asrs.arc.nasa.gov/report/electronic.html

If you feel you need to talk it over with someone higher up

the FAA chain, you can always contact your nearest Flight Standards District Office. While FSDOs do not directly deal in ATC management, they are a starting point for pilots who wish to discuss safety issues at the local level. The listings for all U.S. FSDOs are at this link:

http://www.faa.gov/about/office_org/field_offices/fsdo/

Let's put Tower's standard--and then nonstandard--clarification into context at the Atlanta Town and Country Airport. You are flying a Cessna 172, with a nominal base leg airspeed of 70 to 80 knots. Your final approach airspeed will be around 65 to 70 knots, on average. You can expect to touch down at a typical stall speed of just under 55 knots. That Bonanza behind you? It will probably fly an average of 15 to 20 knots faster in all phases around the traffic pattern.

Even though the Bonanza entered the downwind with you comfortably in the lead, the spacing between you and the Bonanza will reduce due to the speed differences between your aircraft. To avoid letting the gap close between you and the Bonanza, Tower has asked you to turn base leg as early as possible--"Keep it in tight"--to give the Bonanza as little time as possible to catch up to you. Tower's other option would be to ask the Bonanza pilot to extend his downwind leg, as you were directed to do earlier. For some reason, Tower would rather you fly a tight pattern than have the Bonanza fly a long bomber pattern.

Don't think Tower is picking on you. It may be the tower controller has more confidence in your ability to modify your traffic pattern than the other pilot. At least, I hope that's the reason. Maybe he *is* picking on you.

We're Outta There

You fly your slam dunk traffic pattern and plant the main wheels 500 feet down the runway from the threshold. You raise the flaps, push the carb heat lever in, and advance the throttle. We are on our way.

As you lift off, you hear Tower say, "Cessna 30 Delta, left turnout to the southeast is approved. Report clear of the traffic pattern." You acknowledge this with, "Cessna 30 Delta, left turnout. We'll call you clear of the pattern."

By the way, though there is nothing technically wrong with it, I personally cringe when I hear pilots parrot the word "approved," as in, Pilot: "Cessna 30 Delta, left turnout approved." My distaste for pilots saying "approved" has to do with a pilot's role on the radio. A pilot makes requests. ATC makes approvals. I personally believe a pilot shouldn't say the word "approved," even as an acknowledgment to ATC. Again, that's just my opinion. You may disagree, and that's okay.

When you are 5 miles southeast of the airport, you say, "Cessna 30 Delta is clear of the airport traffic area." To which Tower will answer, "Cessna 30 Delta, no reported traffic in your vicinity. Frequency change approved." The transmission, "No reported traffic in your vicinity" is advisory only and should not be repeated. You may respond to "Frequency changed approved" by saying either "Cessna 30 Delta, switching," or simply, "Cessna 30 Delta."

"Switching" means you are leaving the air traffic controller's frequency for another frequency. Acknowledging with your call sign is sufficient because Tower gave you a very general instruction that does not need to be repeated. Normally, you would want to parrot ATC instructions so the controller can listen to your read back and ensure it is accurate.

For very general instructions, with limited or no impact on flight operations, it's not necessary to have ATC quality-assure your read back. Let's face it. You know you no longer need to talk to Tower outside of the airport's airspace boundary. Tower knows it too. Of course you are going to switch frequencies. The call to change frequencies from Tower is a formality with virtually no impact on operations. I know this advice covers a gray area. If in doubt, repeat the controller's instructions.

That said, it's time to switch frequencies to Atlanta Center for flight following. We went over how to do that in a previous chapter, so I won't repeat it here. We do need to quickly go over the term "Common Traffic Advisory Frequency," or CTAF.

The Part-Time Tower

CTAF is exactly what we discussed earlier when we talked

about UNICOM operations. You get an airport advisory as you are approaching the airport, but still outside of the traffic pattern, or before taxiing for takeoff. Once you are inside the airport traffic pattern, or taxiing out the runway, you self-announce your position on the CTAF.

CTAF an be accomplished on UNICOM, MULTICOMM, a discrete Flight Service frequency, or on a non-operating tower frequency. There is virtually no difference in how you get an airport advisory on CTAF. The only difference is who may give you the advisory. If the Flight Service Station serving your airport is open, a Flight Service specialist will give you advisory. If Flight Service is closed, but an FBO operator responsible for the UNICOM frequency is open, you will get your information from them. Some airports have an automated airport advisory service.

The only reason I am bring up CTAF now is because it relates to airports that have a tower which is not open 24 hours per day. You will almost always see "CTAF" listed in the frequency lineup for airports with part-time towers. The CTAF frequency will usually be the same as the tower frequency. (See the airport diagram for Atlanta Town and Country, next page.)

This means, when the airport's tower is closed, you use the tower's frequency for airport advisories and self-announce procedures. If there is no CTAF listed, use the listed UNICOM, MULTICOM, or nearest Flight Service Station frequency for traffic advisories.

If you happen to be on the airport tower's frequency exactly at closing time, you will hear the tower controller say the tower is closed and CTAF is now in effect. At that point, you should consider the airport uncontrolled and switch to self-announce procedures.

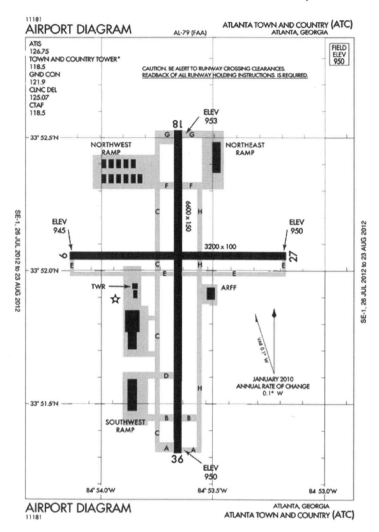

Note the frequency list (upper left). CTAF is 118.5, the same as Tower frequency.

Up next in the following chapter, I'm going to throw some curve balls at you. They might just ruin your day. I know, it's something to look forward to. You can thank me later.

Take Action

It's time to challenge yourself by flying into a tower-controlled airport. My recommendation is to fly into a busy airport at an off-peak hour when the airport's traffic load is light. Beat up the airport traffic pattern for a while by flying multiple touch-and-goes.

When you feel comfortable working the airport traffic pattern when it is not busy, challenge yourself further by flying into the airport during busier times of the day. I would also recommend landing to a full stop and taxiing to a parking area on the airport. After parking, take a break for a half-hour to an hour.

Following your break, fire up the aircraft engine and taxi back to the active runway for departure. The reason I would like you to taxi into and out of parking is to get used to working with the ground controller at the airport. If you only do touch-and-goes, you won't get the full experience of working with the two major players in the airport tower.

Chapter 11: How to Get Lost on the Radio with Little Effort

Let's say today you are flying VFR and you want to pick up flight following from an enroute air traffic control center. What a coincidence. That's exactly the situation you find yourself in as you depart the traffic pattern at Atlanta Town and Country.

Where can you look to find an enroute center (ARTCC) frequency? It depends on what you have on hand. If you have FAA-printed enroute charts, such as Enroute High or Enroute Low charts, you will find the nearest enroute sector frequency in little "postage stamp" boxes scattered on the chart. Take a look at the illustration of a low enroute chart below, or pull out your own low enroute chart, if you have one. Simply find the box nearest your location on the chart and dial in that frequency.

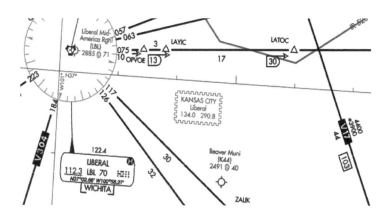

Kansas City Center can be reached on frequency 134.0.

If you are using Jeppeson products, the Enroute Low charts have the frequencies in boxes on the chart, same as the government-issued charts. The Enroute High charts have no frequency boxes on the chart, but there is a table of enroute frequencies in the margin of the chart. This table is just about worthless. It lists frequencies by enroute center, Chicago Center, for example, but there are no locations associated with each frequency. You might pick a sector frequency for Chicago Center that operates from an antenna in Central Illinois, while you are flying in Southern Wisconsin. You have no way of knowing where the sector is located, that is until you try to reach it on the radio. The silence will tell you that you are too far away to be heard, but that is all it will tell you.

Sectional charts don't even have enroute center frequencies on them. If all you have in the cockpit is a sectional, and you want to get in contact with a center controller for, let's say flight following, you will have to do what I did one time in a Boeing 757.

There we were, flying along in flight at 37,000 feet, going from, uh, maybe I shouldn't say that. Albuquerque Center said, "Airliner 1445, contact Albuquerque Center on one two . . ."

Oh damn! I just made a big mistake! The captain was flying. I had the radios. When Albuquerque started to give me the new frequency, I reached for the wrong radio tuner and started to spin in the new frequency.

Most aircraft radios have a window to hold a standby frequency and a window to hold the active frequency. Normally, you tune the new frequency into the standby window and then hit the transfer switch to move the new frequency to the active side. When you hit the switch, not only does the new frequency go active, the formerly active frequency moves into the standby window. This is a great feature, because if the new frequency that goes active does not work, you can always hit the transfer switch again and restore the old, working frequency.

Not so on the Boeing 757. On the Seven Five, each radio control head has two windows, but you can tune a new frequency into either one. Instead of a transfer switch, the Seven Five has a flip-flop switch. The flip-flop is a toggle switch that points to either the left frequency window or to the right frequency window. Whichever side the toggle points to is active.

Normally, a smart pilot will put a new frequency into the

window that's not currently active, and then push the flip-flop toggle towards that window. A smart pilot will also take note of which side the toggle is pointing to, and then put the new frequency in the side the toggle is not pointed to.

For some reason, though I've done it correctly a bazillion times, this time I rolled the first couple of digits into the active window. My intent was to roll the new frequency into the non-active side as the controller gave me the frequency. But Head-Up-Butt syndrome was in effect and I ended up trying to enter the new frequency into the window currently in use. Because of my special trick, I immediately cut off the controller before he could give me the rest of the new frequency.

Bye bye Albuquerque Center. I hardly knew ye. And I couldn't remember ye. Which means,

- I had a non-working frequency tuned in.

- The non-active radio frequency was also worthless because it was tuned to an enroute sector we left about 200 miles ago. (That's the problem with flying at the speed of stink. Things move away from you real fast!)

We use Jeppesen Enroute High charts which don't have center frequencies listed by location, as I mentioned earlier. However, comma, there was a way out. I want you to know about it should you ever run into a situation where you need to get ahold of Center and you don't have a chart that shows the frequency you need.

On the Jeppesen chart, just above that worthless table of non-located frequencies, over in the margin it says, "For the correct enroute frequency contact any flight service station on 122.55."

Aha! I tuned up 122.55, and played with the #2 VOR tuner to determine our position by radial and DME. (The flight service station specialist will ask you for your radial and DME so he can determine the correct frequency for your location.)

Just as I was about to press the radio transmit button, I heard this on 121.5 on radio #2:

"Airliner 1445, this is Albuquerque Center on Guard. Contact Albuquerque Center on 120.95."

Great. Now the whole world knows I messed up. But, swallowing my pride, I rolled 120.95 into radio #1 and checked in. The controller gave me a new frequency to contact. This time I double-checked the flip-flop switch's position and put the new frequency into the opposite window. (Fool me once, and all that.) Problem solved, almost.

About 5 seconds later, our ACARs box (that's the digital touchscreen display we use to get and send inflight data over a discrete network) chimed. There was a message from our dispatcher on the ACARs screen. It said, "Contact ATC on 120.95."

Hard to get lost on the radios for very long when you are scooting along at .80 Mach with 185 people on board. Everyone keeps an eye on you, and lets you know the second you are off track.

Point is, keep 122.55 in mind. If you cannot raise Flight Service on 122.55, the frequency 122.2 is also widely used. Try it. It comes in really handy when you need it. Oh, the radio call I would have made?

"Any flight service station, Airliner 1445 on 122.55, two zero miles northeast of Saint John."

"Airliner 1445, this is Prescott Radio. Go ahead."

"Airliner 1445 is a Boeing 757, on the Saint John 040-degree radial for twenty-two DME at flight level 370. We are looking for the correct Center frequency."

"Airliner 1445, give Albuquerque Center a try on 120.95." And so on. . .

Situational Lost Comm

The type of situation I just described is self-induced. You make a mistake with the radio switches and force yourself to break contact with ATC. Some day, you are going to lose contact with your air traffic controller, and at first, you aren't going to know the reason why you lost contact. That situation is called lost communication, or lost comm, for short.

Lost comm is not the same as "No radio," or NORDO. Lost

comm is a temporary situation in which you do not have a connection to ATC. The other situation, NORDO, is a permanent condition, in which the radio (or radios), is/are deader than than a mummy of an Egyptian pharaoh. The difference between lost comm and NORDO is an important distinction. Knowing which of the two situations you are in is equally important.

Before you can officially declare your airplane NORDO, you have to determine: Are my radios truly dead (NORDO), or, have I accidentally done something to break contact with ATC (lost comm)?

Before you attempt to answer this question, do this first if you have just switched frequencies: Make sure you have the frequency tuned in correctly. Tuning a radio frequency incorrectly is the number 1 cause of lost communication. Verify you did not transpose a pair of digits in that frequency. For example, if your intended frequency was 120.75, make sure you didn't accidentally tune 120.57. Sometimes looseness in the frequency selector knob will cause a digit in the frequency to change. For example, if you tuned 121.9, and the frequency selector is loose, you may look down and see the frequency has jumped to 122.9. If the frequency looks correct, it's time to do a quick check to determine whether your radio is dead or alive.

There is a reliable and quick way to determine your circumstance. If your radio has died, you should hear absolutely nothing over your headset or speakers, even when you key your microphone. When you turn the radio's squelch control all the way down, you won't hear static. If your radio has an electronic display, the frequency windows will be blank. If your radio has a transmit light, it will not light up when you key your microphone. If you can hear transmissions from other pilots on the frequency, your radio is not dead. If there is no radio traffic on the frequency, but your radio appears to be powered, you may simply have situational lost communication.

"Situational lost communication" is a term I created, and here's what it means. It means you've done something to create a situation in which you can no longer communicate with air traffic control by radio. It doesn't mean your radio is not working. It means you've either flown out of radio range of the person you were speaking to, or you did something to the radio's switches that makes communication with that person impossible.

Let's look at some examples. There you are, flying along in flight, talking to an air traffic controller at Cleveland center. It's a clear and beautiful day and you've got no worries. So you occupy your time by talking to the person riding along with you in the airplane. The two of you are into a deep and long conversation. The radio chatter in the background is just so much noise, so you turn the volume of your radio down slightly so it won't interfere with your conversation with your flying buddy. Twenty minutes later, you see another airplane fly past you, and you realize maybe you better pay more attention to the radio. Again, you hear nothing but chatter and no one is saying your aircraft's callsign. You notice some clouds ahead that appear to be at your altitude, and since you are flying VFR, you decide to descend a little bit to maintain VFR cloud clearance. Being a good pilot, you announce to Cleveland center your intention to descend: "Archer 373 Victor Zulu departing five thousand five hundred for three thousand five hundred VFR."

There's no response. So you try again:

"Archer 373 Victor Zulu passing five thousand for three thousand five hundred."

No answer.

"Cleveland Center, Archer 373 Victor Zulu."

No answer.

"Cleveland center, Archer 373 Victor Zulu, how do you copy?"

Cleveland Center does not answer. You check your radio. It's on. You check the frequency. It's the right one. You check the settings on your comm panel. They look good. You check your headset plugs to make sure they haven't pulled out of the jacks in the cockpit audio panel. Yes, the headset is plugged in correctly. You turn the squelch switch to low and hear plenty of static.

"Cleveland Center, how do you read Archer 373 Victor Zulu?" Nothing.

Here's what happened. You got so busy talking to your flying buddy that you failed to hear the controller at Cleveland Center tell you you were reaching the limit of his sector and to contact the next controller on 127.35 for further flight following.

Cleveland Center tried calling you a couple more times, and getting no response, assumed you no longer wanted flight following and had left his frequency. So, now you are out of radar contact, out of radio contact, and out of luck. That is, until you discover the true nature of your lost communication error and do something about it.

Here's another example. New day, new airplane, and you're flying along in flight when you decide you'd like to leave the active air traffic control frequency to talk to someone at the nearest flight service station.

You: "Kansas City Center, Tomahawk 887 Juliet Tango would like to leave your frequency for 2 minutes."

KC Center: "Tomahawk 7 Juliet Tango, frequency change approved. Report back in 2 minutes or less."

You: "Tomahawk 7 Juliet Tango." At this point, you tune in the Flight Service station frequency on your secondary VHF radio and switch your transmit selector on the audio control panel to Radio #2. You also deselect the Listen button for your speakers and headset for Radio #1 so you won't have any interference from Radio 1 as you talk to Flight Service.

Being the steely-eyed pilot you are, you hack the cockpit clock, to time yourself, knowing you need to get back to Kansas City Center in 2 minutes. With everything set, you call Flight Service and get an update on the weather at your destination. After writing the details on your clipboard, you finish with a quick inflight report to flight service and say your goodbyes. Checking the clock, you see that you've managed to get your work done in 1 minute and 45 seconds. Because 2 minutes are almost up, you quickly switch your transmit selector back to Radio 1 and call: "Kansas City Center, Tomahawk 7 Juliet Tango back on your frequency."

Nothing.

You: "Kansas City Center, Tomahawk 887 Juliet Tango is back up." Nothing.

You try again. "Kansas City Center, how do you read Tomahawk 887 Juliet Tango?" Dead silence. Uh oh. It seems you have just gone lost comm. You do all the things a good pilot should do. You check the radio. You turn the squelch down. You check your comm cord connections. All is well.

It turns out Kansas City Center is hearing your just fine. In fact, the controller is starting to get annoyed because she is calling you back and you aren't answering. Until you see that the Listen switches are still set for Radio 2, the only person you might hear is the flight service station specialist, if he happens to get a call from another airplane. Until then, and until you recognize your switch error, you are situationally lost comm.

There are maybe a dozen ways to create a situation that produces lost comm, but all those ways really fall into just 2 categories: Either you got preoccupied and flew yourself out of radio range without realizing it, or, you've got the radio switches set incorrectly. The reason why you cannot reach someone on the ground may not be obvious. It's like proofreading your own writing. The error might be staring you in the face, but you just can't see it from where you are sitting.

No matter how you created your own lost comm situation, here's how to fix the problem. First, take a breath and fly the airplane. Airplanes don't crash due to simple lost comm. Don't get so caught up in a minor problem that you create a major problem by failing to fly. Second, continue to navigate. If you were on a published airway, stay on it. If you were avoiding obstructions and bad weather using your eyeballs, continue to do so. Don't hit a rock or a tower because you are heads down tinkering with the radios.

If you are flying under instrument flight rules, stay on the instruments and continue to fly. The regulations spell out the altitude and route to fly.

If you have an autopilot or a second person qualified to fly, transfer control of the airplane to lighten your load while you troubleshoot, but don't ever forget to fly. That means, even if the airplane is on autopilot, someone still needs to monitor the flight path as though he or she is still flying. If another person takes control of the aircraft, that person's only job is to fly the aircraft. Don't allow the other person to help you troubleshoot. Make sure the other person does nothing but fly. Once the flying and navigating are under control and remain priorities one and two, then you can troubleshoot.

First, make sure the frequency you intended to tune in is tuned in. Next, determine if your radio is alive or dead. The easiest way to do this is to listen. If you hear other pilots talking on the frequency, bingo! You've got the answer to your question. If the radio sounds dead, look at your radio. Is it on? If the radio has LED digits showing the frequency, and you can see those digits, the radio is working. If you have an older model, without an LED display, key your microphone and see if the transmit light illuminates, or if you hear the pop in your headset or speaker as you key and unkey the mic. If the radio has died, and you don't have a backup, you are truly lost comm. But wait, there's more, as they say on those TV commercials.

Next, check the position of each switch on your master communication panel. I'm talking about the panel that controls which radio takes input from your microphone and which radio feeds your headset and cockpit speakers. As I said before, sometimes it's hard to spot the error on the comm panel, so talk out loud as you review the switch positions. If you intended to talk and listen on Radio 1, make sure all the switches you need to talk and listen are set to Comm 1. Even better, if you have a flying buddy on board, let him or her review the switch positions for you--sort of like having someone else proofread your work--but make sure, if you get your buddy involved, someone is paying attention to aircraft control. Assuming all that is okay, let's move on.

What's the first thing technical support tells you to check when you call them to troubleshoot your non-working computer? First they ask you if the computer is turned on. It's seems obvious and stupid, but it is a good idea to check to make sure the master avionics or comm switch didn't get bumped to the off position. Hey, it's happened before! While you are at it, you might as well check the circuit breakers to make sure the breaker for the radios hasn't popped.

What's the next thing tech support tells you when you call about your computer? Is it plugged in? Doh! What a stupid question, right? Of course it's plugged in, but . . . just to be sure, check your headset plugs if you are using a headset, and make sure the plugs haven't unplugged. It's even a good idea to unplug and reset your headset plugs just to be sure. You are remembering to fly the airplane as you do all this, right?

Make sure the radio volume is turned up, and rotate the radio's squelch knob towards low if you have a squelch knob.

If there is no mechanical reason why you can't speak to the last person you were talking to on the ground, you are in a situational lost comm. Time to do something about that, and what you'll do depends on whether you are VFR or IFR.

If VFR, obviously maintain VFR cloud clearances and fly where the inflight visibility is at least 3 miles. As long as you remain VFR and can stay out of controlled airspace and airport traffic patterns, you can continue without speaking to anyone. If you want to get back in touch with a controlling agency, you have many choices.

Let's start with the easiest solution. It assumes you can hear other aircraft on your frequency. Try this. Key the microphone and say, "Any aircraft this frequency, Tomahawk 887 Juliet Tango." I guarantee you, if any airliners are on the frequency with you, at least one airline pilot, who is bored to tears as he drones along, will answer your call with great enthusiasm. Even if there are no airliners on your frequency, some other helpful pilot will usually answer.

Other Pilot: "Aircraft calling on this frequency, this is Airliner 356, go ahead."

You can then tell him your situation, and be prepared to give your location to the pilot who answered. It might sound like this:

You: "Airliner 356, this is Tomahawk 887 Juliet Tango. I was talking to Kansas City Center on this frequency but I can't reach him anymore."

Other Pilot: "Tomahawk 887 Juliet Tango, Airliner 356 copies. Say your position."

You: "Tomahawk 887 Juliet Tango is on the Springfield three two zero degree radial for four three DME at six thousand five hundred."

Other Pilot: "Tomahawk 887 Juliet Tango, Airliner 356 copies. Standby. Kansas City Center, Airliner 356. . ."

ATC: "Airliner 356, Kansas City." (You will not hear ATC's end of this conversation if the controller's radio station is out of range.)

Other Pilot: "Airliner 356 is talking to a Tomahawk 887 Juliet Tango. He's on the Springfield three two zero for four three DME at six thousand five hundred. He's looking for a center frequency."

ATC: "Roger Airliner 356. Have Tomahawk 887 Juliet Tango contact Kansas City Center on one two seven point five."

Other Pilot: "Airliner 356 copies, break break, Tomahawk 7 Juliet Tango, Kansas City says give them a call on one two seven point five."

You: "Tomahawk 887 Juliet Tango copies one two seven point five. Thanks for your help." And you are on your way like nothing happened.

If you can't reach anyone else on your frequency, all is not lost. You can look at your sectional map and find a frequency for the nearest terminal radar approach control, or airport tower. Those frequencies, plus enroute center frequencies, are even easier to find on an enroute map for IFR flight, if you happen to be carrying one. You can call the nearest flight service station or flight watch and let the station specialist help you figure out who to contact on an appropriate frequency. Just like earlier, when we talked about contacting another aircraft on your frequency, before you contract flight service or flight watch, work out your location because the specialist is going to need that to give you a frequency.

If you are unsure of your location, the flight service specialist will be able to walk you through the steps to work out your location.

One last idea before I wrap this up. Sometimes what appears to be lost comm is nothing more than tuning the wrong frequency when switching from one controlling agency to another. For example, Oakland Center tells you to contact the next sector on one three two point two five, and you either mishear or accidentally tune one three two point five. When you get no reply from the controller on the new frequency, simply switch frequencies back to the controller you just left and ask him or her to repeat the new frequency. Problem solved.

It basically boils down to this. There are two ways to go lost comm: mechanical radio failure, or situational radio failure. If the radio is working, you are in situational radio failure. To get out of situational radio failure, change your situation. Check the radio. Check your switches. Check your connections. If those are all good, get in touch with anyone on the ground or in the air. Use your map. Use other pilots on the frequency. Use flight service. You will eventually work it out. But remember, lost comm is not an emergency. Fly the airplane first and always. Navigate to stay out of trouble. Then, and only then, work out your lost comm problem. Your priorities should always be, in this order:

1. Aviate

2. Navigate

3. Communicate

We have covered a lot of ground in this chapter. It would be easy to forget most of the information, especially if you encounter a lost comm situation 2, 5, 10 or more years from now. Never fear, I've created a lost comm checklist you may print and hang on to for that inevitable day when your radio goes dead. I've included an expanded checklist that covers every step in detail. Then there follows an abbreviated checklist that contains the essential steps to recovering communications without an explanation for each step. If you ever misplace this book (say it ain't so), you can always snag printable copies of VFR and IFR lost communication checklists at ATCinsider.com.

They say a person should never assume anything. In this case I'm going to assume you made tracks over West Georgia in your trusty Cessna without losing contact with ATC. Now, it's time to return for a landing at the Atlanta Town and Country Airport.

After you have had a chance to read through the lost comm checklists for your personal amusement, and to get a snack from the refrigerator, flip over to the next chapter. We will make the transition from flight following with Atlanta Center back into the good hands of the controllers at Atlanta Town and Country Airport.

Lost Communication (VFR) Expanded Checklist

Note: This checklist is not an FAA-approved checklist. It is presented as an educational device only. Pilots are cautioned to apply guidance on lost communication from the current Aeronautical Information Manual, and are required to follow the Federal Aviation Regulations when operating aircraft in the U.S. Nothing in this checklist supersedes this requirement.

Note:
Before beginning this checklist, verify you have the intended frequency tuned into the radio, i.e. the frequency digits are not transposed, and the displayed frequency did not jump off of the frequency you originally tuned.

Radio Working?

1. Look--Does the radio appear to have power?

    a. LED frequency digits lit (if electronic frequency display).

    b. Transmit light illuminates when mic keyed.

2. Listen--Can you hear other communication?

3. Test--

4. Volume turned up.

5. Rotate squelch knob to low and listen for static.

6. Check Avionics or Radio Master Switch--On.

7. Check Radios circuit breaker--In.

Communication Master Control Panel set correctly?

1. Is the Transmit Selector Switch set to the radio in use?

2. Is the Listen Selector Switch set to the radio in use?

Headset

1. Connectors--Plugged into headset jacks.

2. Headset Volume Knob (if applicable)--Rotate towards louder.

Note: If any of the preceding steps restores 2-way radio communication, STOP HERE and proceed with: Situational Lost Communication Checklist. Otherwise, continue with the next item.

Land

1. Squawk 7600.

2. Avoid controlled airspace to the maximum extent practicable.

3. Continue to your planned destination or land at the nearest suitable airport.

> a. If landing at an airport with a control tower, follow light gun signals for landing clearance and taxi.

> Or,

> b. If landing at an uncontrolled airport, scan the

entire airport traffic pattern from at least 500 feet above pattern altitude. Enter the traffic pattern when you are sure you will create no conflict with other aircraft.

----End of Checklist----

Situational Lost Comm (VFR) Expanded Checklist

(Assumes radio is operational but contact lost with ATC.)

1. Return to your last assigned frequency and try to establish contact.

2. Contact other aircraft on the frequency:
"Any aircraft this frequency, this is [your call sign]."

3. Once contact is made with another aircraft:

    a. State your lost comm situation.

    b. State your position.

Note: Other aircraft will contact air traffic control and give you a new radio frequency to try.

4. If unable to contact another aircraft on your current frequency: Find the frequency for the nearest ARTCC on your map and contact an air traffic controller on that frequency.

    a. Be prepared to give the air traffic controller your position.

    Or,

    b. Find the frequency for the nearest Flight Service Station or Flight Watch on your map and contact the station specialist to get an appropriate frequency. Be prepared to give the specialist your position.

----End of Checklist----

Lost Communications (VFR)
Abbreviated Checklist

Note: This checklist is not an FAA-approved checklist. It is presented as an educational device only. Pilots are cautioned to apply guidance on lost communication from the current Aeronautical Information Manual, and are required to follow the Federal Aviation Regulations when operating aircraft in the U.S. Nothing in this checklist supersedes this requirement.

Note:
Before beginning this checklist, verify you have the intended frequency tuned into the radio, i.e. the frequency digits are not transposed, and the displayed frequency did not jump off of the frequency you originally tuned.

Radio working?

    1. Look--Indications of power.

    2. Listen--Other communication on the frequency.

    3. Test

        a. Volume--Increase.

        b. Squelch--Low.

        c. Listen for static.

Radio Master Control Panel

1. Transmit Selector Switch--Set for radio in use.

2. Listen Selector Switch--Set for radio in use.

Headset

1. Connections--Checked in.

2. Headset volume (if applicable)--Increase.

Note: If radio is WORKING, STOP HERE and proceed with Situational Lost Communication Checklist.

Land

1. Transponder code--7600.

2. Continue--VFR.

3. Avoid controlled airspace as much as practicable.

4. Land at nearest suitable airport.

> a. Uncontrolled airport--clear for traffic and avoid conflicts.

> Or,

> b. Controlled airport--clear for traffic and follow control tower light signals.

----End of Checklist----

Situational Lost Comm (VFR) Abbreviated Checklist

(Assumes radio is operational but contact lost with ATC.)

Attempt contact with:

   a. ATC on last assigned frequency.

   b. Any aircraft on current frequency.

   c. ATC on frequency shown on navigation map for your location.

   d. Flight Service or Flight Watch.

When contact is established:

   a. State your situation.

   b. State your position.

   c. Get correct ATC frequency and make contact on that frequency.

----End of Checklist----

Take Action

Run through this simulation: You are flying VFR across the Great South Plains somewhere southeast of Midland, Texas. You had been talking to Fort Worth Center for flight following, but you notice the radio has been silent for the last 5 minutes. You do not hear any chatter whatsoever on the current radio frequency. You try calling Fort Worth Center but there is no answer.

In the initial steps of the Lost Comm Checklist, listening to the radio for any communication is part of the process to determine if your radio is working. What are the other two steps you should try to determine if your radio is working?

What other components of your radio system should you check?

In this simulation, we'll say you determine that your radio is inoperative. What should you do next?

Chapter 12: Landing with No Radios

It's been more than an hour since you first tuned in the ATIS for the Atlanta Town and Country Airport before your initial radio call to ground control. When you switch Comm Radio 2 back to the ATIS frequency, the Atlanta Town and Country Airport information has changed. The big item that has changed is the active runway. This is because the wind direction and speed has changed significantly.

The ATIS now tells you the surface wind at the airport is 310 degrees at 10 knots gusting to 18 knots. The active runway is now Runway 36 for departures and arrivals. Runway 27 is also available for departures only. The ATIS still contains the reminder for VFR arriving aircraft to contact Town and Country Tower 10 miles from the airport. The ATIS ends with, "Advise the controller on initial contact that you have received information Echo."

You have been talking to Atlanta Center for flight following. As you fly to within 15 miles of the Atlanta Town and Country Airport, the controller at Atlanta Center says, "Cessna 9130 Delta, no observed traffic between you and the airport. Radar service terminated. Contact Town and Country Tower on one one eight point five. Good day."

You acknowledge Atlanta Center with, "Cessna 9130 Delta, switching. Good day." There is no requirement to repeat the radio frequency given to you by Atlanta Center. It's perfectly fine to repeat the frequency if you need verification that you heard correctly. If you don't need verification, you don't have to say the frequency.

Many pilots misunderstand this distinction. They believe repeating every radio frequency is a requirement, when in fact, it is not. Atlanta Town and Country Airport is your home airport. You know the frequencies well, so there is no need to repeat and verify with ATC what you know so well.

Unfortunately, it does not matter that you know Town and Country Tower's frequency, or any frequency for that matter. It looks as though your entire radio stack is toast.

You pull out that Lost Comm Abbreviated Checklist that I created for you in the previous chapter and you run through it to make sure your radio is kaput. Here's a review:

Lost Communications (VFR) Abbreviated Checklist

Note:
Before beginning this checklist, verify you have the intended frequency tuned into the radio, i.e. the frequency digits are not transposed, and the displayed frequency did not jump off of the frequency you originally tuned.

Radio working?

1. Look--Indications of power.

2. Listen--Other communication on the frequency.

3. Test

   a. Volume--Increase.

   b. Squelch--Low.

   c. Listen for static.

Radio Master Control Panel

1. Transmit Selector Switch--Set for radio in use.

2. Listen Selector Switch--Set for radio in use.

Headset

1. Connections--Checked in.

2. Headset volume (if applicable)--Increase.

Everything you try indicates one--and only one--conclusion: Your entire radio suite is stone cold dead. You are certain your transponder has joined the crowd and also kicked the bucket. The problem probably has to do with power not getting to your radio stack, but you aren't a mechanic. You can't fly and repair the system anyway, so you might as well deal with what you have.

Here's how to deal with the problem. First, consider that you are going into Class D airspace without a transponder. Is that a problem? The answer is in CFR 91.129 Operations in Class D airspace:

> **(c)** Communications.
> Each person operating an aircraft in Class D airspace must meet the following two-way radio communications requirements:
>
> **(1)** Arrival or through flight.
> Each person must establish two-way radio communications with the ATC facility (including foreign ATC in the case of foreign airspace designated in the United States) providing air traffic services prior to entering that airspace and thereafter maintain those communications while within that airspace.

As a review, here is the definition of Class D Airspace in the AIM:

> AIM 3-2-5. Class D Airspace
> a. Definition. Generally, that airspace from the surface to 2,500 feet above the airport elevation (charted in MSL) surrounding those airports that have an operational control tower.

Note there is no requirement to have an operating transponder for Class D airspace. The question remains, can you return to Atlanta Town and Country without an operating radio, since Class D airspace requires two-way radio communications? Back to CFR 91.129:

> (d) Communications failure.
> Each person who operates an aircraft in a Class D airspace area must maintain two-way radio communications with the ATC facility having jurisdiction over that area.
> If the aircraft radio fails in flight under IFR, the pilot must comply with Rule 91.185 of the part.
> If the aircraft radio fails in flight under VFR, the pilot in command may operate that aircraft and land if--
> > (i) Weather conditions are at or above basic VFR weather minimums;
> > (ii) Visual contact with the tower is maintained; and
> > (iii) A clearance to land is received.

Before your radios quit, the ATIS indicated the weather was well within VFR limits for the airport. Of course, with unlimited visibility, you will have no problem keeping visual contact with the tower. In fact, you can see the tower at the airport already, and you are still 10 miles away.

Before we talk about what happens next, I want to consider transponder operations when you are NORDO. Let's say your situation was slightly altered. Let's say you are radio out, but your transponder still works. This changes your procedures slightly.

If you are NORDO, but the transponder works, you should set the code 7600 into the transponder, per the procedure stated in the AIM. This action will set off alarms at every ATC facility within radar range of your aircraft. It also highlights your aircraft as NORDO on all radar displays that show your aircraft. Air traffic controllers in the area will move all aircraft with potentially conflicting flight paths out of your way. At that point, you are like Moses parting the Red Sea. Wherever you go, other airplanes under radar control will get the heck out of your way.

The Value of 7600

Squawking 7600 doesn't guarantee you safe passage. Pilots not talking to ATC have no idea about your location or situation. Additionally, if you are in an area without radar coverage, squawking 7600 is irrelevant. Regardless of the situation, squawk 7600 and let ATC worry about what that means for other aircraft in the area. Do keep your eyeballs open for other aircraft no matter where you are.

As you approach your destination airport, the 7600 code your transponder is squawking may also highlight you to the controllers in the airport's tower if the tower has a Bright Display. They will be better prepared for your arrival than if you had shown up without squawking 7600.

In your current situation, with no transponder, all is not lost. Town and Country Tower's Bright Display repeats all air traffic picked up from a remote radar site. Even though your transponder is dead, your airplane will still show up on the bright display. It will appear as a primary radar target without any flight data. That means the tower controllers will see the radar blip of your airplane, but they won't be able to tell if you are at 500 feet or 25,000 feet. In any case, they will see an airplane on radar, approaching their airport.

Look at the Pretty Lights

The only question remaining is, how are you going to receive clearance to land from Tower without an operating radio? After all, receiving clearance to land is one of the requirements to arrive at a Class D airport with radio failure.

If you will recall from a previous chapter, I said the controllers in Town and Country Tower have a light gun hanging from the ceiling of the tower cab. They can use the light gun to signal a NORDO airplane. Different lights, emitted from the light gun, have different air traffic control meanings.

ATC light signals have the meaning shown in the following table, as described in CFR 91.125 ATC Light Signals:

Meaning			
Color and Type of Signal	Movement of Vehicles, Equipment and Personnel	Aircraft on the Ground	Aircraft in Flight
Steady green	Cleared to cross, proceed or go	Cleared for takeoff	Cleared to land
Flashing green	Not applicable	Cleared to taxi	Return for landing, (followed by steady green)
Steady red	STOP	STOP	Give way to other aircraft and continue circling
Flashing red	Clear the taxiway/runway	Taxi clear of the runway in use	Airport unsafe, do not land
Flashing white	Return to starting point on airport	Return to starting point on airport	Not applicable
Alternating red and white	Exercise extreme caution	Exercise extreme caution	Exercise extreme caution

Know the Flow

Before entering Class D airspace while NORDO, the AIM says, "Remain outside or above the Class D surface area until the direction and flow of traffic has been determined." You won't know the flow of traffic until you get close to the airport.

The AIM instructs you to determine the flow of traffic before entering Class D airspace so you can avoid disrupting other airplanes already in the airport's pattern. The last thing you want to do is dive bomb into the airport traffic pattern and send other airplanes scattering to avoid a mid-air collision with you. If you have ever seen the aerial demonstration teams-- Thunderbirds or Blue Angels--do their bomb burst maneuver, you know what I'm talking about. Ooh, aah! Look at the airplanes scatter!

The AIM says to remain above or outside of the Class D surface area. Remaining outside Class D--more than 5 miles from the airport's center--will probably not let you see what is going on in the pattern. My suggestion would be to get a bird's eye view of the pattern by flying above Class D.

The Atlanta Town and Country Airport's elevation is 950 feet MSL. Call it 1000 feet to make your job easier. Add 2,500 for the vertical limit of Class D airspace. If you fly above 3,500 over the airport, you are outside Class D. From that vantage point, you should look for airplanes taxiing out to the runways, and for airplanes in the rectangular traffic pattern for the active runway. It's also a good idea to look out on the extended approach path for the active runway to see if any airplanes are approaching the airport from a long, straight-in approach.

As you know, the flow of traffic at an airport changes minute by minute. What you see on and around the airport, right now, will change by the time you enter the downwind leg of the traffic pattern. When you feel like you have a grip on the traffic flow at the airport, waste no time heading for a downwind entry for the landing runway.

Look Out, I'm Coming In

I recommend, as you set up for your downwind entry, you aim for a point 2 to 3 miles outside of the entry point at midfield for the landing runway. Continuously scan for traffic in the pattern and outside of the pattern. I mean, clear like your life depends on it. It does. Watch carefully for other airplanes headed for the downwind entry point from any direction. Strive to be at pattern altitude or just slightly above as you make your turn to enter the downwind entry point.

Which downwind entry point should you strive for at the airport? If the airport has a published direction for its traffic pattern--a left-hand pattern for the active runway, for example--set up for an entry that complies with the published pattern. If there is no published pattern, meaning the airport uses both left and right patterns for the active runway, strive for the entry point that matches the flow of traffic.

If other airplanes are using a right-hand pattern around the airport, insert yourself into the right-hand pattern. Why? That is where the tower controller will be looking. Since you are radio out, and transponder out, you want the tower controller to notice your airplane.

If you sneak in the back door, on the side opposite the general flow of traffic, the tower controller may not see you. Or, you may give the controller heart palpitations when you pop up unexpectedly on final approach from his blind side.

We're not as worried about the controller's heart condition as we are about giving him time to plan for your arrival. Try not to surprise the controller.

As you approach the downwind entry, visually clear the downwind like a field mouse at a dinner party for timber wolves. Watch for other airplanes on the downwind leg who are approaching the midfield entry point. If you feel entering the downwind would cut off another airplane approaching the midfield point, break off your entry by turning away from the downwind leg and climbing above pattern altitude.

When you have successfully entered the downwind leg, with good spacing ahead and behind other aircraft, your workload is going to skyrocket. Not only do you have to fly a safe circuit around the pattern, you also have to continuously crosscheck the airport tower's cab. The cab is the room at the top of the tower, surrounded by windows, where the controllers stand.

As you crosscheck the tower's cab, you are looking for a light signal. What you are hoping to see is a steady green light, meaning cleared to land. Don't expect to see the light immediately. The controllers down in the tower are going to be strategizing and sorting traffic to make sure you have a safe path to the runway. It may take them seconds or minutes to sort it out.

If you get the green light, you should rock your wings to acknowledge the signal. You don't have to perform an aerobatic maneuver. Just make a few wing wags left and right to let the controller know you saw the signal. At night, flash your navigation lights or, if you are pointed towards the tower, flash your landing light.

With a green light, you may press on towards a landing; but, don't drop the tower cab completely out of your crosscheck. Circumstances may change at the airport. The controller may feel it is unsafe for you to land right now. As a radio-out airplane, you will be given priority. That doesn't mean ATC can prevent anything and everything from getting in your way.

Going Around

Let's say it's just not your day. After you are given the green

light to land, a coyote decides to wander onto the active
runway to do whatever coyotes do in the middle of an airport.
In that case, the tower controller is going to shine a steady red
light at you, meaning "Give way to other aircraft and continue
circling." Give the tower a wing rock and climb to, or maintain,
traffic pattern altitude. If you are on final approach, simply go
around. You don't need to rock your wings. The controller will
know you got the message when you initiate your go-around.

Clear for other airplanes like a golfer looking for shelter in a
lightning storm. That red light from Tower might mean there is
a serious traffic conflict. Also, don't forget to check the status of
your own airplane. Maybe that red light from Tower meant
there was something wrong with your airplane. For example,
perhaps you got so caught up in your radio-out predicament
that you forgot to lower the landing gear on your retractable
gear airplane.

In unusual circumstances, such as a radio out situation, it's
not the unusual problem that will bite you; it's the normal
procedures that often get overlooked because your habit
patterns are disrupted by the problem. The National
Transportation Safety Board has reams of files in which pilots
destroyed perfectly good airplanes because they were
distracted by unusual events.

What follows is a brief digression, but it is a good example of
how mis-prioritizing can turn a minor problem into a major
emergency. Eastern 401 was a perfectly functional Lockheed
1011 that crashed into the Florida Everglades on a clear, calm
winter night in 1972. The flight crew devoted all their attention
to fiddling with a burned out light bulb in one of their landing
gear indicator lights. Except for the burned out light bulb, the
jet was 100% normal and flyable in all respects. The pilots let
the plane descend and crash into the swamp while they were
distracted by something slightly out of the ordinary--a burned
out light bulb.

A red light from Tower means something is wrong. What's
wrong may be inside your own airplane or even inside your
own head. If you were distracted, pull your head out of your
butt and get back in the game.

You've Been Green-Lighted

Good fortune is on your side because you get a flashing green light from tower, meaning "Return for landing." As you press in for landing you see a steady green light from Tower. On final approach, you can see your runway, Runway 36, is clear of traffic (and coyotes.) So you land.

After slowing and then clearing the runway onto the parallel taxiway, you see a flashing green light coming from the tower. This means you are cleared to taxi. You push the throttle and begin to head for your parking area on the airport.

Approaching the intersection of your taxiway and Runway 27, you keep an eagle eye on the tower. You are watching to see if the ground controller gives you a steady red light, meaning stop. In the absence of any light at all, you can continue across Runway 27 after clearing both ways for traffic. In this case, the ground controller read your mind and gave you another flashing green light to reassure you it is safe to cross the runway. Again, you may or may not get a flashing green light at intersections, so clear the area and press on in the absence of a red light.

After crossing Runway 27, it's a clear shot back to your parking area on the Southwest Ramp. You pull into your parking spot, set the brakes, and shut down. Job well done, considering the circumstances.

Getting Lit in Florida

Many years ago, I had a personal experience with light signals from a control tower. I was invited to ride along in a friend's airplane. We were flying into an airport in southern Florida--one that I had never been to. My friend's sectional chart showed this airport was uncontrolled and used a UNICOM frequency.

As we entered the downwind for this airport, with my friend making the appropriate self-announce reports on UNICOM, I saw a very tall building near the center of the airport. It looked like a control tower. I pointed the tower out to my friend. He said, "It must be under construction, or something."

The right answer was, "Or something." Shortly after he said this, as we were approaching base leg, I saw a steady green light coming from the tower. Uh oh.

My friend landed and taxied to an FBO. As we set brakes, a guy comes jogging out of the FBO's building. My friend noticed how quickly the FBO sent someone out to meet our airplane and remarked, "Good service." I said, "I've got a feeling he is about to serve you."

As soon as our airplane's propeller stopped, the man from the FBO approached the left side door and held up a piece of paper. My friend opened the door and the guy said, "Tower wants you to give them a call. Here's the phone number." He handed my friend the paper with the number on it.

I said to my friend, "Let me look at your sectional again." He handed it to me. The date on the chart was 4 years old. Apparently, in the preceding 4 years, this airport had a control tower installed and had become a controlled field.

The supervisor in the control tower gave my friend a stern lecture on the phone. At least, that is how my friend described it. I think it was more of an ass chewing.

He learned something from the lecture. Mainly, don't fly with out-of-date charts. I learned that light signals from a control tower show up very well on a sunny day.

It's time to get your airplane's radios fixed because your next flight will take you into Class C airspace. You will definitely need the radios and your transponder to work with the radar controllers at a Class C airport. When you have your avionics fixed, and you've dropped a few coins in your mechanic's cash drawer, we'll meet back here and discuss airport radar services. Such a deal!

Take Action

Answer the following questions. (Correct answers are on the last page of this chapter.):

You have determined your airplane is NORDO. You want to land at your home airport, which is in Class D airspace. As you enter the airport's downwind leg for the landing runway, you look at the airport tower and see a flashing red light. What do you do next?

You are established in an airport traffic pattern at a tower-controlled airport while NORDO. As you turn your aircraft from the downwind leg to the base leg, you see a steady green light shining from the tower. What are you cleared to do?

After landing your NORDO aircraft, you see a flashing green light from the tower. What are you cleared to do? How would your action differ if you saw the flashing green light while flying around the airport traffic pattern?

Answers:

If you see a flashing red light while in the airport traffic pattern, the light tells you the airport is unsafe. You should not land. Divert to another suitable airport within range, taking into account your airplane's remaining fuel quantity.

A steady green light from Tower means you are cleared to land.

A flashing green like from Tower, while your aircraft is on the ground, means you are cleared to taxi.

Chapter 13: Emergent Emergencies

While your airplane is in the shop for repairs to its avionics suite, let's talk. It will keep you from thinking about the repair bill you are going to get. Let's talk about those days when it would be better to be on the ground wishing you were up there, rather than being up there wishing you were on the ground. Let's talk about emergencies in the air.

You might notice we are in Chapter 13 of this book. This is as good a place as any to talk about those times when a pilot's luck runs out.

You will remember earlier, I suggested when it comes to aviation, we pilots strive to be good, rather than lucky. There is no doubt, some days, no matter how good we try to be, good luck runs out. On those days, a pilot has to call on skill and experience to overcome circumstances. A pilot can also call on ATC to help.

First, emergency or not, an air traffic controller cannot fly your airplane for you. I know you have heard stories, and perhaps watched a movie, in which an air traffic controller talks to an inexperienced pilot, or a non-pilot, and coaches that person to a safe landing. There are also many instances in which an air traffic controller has managed to calm a pilot who panicked in an emergency.

The National Air Traffic Controllers Association (NATCA) has an annual ceremony in which they present something called The Archie League Award. The award goes to the controller who performed the best save of the year. A save occurs when the actions of an air traffic controller help a pilot bring a flight to a safe conclusion in the face of bad or dire circumstances. You can listen to audio recordings of air traffic controllers performing these dramatic saves by going to http://www.natca.org and selecting Archie League Awards from the navigation menu at the website.

Oh great. Now I've given you a distraction. Okay, go ahead

and investigate that website. I know you want to. I'll wait here while you listen to some of those recordings. Do me favor though, don't get so lost on the internet that you leave me hanging here for days.

You're back? You got lost on the internet didn't you. Figures. That's okay. It gives us an opportunity to talk about getting lost--in an airplane.

Lost in Space

Getting lost is one of several self-induced predicaments that can occur in an airplane. Being lost does not begin as an emergency, if your airplane has plenty of fuel in the tanks. The less fuel you have on board, the less flight time you have remaining to resolve your situation. The less flight time you have remaining, the less distance you can travel. The less distance you can travel, the less number of suitable airports are within range of your present position. If you wait too long to seek help, you may put yourself out of reach of a suitable airport. Now, you have an emergency.

Here's how to avoid converting your predicament into a full-blown emergency. When you can no longer determine where you are, admit to yourself, "I am lost." Then, if possible, climb. Higher altitude equals better radio reception both for communication and for navaid signals. A higher altitude gives a wider field of view, meaning, you will be able to see more landmarks if the inflight visibility is good. Climbing puts more space between your airplane and obstacles on the ground. A cushion between you and obstacles is always a good thing to have while you are trying to troubleshoot a problem.

Right after that, get on the radio and say to ATC, "I am lost." Don't wait, because the longer you wait, the fewer options you will have.

If you were already in contact with ATC for flight following, your lost situation will only amount to temporary disorientation. If ATC has your airplane in radar contact, the controller can instantly advise you about your current position. End of emergency.

If you are not in contact with ATC, and you admit to yourself that you are lost, it's time to get in touch with someone on the ground who can help you identify your location. There are several ways to do that. I'll cover your options.

Calling Flight Service for help is your easiest option. While there are many discrete frequencies for Flight Service, the universal frequency, 122.2, should work anywhere there is a Flight Service radio antenna within range. Keep 122.2 locked in your memory. You might need it someday.

Dial 122.2 in Comm Radio 1 and make this radio call: "Any flight service station on 122.2, Wayward 752 Romeo Mike." As soon as you make that radio call, one or more flight service station specialists will answer your call, and help you identify your location.

Of all your options, calling Flight Service is easiest because:

- The frequency 122.2 is easy to memorize. You don't have to hunt for it on a map. It works everywhere in the United States.

- A flight service specialist is not busy controlling traffic like an air traffic controller. He can devote his full attention to your predicament.

- A flight service specialist is an expert in helping lost pilots become un-lost.

If I ever found myself lost in an airplane, and my airplane's fuel state was not critical, I would choose the flight service station option.

As a second option, you may call ATC for help. If you have a navigation chart on board, unfold it so you are looking at the general region in which you believe you are flying. Find the nearest air traffic control frequency on the chart and dial it in. The ease of finding a frequency will depend on the type of chart you have. Sectionals and terminal area charts only list frequencies for airport towers and approach control facilities. Low altitude enroute charts are the best, because they show enroute center frequencies in postage stamp-shaped boxes. The boxes are placed geographically on the map in the general vicinity ofeach control sector's area of responsibility. Note the name of the controlling agency associated with the frequency. For example, Kansas City Center, 133.4. High altitude enroute charts are not relevant for this discussion because they only cover positively controlled airspace. You would not be flying around at Flight Level 210 without talking to ATC. . . I hope.

For example, you are flying in central Iowa, VFR, and every farm field you see below looks like every other farm field. You admit to yourself you are lost. You still have more than 2 hours of fuel on board, so you have time to resolve your problem. My recommendation is to fix the problem right now. Don't burn more fuel than is necessary to get reoriented.

You know you are flying somewhere between Mason City and Fort Dodge. You find a postage stamp box for Minneapolis Center on your low altitude enroute chart for the general area where you believe you are flying. (See the enroute low chart.)

The frequency for Minneapolis Center near Fort Dodge, 134.0, can be found in the "postage stamp."

You dial in 134.0 and say, "Minneapolis Center, Wrongway 752 Romeo Mike." At this point, one of two things is going to happen. Either a controller at Minneapolis Center is going to answer you and say, "Wrongway 752 Romeo Mike, Minneapolis Center, say your position and go ahead," or, there's going to be no answer at all. If there is no answer, it's likely you are out of radio range of the ATC facility you picked off of your map.

Let's say, in this case, the controller at Minneapolis Center does answer your call. The controller will ask you what type of navigation equipment you have on board. She will ask you to tune one or more of your navigation radios to navaids in her working sector. She will also assign a transponder code to you and ask you to hit the ident button on your transponder. If she can grab your airplane on radar, your lost situation will be over. Once in radar contact, she will advise you of your exact location. For example, she might say, "Wrongway 752 Romeo Mike, radar contact three seven miles northeast of the Fort Dodge VOR."

If she can't get you in radar contact, she will help you work the navigation radios to try and determine your general position. Once the two of you have worked out your general position, she will push you over to another frequency which is used by an ATC facility with radar coverage for your position.

After switching frequencies, you will establish radar contact with the controller on the new frequency. That controller will help you get oriented and give you whatever direction you need to continue enroute or land.

If all else fails, or if you feel you need help right now, dial 121.5, the VHF emergency frequency, into Comm Radio 1. If fuel is not critical at this stage, being lost is not an emergency. You are still free to use 121.5 because there is potential for this to become an emergency.

When you need immediate assistance without declaring an emergency, you should use the word "Pan" on the radio. Dial in 121.5 and say, "Pan, pan, pan. Any air traffic control agency on this frequency, Wrongway 752 Romeo Mike." Then listen. You should get at least one air traffic controller to respond. If more than one controller responds, pick the call sign of one and respond: "Wrongway 752 Romeo Mike is lost and needs your assistance." I know it may be a little embarrassing to admit this on the radio, but no one is going to laugh. The air traffic controller will take your situation very seriously.

If you are out of radio range of any ATC facility, or if you are in a radio blind spot created by high terrain, you may get a response on 121.5 from another airborne pilot. Ask the pilot who answers your call to relay your request for assistance to ATC. You should be able to nail down your position and get additional assistance using this relay method.

Before we wrap up this segment on getting lost, let's address fuel one more time. If you become lost and you are running low on fuel, bear this in mind: Talking on the radios will not improve your fuel state. If fuel is low, get on the ground using the sailor's motto, "Any port in a storm."

No matter where you think you are, and no matter where you actually are when you become lost, if your airplane's fuel quantity has reached the point where landing immediately is your only option, then land.

Forget about trying to reach someone on the radio. Look around and spot an airport close by, with enough runway on which to land. Land there, even if it isn't your intended destination. Land there, even if it's a grass strip and you were planning to land on concrete or asphalt. Just land, and then worry about what happens next. Don't be the next pilot who overflies a good airport because it doesn't look like it has an FBO or a town nearby. Just land.

Any Mountaintop Air Patch Will Do

One time, when I was ferrying a Mooney for a friend, the airplane's engine started running rough. I was over the mountains of West Virginia when this happened. If you have ever flown in this area, you know it is not the most hospitable place for a forced landing. Fortunately, I spotted what looked like a dirt landing strip on the top of a mountain. It was nothing more than a lane of dirt on the bald top of a forest-covered peak. There was nothing else around the strip except trees.

I would never consider landing on a mountain top under any other circumstance. You cannot be choosy about where you land when your airplane needs to be on the ground, right now. I landed, and worried about where I had landed afterword.

Becoming lost can be just another story you can tell, if you admit you are lost well before your fuel quantity gets critically low. (Or, it can be a story you can keep to yourself if you don't care to tell your friends you got lost.) Air traffic control, Flight Service, and even other pilots can help you out on the radio. As pilot in command, you are the final decision maker when it comes to flight safety, so don't let jabbering on the radio take priority over landing before your plane runs out of fuel.

Feeling Fuelish

While we are on the subject of fuel, remember those four words you are never supposed to say to passengers in your airplane? Our first "F" is fuel. Now is a good time to explain why, in the context of emergencies. Just a moment ago, we looked at how your airplane's fuel quantity can influence your actions during the time you are lost. Let's look at a low fuel state for its own sake.

When you are in contact with ATC, and fuel is getting critically low, there are words you can say to air traffic control that will influence how quickly you can get your airplane on the ground. First, you can whine on the radio about how low your fuel is getting. I hear pilots make this mistake every once in a while.

"Approach, Airliner 894's fuel is getting kind of low. How much longer do you think it will be before you can fit us in for landing?" Or, "Hey Approach, Private Aircraft 536 Lima Zulu, we're starting to look at our low fuel situation. Where are we in the sequence for landing?"

These kinds of statements might get an air traffic controller's attention. They might also influence an air traffic controller to move the pilot who moans about his fuel state a little further up the line for landing. Then again, whining about fuel might just fall on deaf ears.

If you really want air traffic control to sit up and take notice of your low fuel situation, there are two specific code phrases you can use. The first is "Minimum fuel." The second--and more urgent--is "Emergency fuel."

When an air traffic controller hears a pilot declare "Minimum fuel," it means the pilot cannot accept any further delay before landing. Minimum fuel does not mean the pilot needs priority to land. It does mean ATC should keep the pilot in the normal landing sequence without further delay.

Although not specifically defined, "further delay" might include intentionally moving the affected aircraft further back in the sequence of aircraft lined up for landing. It may also mean putting an airplane into a holding pattern, asking the pilot to circle, or giving the pilot extensive headings off course, thus delaying landing. ATC will not take these actions after a pilot declares minimum fuel, except to give a higher priority to an emergency aircraft.

Speaking of emergency aircraft, if you declare "Emergency fuel," you are telling ATC to give you priority to land, stat! Emergency fuel means, if ATC does not allow you to jump to the head of the line of aircraft, and land immediately, your airplane may run out of fuel before landing.

If your airplane's fuel quantity is getting critically low, which statement should you make to ATC? Here is the guidance I use to determine whether I should declare "minimum fuel" or "emergency fuel." These are only my techniques. They are not written in the AIM or the CFRs. You and your flight instructor might use different guidance.

Given your aircraft's rate of fuel burn, if you feel your current fuel state will allow an attempted landing, with just enough fuel to make a go-around and one more landing attempt before the fuel tanks run dry, it's time to declare minimum fuel.

If landing conditions at your intended destination are questionable and you think there is a possibility you might have to divert to another airport, minimum fuel changes slightly. Your fuel state should allow an attempted landing at your original destination, followed by a go-around, followed by a divert to a landing at another airport. If you feel you have just enough fuel to do all of this, and no more, it's time to declare minimum fuel.

If your aircraft's fuel quantity is low enough that you believe you have only enough fuel to fly directly to a final approach and land, with no go-around option, it's time to declare emergency fuel. Simple enough. Again, this is my technique. You may have different criteria.

It doesn't matter which criteria you use, as long as you make the minimum fuel or emergency fuel radio call when your personal criteria are met. Pilots worry about declaring minimum or emergency fuel with ATC. That's why you hear pilots hemming and hawing about their fuel to ATC without actually declaring anything.

Pilots believe if they make a declaration, they will be investigated by the FAA. They believe their judgement will be questioned for letting their fuel get so low. Or, perhaps they believe the investigation will show they had enough fuel, making the emergency declaration unnecessary. They worry that one thing will lead to another and they might lose their pilot license.

All of this worry is utter nonsense in the context of an emergency. To these pilots I say, if you run out of fuel before landing, you will definitely lose something. I say, make your declaration and land safely. Worrying about anything other than a safe landing is not worthy of a pilot in command.

Fire!

Fire is the next "F" in our hit parade. You don't have to actually see fire in the cockpit or cabin of your aircraft to know it's there. Where there's smoke there's fire, or the potential for fire. At the first sign of smoke, declare an emergency with ATC and get on the ground now. There are only a few emergencies that require quick action and a clearance direct to the threshold of a runway. Fire, or the indications of fire, is one of those emergencies.

While you are declaring your emergency, be sure to tell ATC you want the fire trucks standing by for your arrival. If you use the word smoke or fire in your emergency radio call, ATC will almost certainly forward a request for rescue and fire fighting service at your destination. Still, it's a good idea to make the request.

When you declare an emergency, ATC is going to need some basic information to pass along to the airport rescue and fire fighting service. The controller will want to know how many people are on board your aircraft.

The reason for this is obvious. He'll also want to know how much fuel you have remaining. You should tell ATC how much fuel you have in hours and minutes. You don't have to calculate the time to the second. Make a general calculation and pass it on.

Relaying your fuel on board helps two ways. First it tells ATC how much time aloft you have remaining, should your emergency require some sort of delay before landing.

For example, if you cannot get your retractable landing gear to extend and lock, fuel on board becomes very important. An emergency for failure to extend landing gear looks very different if you have 3 hours of fuel remaining versus 30 minutes of fuel remaining.

Second, fuel on board is an item of special interest to fire fighters. An airplane loaded with fuel may present a much larger problem for fire fighters than an airplane with very little fueling remaining in the tanks. More fuel on board equals a bigger fire if your emergency leads to a fire. They need this information in order to calculate how much manpower and equipment might be needed.

ATC may also ask if you are carrying any hazardous materials on board. Hazardous material, or HAZMAT, gets special attention from the fire and rescue service. If ATC doesn't ask, and you are carrying HAZMAT, let ATC know. If HAZMAT is on board, fire and rescue has to plan for containment and decontamination if the material's container is compromised as a result of your emergency.

I sugar-coated what might happen to the HAZMAT container. What I meant to say was, the fire department has to plan for containment and decontamination when the container disintegrates in the fiery crash of your airplane. Better?

As you can see, when you declare an emergency, your workload on the radio will probably go way up. First, remember your priorities:

1.   Aviate: Meaning always maintain aircraft control.

2.   Navigate: Meaning, fly where you need to fly and don't hitting anything in the process.

3. Communicate: When the aircraft's flight path is stabilized, and you can keep it that way; and, you are headed where you need to be headed safely, only then allow time for radio communication.

If you are not already in contact with ATC when an emergency arises, squawk 7700 on your transponder. Here's why. When you squawk the emergency code, it alerts every radar control facility that you are a priority aircraft. This will prepare all controllers handling traffic in your vicinity to clear a path for you, whether you talk to these controllers or not. It says, "Get everybody out of my way. I have my hands full!"

When you declare your emergency on the radio, other pilots should yield to you on the radio. Certainly ATC will give your radio calls a priority. In some situations, particularly at very busy airports, your radio calls may have to fit into the general flow radio calls from other pilots.

Several months before I began writing this book, a Delta Boeing 757, taking off from Kennedy International Airport in New York, experienced an engine failure. The pilots handled the emergency calmly and methodically. Their biggest complication was trying to get in a word on the radio when told to contact Kennedy Tower. The tower controller was so busy moving other aircraft out of the way of the emergency aircraft's path that the radio was completely tied up. The pilot handling the radio in the 757 with the emergency had to make 5 radio calls to Tower before he could establish contact and get landing instructions.

There might be a way to simplify your radio workload. If you are working with approach controller, you may request to remain on that controller's frequency through the approach and landing phase. The approach controller should be able to coordinate with the tower controller at your destination and obtain landing clearance for you. This might not work in every situation. It's worth asking, especially if you cannot afford the distraction of making contact with a new controller during your emergency.

In the Soup

Fog, another "F" to avoid, may or may not constitute an emergency. Fog is relevant to this discussion because it has bitten so many VFR-only pilots in the past. History has shown, when a non-instrument rated pilot enters fog, cloud, or any other weather phenomenon that prevents a pilot from distinguishing up from down, disorientation can be minutes or seconds away. Disorientation almost always leads to loss of aircraft control. Here's how ATC can help.

In general, VFR pilots are good at maintaining VFR cloud clearances and inflight visibility. They rarely wander into instrument meteorological conditions (IMC) without doing their best to avoid it. More often than not, if a problem with IMC is going to occur, it happens when a VFR pilot scud runs below a cloud deck or when he attempts to maintain VFR above a cloud deck or fog bank.

If you ever find yourself trapped above or below a cloud layer, and it seems like there is no place to go to avoid IMC, get on the radio with ATC. Air traffic controllers, while not equipped with dedicated weather radar, have a lot of useful information at their fingertips. In general, an air traffic controller has access to almost all of the weather data available to a specialist at a flight service station. Unlike a flight service station specialist, an air traffic controller can steer you toward better weather conditions most of the time.

ATC does have its limits when it comes to weather. While ATC can look at weather charts depicting broad areas of good and bad weather, air traffic controllers cannot pinpoint areas of IMC and visual meteorological conditions (VMC) (with a few exceptions that I'll discuss in a moment). Some approach control facilities at the biggest airports have doppler weather radar overlaid on their air traffic control displays, but doppler radar is rare elsewhere. If an approach controller uses integrated doppler radar, he can steer your aircraft around areas of precipitation with amazing accuracy.

Enroute center controllers can only tell you where general areas of precipitation are occurring, with only broad indications of intensity. You will often hear statements from center controllers, such as "Light to moderate to extreme precipitation along your route of flight." Well, thanks for nothing Mr. Controller. That helps a lot. It is better than a stick in the eye;

and it might help you from entering a downpour of rain.

ATC does excel at telling you which airports in your area have the best weather for landing. Controllers have access to surface weather depiction charts, as well as the specific weather conditions for the airports with weather-reporting systems. When you need a place to land with suitable weather for your pilot rating, ATC has the quickest answer.

While we are on the subject of suitable airports, air traffic controllers can call up displays of the charts for every airport within their area of responsibility. Need to know how long the runway is at XYZ Airport? ATC can tell you. Need to know if there is an airport fire and rescue service at the airport? ATC can tell you. Need to know if there is emergency medical service at or near the airport because you have a medical emergency on board? ATC can tell you.

Chest Pains

Speaking of medical emergencies, let's go there now. Yes, I know we were supposed to be talking about the four "Fs." The last "F", which I refuse to put into print into this book, is not an emergency anyways. At least it isn't an emergency for most sane people.

When you do have an actual medical emergency on board, you should state "Medical emergency" to ATC. Using those words still gives your airplane priority, and they do something else. They signal the air traffic controller to alert emergency medical services to meet your airplane on arrival.

Typically, in a medical emergency, ATC will want to know something about about the person in distress. Be prepared to pass along basic information about the victim, such as gender, age and known medical issues or history. ATC has access to anyone you could reach by phone call if you were on the ground. If you have another passenger on board who can administer first air or other treatment for the patient, don't hesitate to ask ATC to give medical personnel a call for guidance.

Let's finish up our overview by covering our last "F": Final. When you declare an emergency, you can do whatever you feel is necessary to arrive safely on final approach as quickly as necessary. The CFRs say you may go so far as to disregard any aviation regulation that stands between you and resolving your emergency safely.

91.3 Responsibility and authority of the pilot in command.

(a) The pilot in command of an aircraft is directly responsible for, and is the final authority as to, the operation of that aircraft.

(b) In an in-flight emergency requiring immediate action, the pilot in command may deviate from any rule of this part to the extent required to meet that emergency.

For example, in the past, when I have been a pilot with a medical emergency on board, I have disregarded the normal arrival pattern for an airport and flown directly to a short final approach. In a very dire situation, such as having a passenger in the midst of an apparent heart attack, I have disregarded the requirement to fly no faster than 250 knots indicated airspeed below 10,000 feet in North America.

One time, with an apparent heart attack victim on board my aircraft, I flew directly towards the runway at Mexico City, doing 300 knots indicated. I extended the aircraft's speed brakes, and dumped the landing gear, slowing just in time to reach a stabilized final approach at 1000 feet above the ground. After landing, the Mexico City tower controller approved a 180-degree turn on the runway. The captain taxied on the runway towards the terminal at a rate of speed that would not have been possible on the taxiways at Mexico City.

With emergency priority, we shaved at least 10 minutes off our travel time from the time we were made aware of the passenger in distress until we reached the jetway at the airport terminal. When someone is possibly dying in the passenger cabin, saving 10 minutes may be the difference between life and death.

The heart attack victim? It turned out to be gas pains. He walked off the jet, smiling. Son-of a- . . . I mean, I'm happy for the guy!

Mayday!

Still under the F-word "Final," let's talk about what to say on the radio when your emergency is extreme. I'm talking about an emergency in which a crash seems inevitable. That's the time to call "Mayday."

A Mayday radio call should be reserved for life threatening situations. These may include, but are not limited to:

- Loss (or imminent loss) of aircraft control for any number of different reasons

- Control surface or structural failure

- Engine failure leading to a forced landing/ditching/ejection/bailout

- Spatial disorientation

- An out-of-control onboard fire

There are probably more examples, but let's not stress ourselves any further by thinking about them. Instead, let's look at what the Aeronautical Information Manual has to say about using Mayday on the radio:

6-3-1 Distress and Urgency Communications

c. The initial communication, and if considered necessary, any subsequent transmissions by an aircraft in distress should begin with the signal MAYDAY, preferably repeated three times. The signal PAN-PAN should be used in the same manner for an urgency condition.

d. Distress communications have absolute priority over all other communications, and the word MAYDAY commands radio silence on the frequency in use. Urgency communications have priority over all other communications except distress, and the word PAN-

PAN warns other stations not to interfere with urgency transmissions.

Note the difference between Mayday and Pan-Pan. Mayday commands radio silence. No other pilots or controllers should speak while the distress situation is under way. Pan-pan gives the pilot in an urgent situation top priority on the radio. Other conversations may continue as long as they do not interfere with communication between the pilot making the Pan-Pan call, and the agency contacted.

A Simulated Emergency

Let's tie all this together by running through a simulated emergency. We'll say you are inbound for landing at Atlanta Town and Country Airport, about 30 miles out, when all of a sudden, you smell oily smoke in the cockpit. You are currently talking to Atlanta Approach under VFR flight following.

"Cessna 9130 Delta is declaring an emergency for smoke in the cockpit." As you say this, you dial 7700 into your transponder. There is good reason to do this. Even though the controller you are working with knows about your emergency, right now he is the only one who knows. By squawking the emergency code, you alert every other controller in the area as to your situation.

ATC: "Cessna 30 Delta, Atlanta copies. Say your intentions."

You: "Cessna 30 Delta needs to land immediately."

ATC: "Cessna 30 Delta, Atlanta Town and Country airport is at your 1 o'clock and 30 miles. Fulton County Airport is at your 5 o'clock and 7 miles. Fulton County has a 6,800 foot long runway and full fire fighting service. What would you prefer?"

You: "Cessna 30 Delta will go for Fulton County."

ATC: "Cessna 30 Delta, roger. Turn right heading one two zero. Descend at your discretion to traffic pattern altitude, which will be one thousand eight hundred feet for Fulton County."

You: "Cessna 30 Delta, heading one two zero. Pilot's

discretion to one thousand eight hundred."

ATC: "Cessna 30 Delta, runways available are 8 and 26 or 15 and 33. As you roll out on the one two zero degree, Runway 26, the longest runway, will be at your one to two o'clock and 5 miles. The Fulton County winds are three one zero at ten knots. Altimeter three zero, zero one. I've called ahead to the airport and you are cleared to land on any runway."

You: "Cessna 30 Delta. Runway 26 will work. I have the runway in sight."

ATC: "Cessna 30 Delta, I copy. You can remain this frequency. When you are able, can you give me number of people on board and your fuel remaining?"

You: "Cessna 30 Delta has 2 people on board and one hour plus four five on the fuel."

ATC: "Cessna 30 Delta, Atlanta copies 2 on board. Fuel, one plus four five."

You: "Verify for Cessna 30 Delta that the fire department has been alerted."

ATC: "Cessna 30 Delta, the emergency equipment is standing by and the fire chief has been notified of your situation."

Declaring an emergency with ATC will move you to the front of the line for landing. It will also get you almost any type of help you need from people on the ground. The only thing ground personnel--including air traffic controllers--will not be able to do is fly the airplane for you. ATC can provide a lot of assistance, but it's ultimately up to you to maintain aircraft control. With that in mind, never sacrifice aircraft control to talk on the radio. Further, don't waste time talking on the radio if your situation requires immediate action to land.

Finally (there's that word again), if you think you should declare an emergency, declare an emergency. Do not let your concern about a post-emergency investigation cloud your judgement. As pilot-in-command, your top priority is safety. Do what it takes to get safely on the ground.

Emergencies are serious stuff. That's why I didn't joke around very much with you in this chapter. We'll get back to happier subjects in the coming pages. It's time to get airborne and shoot the breeze with Approach Control. Let's do it!

Take Action

Calculate the fuel quantities at which you would declare Minimum Fuel and Emergency Fuel to ATC in the following situation. (Answers are on the last page of this chapter.):

Let's say you are flying an aircraft that has fuel tanks in the left and in the right wing. The fuel capacity of each wing tank is 20 gallons. Let's also assume the left wing tank is empty and the fuel level in the right wing fuel tank is getting very low. You know your airplane burns, on average, 1 gallon of fuel to make 1 complete circuit around an airport traffic pattern.

Let's assume there is 20 minutes of flying time from your present position to touchdown on the runway at the nearest suitable airport. You calculate it will take 3 gallons of fuel to cover the distance to the runway and to land. Assuming your aircraft's fuel gauges are accurate to + or -2 gallons of fuel when the fuel indicator is at or below the 1/4-tank mark, at what fuel indication would you declare Minimum Fuel to ATC?

At what fuel indication would you declare Emergency Fuel to ATC?

Let's say you have declared Minimum Fuel to ATC. When you roll your aircraft out on final approach to the airport's one and only runway, the aircraft landing ahead of you blows a tire and stops on the runway. Tower tells you to discontinue your approach and go-around. Tower also says the runway will be closed for at least 20 minutes while the other airplane is cleared from the runway and the runway is checked for debris. There is another airport with a suitable runway, 10 minutes flying time from your present position. What would you say to ATC?

You are flying a twin-engined aircraft capable of cruising at 280 knots indicated airspeed (KIAS) at 5,000. You are presently at 5,500, 20 miles northeast of the Bismarck Airport in North Dakota. You are in contact with Minneapolis Center for VFR flight following. You have 4 passengers on board.

Suddenly, one of your passengers clutches his chest, groans loudly, and then slumps over in his seat. The passenger sitting next to this man says, "I think he is having a heart attack." Write down what you would say to ATC and what you would do with your aircraft from this point forward.

Answers

At what fuel indication would you declare Minimum Fuel to ATC? At just above 1/4 tank remaining in the right wing tank. Here's the calculation: 3 gallons to fly from present position to landing + 1 gallon to reject the first attempt at landing and fly another circuit around the pattern = 4 gallons total.

Your fuel gauge indicates full at 20 gallons, so a quarter tank = 5 gallons +/- 2 gallons. Add in the error factor of 2 gallons to your previous calculation of 4 gallons and you arrive at 6 gallons of fuel remaining, or an indication of just slightly above the 1/4 mark for the right wing tank.

You would declare Emergency Fuel at 5 gallons remaining (3 gallons to reach the runway + 2 gallons margin of error on the fuel gauge). Realistically, since the indicator needles on most fuel gauges for light, single-engine aircraft bounce up and down in turbulence, I personally would declare Emergency Fuel as my fuel remaining approached 1/4 tank for this example airplane.

Caution: The preceding fuel exercises are designed to get you thinking about when to declare Minimum Fuel or Emergency Fuel. They should not be taken as absolute guidance for your airplane. Consult your flight instructor for guidance on fuel calculations that would apply to your airplane.

If you had previous declared Minimum Fuel and the runway closed at your intended destination as you reach final approach, you should change your declaration to Emergency Fuel and immediately begin your divert to your alternate airport. ATC estimates for runway closure times can be way off the mark. Talk to your flight instructor about all of your options in this type of situation.

You would say, "Minneapolis Center, Twin Cessna 9130 Delta

is declaring a medical emergency. I need to proceed direct to the active runway at Bismarck." You would then fly at your aircraft's maximum forward airspeed toward the tower-controlled airport. ATC would ask you basic questions about your medical emergency, such as the patient's name, approximate age, and your best estimate of the patient's condition. You would fly your aircraft to a short approach for the landing runway, slowing early enough to make a normal, un-rushed landing. Think about the radio calls you would make in this situation. Chair fly the entire arrival, landing, and the taxi to an area where paramedics could meet your aircraft.

Chapter 14: Skipping out of Charlie's Class

In a previous chapter I said, when you are flying VFR and request flight following, you are free to do as you please in your airplane. Of course, you are still obligated to maintain VFR cloud clearances and inflight visibility, and, to follow the Consolidated Flight Rules for general aviation. Flight following is a passive service. ATC will not attempt to direct your airplane unless you request specific directions. Even when there may be a flight path conflict with another aircraft, ATC will only suggest a heading to avoid the other aircraft. You are not required to follow ATC's suggestion. (My guess is, Mr. T would say, "I pity the fool who does not follow ATC's suggested heading to avoid traffic.")

When you enter Class C airspace--airspace controlled by a Terminal Radar Approach Control (TRACON)--you are not required to accept control by radar. All that's required to enter Class C airspace is radio contact with TRACON. Even that is not a big deal.

For example, you are approaching the lateral boundary of Class C airspace. You tune in the approach control frequency for the TRACON serving your destination airport. You make your radio call to the approach controller like this:

"Humidor Approach, Sky Goddess 779 Uniform Whiskey, two zero miles east of Humidor, with information Tango." Humidor approach comes back with "Sky Goddess 779 Uniform Whisky, standby. Break, break. Ridiculously Large 290 Heavy, descend and maintain niner thousand."

Humidor Approach told you to stand by. Does that mean you have to hold outside of Class C until the approach controller has time for you? Let's go to the Aeronautical Information Manual:

3-2-4. Class C Airspace

3. Arrival or Through Flight Entry Requirements.

1. Arrival or Through Flight Entry Requirements. Two-way radio communication must be established with the ATC facility providing ATC services prior to entry and thereafter maintain those communications while in Class C airspace.

NOTE--
If the controller responds to a radio call with,"(aircraft callsign) standby," radio communications have been established and the pilot can enter the Class C airspace.

[Ed.: Underline added for emphasis.]

2. If workload or traffic conditions prevent immediate provision of Class C services, the controller will inform the pilot to remain outside the Class C airspace until conditions permit the services to be provided.

3. It is important to understand that if the controller responds to the initial radio call without using the aircraft identification, radio communications have not been established and the pilot may not enter the Class C.

In our example, the controller responded to you with your aircraft call sign and "standby," so you are welcome to enter the Class C airspace. Isn't VFR flight a hoot? There's almost nothing you can't do, and you still get the benefit of working with ATC.

Once inside Class C airspace you are not required to take direction from TRACON. You may do all of your coordination with the airport tower controller at your destination airport. I didn't make that up. Here it is in black and white in the Air Traffic Controllers Manual J.O. 7110.65:

Section 6. Basic Radar Service to VFR Aircraft-Terminal

7-6-2. SERVICE AVAILABILITY

Aircraft which do not desire radar service may be fitted into the landing sequence by the tower. Coordination of these aircraft shall be accomplished with the approach control unless a facility directive/LOA [Letter of Agreement] prescribes otherwise. Nonparticipating aircraft shall, to the extent possible, be given the same landing sequence they would have received had they been sequenced by radar vectors.

There are many reasons why you might not want radar control inside Class C. If you don't intend to land at an airport inside Class C, you might not desire radar control. For example, let's say you want to poke your head inside of Class C to sight-see; or dust crops; or do a photographic mission; or do an aerial inspection of a power line; or do search and rescue; or hunt down a criminal operation. Any of these missions would require more freedom of movement than a radar controller would provide.

When you need to accomplish free flight inside of Class C, you still need to establish communications with the controller and place your airplane in radar contact. That means you must have an operable transponder with Mode C. The air traffic controller will assign a code to your transponder, or ask you for your transponder code if one was assigned by another controller. The controller will then ask you where and at what altitudes you will be operating. The format is similar to flight following, except inside Class C, the flight following is mandatory.

AIM 3-2-4. Class C Airspace

c. Operating Rules and Pilot/Equipment Requirements:

Pilot Certification.
No specific certification required.

Equipment.

(a) Two-way radio; and

(b) Unless otherwise authorized by ATC, an operable radar beacon transponder with automatic altitude reporting equipment.

Example of operations inside Class C when landing is not desired:

Pilot: "Pipeline 401 Hotel Bravo will be flying north along the pipeline next to I-95, at or below 2,000."

ATC: "Pipeline 401 Hotel Bravo, roger. Advise me before you climb above 2,000 at the end of your inspection run."

That's an overview of Class C operations. We'll get further into the details as we fly in your airplane. That's right. I'm going to scam more flying hours from you, in your airplane, on your dime.

The Big Upgrade at the Home Drome

More news for you. While we have been shooting the breeze during the last couple of chapters, those crazy cut-ups at the Department of Transportation expanded the budget for Atlanta Town and Country Airport.

Let's see what your tax dollars and landing fees hath wrought. KATC now has its very own TRACON, called Town and Country Approach, or Town and Country Departure, depending on whether you are inbound or outbound to the airport. The facility has two radar positions. One controller handles arrivals and departures to and from the north. The other controller handles traffic inbound and outbound to the south.

KATC's approach control sectors are divided along an east-west line, illustrated in the airport's charts. At KATC, an airplane arriving from any bearing between the ATC VORTAC 271-degree radial clockwise to the 090-degree radio would use the frequency for the North approach controller. If arriving from a bearing of 091 degrees clockwise to 270 degrees, South approach control frequency would be used.

Even though the TRACON sectors are divided into north and south segments, both controllers are referred to simply as "Town and Country Approach," or "Town and Country Departure."

The installation of a dedicated airport surveillance radar system allowed the airport authority to add a Minimum Safe Altitude Warning (MSAW) system in the airport tower. A computer monitors the altitude reports (Mode C) coming in from the transponders of aircraft working around the airport. The computer compares the airplane's altitude report against the height of the terrain over which the airplane is flying. When the computer detects an airplane is flying too close to terrain or ground-based obstructions, the computer will trigger an alarm in the airport tower. The tower controller then relays this information to the descending aircraft by saying, "Low altitude alert. Check your altitude." The AIM says pilots of VFR aircraft have to request MSAW monitoring to receive the service. The service is automatically provided for pilots operating under IFR.

There is a less-sophisticated version of MSAW, called Low Altitude Alert System, or LAAS. This system triggers an alert at the controller's position when an airplane descends below a preset minimum safe altitude for the area in which it is flying. Like MSAW, LAAS is automatically provided to pilots flying IFR, but must be requested by pilots flying VFR.

This is another case where the FAA knows not to load VFR pilots up with services they don't want. It's really a good deal when you get to pick and choose the level of service you want.

There are other, new services at Atlanta Town and Country. The airport has gotten busy enough to justify a third air traffic control position in the tower. There is now a controller who handles clearance delivery on frequency 125.07. Clearance Delivery relays route clearances to pilots departing on IFR flight. Clearance Delivery also assigns transponder codes and departure instructions to VFR aircraft.

The Airport Improvement Project also allowed KATC to get Airport Surveillance Detection Equipment with X-band radar. The ASDE-X system is a ground-scanning radar that depicts the position of aircraft taxiing on the airport. The system also provides a data block for each taxiing aircraft that shows the aircraft type and its call sign. I'll have more on how this affects you in a moment.

After all of the money outlay for these improvements, there were still a few coins left over to install an airport windshear detection system. The windshear detection system is a series of sophisticated weather vanes and anemometers on towers scattered around the airport. These towers relay wind speed and direction to a central computer that compares the readings. When the computer detects a sudden shift in wind direction or speed over a certain threshold, it will trigger an alarm in the control tower along with relevant wind data. The tower controller will pass this information along to pilots with the warning, "Windshear alert!" along with the location and degree of wind shift. For example, "Windshear alert! North field boundary winds are three three zero at two five. South field boundary winds two one zero at one six." (You can tell Atlanta Town and Country airport is a true work of fiction. Only the largest airports, with significant landing fees, can pay for this level of air traffic control technology. I threw all of this into KATC to illustrate what is possible in air traffic control.)

Let's Work the New System

Lucky you. You get to try out all of this whiz-bang technology on your next flight, which happens to be right now. Your first indication of all the improvements at KATC is in the new messages contained in ATIS:

"Atlanta Town and Country Airport information X-ray. One nine five three Zulu weather. Seven thousand scattered. Visibility seven miles. Temperature two one. Dewpoint one seven. Wind, two zero zero degrees at one two, gust two zero. Altimeter three zero one three. Runway One Eight in use. Landing and Departing Runway One Eight. Departing Runway Two Seven. All aircraft contact Clearance Delivery on one two five point zero seven prior to taxi. All aircraft operate transponder with Mode C while taxiing. Read back all hold short clearances. Advise that you have received information X-ray."

Just as we expected. For the airport's ASDE-X radar to work, you have to run your transponder, with altitude reporting feature on, while taxiing. Let's add that to our Before Taxi checklist. Also, we'll have to call Clearance Delivery before we taxi, even though we are departing VFR.

Clearance Delivery has one other function that I haven't mentioned yet. If there are any departure delays, for any reason, Clearance Delivery will let you know about the delay. With this in mind, there is no sense starting your aircraft's engine before calling Clearance Delivery. If there is a delay, it would be better to wait it out without burning fuel.

Get Your Clearance

I've tuned Comm Radio 1 to 125.07 and I'll get the clearance, Clarence. "Town and Country Clearance, Cessna 9130 Delta. On the Southwest Ramp. VFR to the northwest with information X-ray."

ATC: "Cessna 9130 Delta, Town and Country Clearance, right now you are number twenty in line for departure. Do you plan on taxiing right now, or would you like to wait out the delay on the ramp?"

"If we wait on the ramp," I ask, "will it affect our place in line for departure? Cessna 9130 Delta."

ATC: "Cessna 30 Delta, negative. Monitor this frequency and I'll call you in about one zero minutes. I should be able to fit you into the sequence with no further delay about then."

"Cessna 30 Delta. We'll call you in one zero minutes."

This is one of the great advantages of having an on-airport clearance delivery. The controller at that position usually has his finger on the pulse of ground traffic and departures. His advice can help you save gallons of fuel.

Some of the larger airports, especially those that handle large amounts of commercial air traffic, have a radio frequency dedicated to metering. The controller in the metering position is there specifically to tell you how long you will be delayed on the ground. Metering may give you a specific time to call for your taxi clearance. Metering is designed to relieve taxiway congestion and conserve fuel. It's a great program, though it can be frustrating to be told your expected taxi time is 3 hours from now.

The Big Picture

While we are waiting for our delay to end, here's the plan. I suppose we should have talked about this earlier. While you were busy getting a chicken salad sandwich from the refrigerator, or doing who-knows-what, between chapters of this book, I filed a VFR flight plan from here to Lovell Field. That's the name of the Chattanooga Airport (KCHA) in southern Tennessee. It lies inside Class C airspace.

Our filed route of flight is direct to the Rome VOR, which is 20 nautical miles northwest of here. From over Rome, we'll fly north on the Victor 333 airway to the Choo Choo VORTAC, which is 5 miles southeast of the airport. From there, we will make our approach and landing at Lovell Field.

On the flight plan, I said it would take 35 minutes to fly to KCHA. We are planning a cruising altitude of 6,500. We'll activate our flight plan with Macon Radio after we get airborne.

I figure after we land at Chattanooga, we can get some lunch at the airport cafe and then head back here. If you are full after eating your between chapters chicken salad sandwich, you can have a soft drink and watch me eat. Sound good? (As if you have a choice in the matter.)

Clearance Read Back/Hear Back

Thanks to the magic of fiction, 10 minutes have passed since we talked to Clearance Delivery. The controller at Clearance Delivery says, "Cessna 9130 Delta, Town and Country Clearance. We can take you right now. Are you ready to taxi?"

"We can be ready in 2 minutes, Cessna 9130 Delta."

"Cessna 9130 Delta, roger. Are you ready to copy your clearance?"

"Cessna 9130 Delta is ready," I answer. Here is a big foot stomper. Don't say you are ready until you have a pen in hand, with the ballpoint poised over a piece of paper. VFR clearances are usually simple and easy to remember, but it pays to get in the habit of writing your clearance on paper. Later, when you work on your IFR rating, and your pre-departure clearance is not so simple, you'll be glad you got into the writing habit early.

ATC: "Cessna 9130 Delta. Departure frequency will be one three four point six. Squawk zero three four seven. Contact Ground, one two one point niner when ready to taxi. Verify you have information X-ray."

"Cessna 9130 Delta, one three four point six. Squawking zero three four seven; and point niner when ready to taxi, and we have X-ray." Notice a few key points in my reply to Clearance.

First, I read back the numbers. He doesn't need to hear me say "Departure frequency," because both of us know the only frequency we are going to get, apart from Ground Control, is a departure frequency. I didn't really need to even repeat the frequency numbers, but this is a new frequency for me, so I wanted him to listen to my read back for verification.

Also, the AIM says, when reading back a ground control frequency, it is not necessary to read back 121 because most ground frequencies begin with 121. (There are exceptions.) The AIM says if I read back the ground frequency, reading back the number to the right of the decimal point is all that is necessary. In this case, I read back, "point niner."

Let me digress for just a second to talk about ATC's hear back policy:

2-4-3. PILOT ACKNOWLEDGMENT/READ BACK

a. When issuing clearances or instructions ensure acknowledgment by the pilot.

NOTE-
Pilots may acknowledge clearances, instructions, or other information by using "Wilco," "Roger," "Affirmative," or other words or remarks.

REFERENCE-
AIM, Para 4-2-3, Contact Procedures.

   b. If altitude, heading, or other items are read back
   by the pilot, ensure the read back is correct. If
   incorrect or incomplete, make corrections as
   appropriate.

   Air traffic controllers do their utmost to listen to your read
back and make corrections when necessary. The ability of an air
traffic controller to hear and respond to every read back
depends on the controller's workload.

   It's a rare occasion when you are the only pilot flying in a
controller's airspace. His attention is usually divided among
many airplanes in his sector. Even as he is giving you a
clearance, he is thinking about his clearance for the next
airplane in his scan, and perhaps, about his clearances for
several airplanes beyond the next.

   An air traffic controller is the the ultimate multi-tasker. In
some situations, multi-tasking is very difficult for a person.
Multi-tasking, while promising in concept, does not always
work as well as we think it does.

   Sometimes, an air traffic controller has too much going on to
fully absorb your read back and check it for accuracy. Don't
depend on an air traffic controller to catch mistakes in every
read back. If you really aren't sure about a clearance, don't just
blurt out what you thought the controller meant, hoping he'll
correct you. If you need clarification, ask for it.

Turn a Wheel

   Alright. I digressed so far, I almost forgot what we were
about to do. Let's spin that prop and get out of here! Our
anticipated taxi route will be the same as the last time we flew:
Taxiways Bravo and Charlie, to hold short of Runway 27. Then
continue on Charlie to the end at Taxiway Golf; or we'll make
an intersection departure from Taxiway Foxtrot. Take a look at
the airport diagram (next page) if you need to review the plan.

   "Town and Country Ground, Cessna 9130 Delta, holding

short of Bravo on the Southwest Ramp. Ready to taxi." Notice I didn't give Ground Control the ATIS information code because I already did that with Clearance Delivery.

Ground: "Cessna 9130 Delta, Town and Country Ground, can you accept Runway 27 for departure?"

"Cessna 9130 Delta, say the current winds."

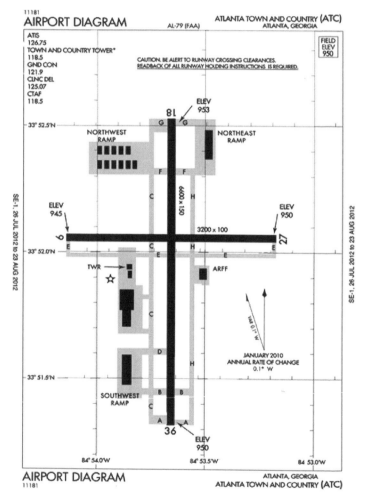

You probably have this diagram memorized by now.

"Cessna 9130 Delta," Ground says, "The winds are one nine zero at one zero, gust one eight."

Huh. I'm not a big fan of having to takeoff with a crossing gusting to 18 knots. Are you?

"Cessna 9130 Delta would prefer Runway One Eight, if it is available."

"Cessna 9130 Delta," Ground answers, "Runway One Eight, taxi via left Charlie. Hold short of Runway Two Seven on Charlie."

"Cessna 9130 Delta, Runway One Eight. Hold short of Runway Two Seven on Charlie." Again, we simply parrot Ground Control's clearance, though we are only required to read back runway assignments and hold short instructions.

As we approach the intersection of Runway Two Seven on Taxiway Charlie, Ground Control says, "Cessna 9130 Delta, cross Runway Two Seven. Hold short of Foxtrot."

"Cessna 9130 Delta, crossing Runway Two Seven. Hold short of Foxtrot."

Ground Control then asks, "Cessna 9130 Delta, can you accept a departure from Foxtrot?" Ground is asking us if our airplane has the performance to make a takeoff on Runway 18 from a point starting at Taxiway Foxtrot. If you look at the airport diagram, Taxiway Foxtrot is approximately 1000 feet from the approach end of Runway 18. (See the diagram on the previous page.)

Runway 18's full length is 6000 feet. We can definitely takeoff on 5,000 feet of runway, which is what will remain in front of us if we depart from abeam Taxiway Foxtrot.

"Cessna 9130 Delta can accept a departure from Foxtrot."

Notice that Ground Control and I both said, "a departure from Foxtrot." We did not say, "a takeoff from Foxtrot." This specific phraseology conforms to the rule that we never use the word "takeoff" on the radio until we are, in fact, cleared to takeoff. We may be thinking about a takeoff, but we make a conscious effort to avoid using it on the radio.

Engage Brain Before Mouth

It brings up another important point. You have to think carefully about what you need to say before you key the microphone to speak. Here's a short story about that concept.

As a former military instructor pilot (IP) the word that I used most often on the radio was: "Disregard!" I had to say this word frequently because my students would often fail to engage their brain before making a radio call.

Student: "Colt 22, uhh, left downwind." (Military call signs use a specific name assigned to each flight, plus two digits.)

Me: "Disregard! Colt 22, right downwind, touch and go."

Student: "Colt 22, flight level 17 for two zero."

Me: "Disregard! Colt 22, climbing through one seven thousand for flight level two zero zero."

When it inevitably reached a point where we instructors could no longer stand the collective mumbling and bumbling on the radio, we would organize a radio drill class. We placed an X on a classroom floor to mark each turning point of a scaled-down airport traffic pattern. We would then have our students march single-file around the pattern, from X to X. As each student reached the next X, he was supposed to say the correct radio call for that point in the traffic pattern. A student who spoke a radio call incorrectly would get immediate and stern "feedback" from one of the IPs.

After an hour or so of this drill, the students' radio calls were much more accurate. There were two reasons for this:

- Practice makes perfect.

- To avoid "feedback" from an instructor, each student would mentally rehearse the next anticipated radio before actually making that call.

While both reasons were in play, reason #2 is the key. Before making any radio call, think about what you plan to say before saying it. Here's a checklist:

1. Brain--Engage

2. Mouth--Open and use

Switching to Tower

"Cessna 9130 Delta," says Ground. "Hold short of Runway One Eight at Foxtrot. Contact Tower one one eight point five when ready."

"Cessna 9130 Delta, will hold short of Runway One Eight at Foxtrot. Tower when ready," I answer. Here we are on Taxiway Foxtrot, holding short of the runway. I see you have turned the airplane into the wind. Time for the pre-departure checks. While you are doing that, I'll flip the radio to Tower's frequency, 118.5.

As soon as I tune in Tower's frequency, we hear, "Cessna 9130 Delta, Town and Country Tower, can you take an immediate?" Tower is asking us if we are ready for an immediate takeoff. I see you aren't quite done with your pre-departure checks.

"Cessna 9130 Delta, negative. We'll need a minute before we are ready," I answer.

"Cessna 9130 Delta, roger," Tower says. "Baron Four One Zero Mike Oscar, Runway One Eight line up and wait. Traffic crossing downfield."

Here is an important point. Don't let an air traffic controller's sense of urgency convince you to do something you are not ready to do. Let me clarify that. If a controller needs you to expedite the movement of your aircraft for safety reasons, such as to avoid a collision, you should immediately comply with ATC's instructions. If a controller needs you to move faster for convenience, don't let the controller rush you if doing so would compromise safety. Many pilot errors result from rushing. If you rush, at ATC's urging, and something goes wrong, it's likely you are going to take the blame, not ATC.

In this case, ATC asked if you could make an immediate takeoff for convenience. An immediate takeoff would have probably helped the controller with his traffic flow. You weren't ready to go because you were still performing your engine run up. Accepting an immediate takeoff might have compromised safety, so I refused the request.

I see you have finished your checklist. I'll make the call to Tower. "Cessna 9130 Delta is ready."

"Cessna 9130 Delta," Tower answers. "Hold short of Runway One Eight." That seemed like a redundant instruction from Tower, but the controller is required to repeat hold short instructions in response to a pilot's ready call on the radio. A repeat of hold short instructions as an acknowledgement to a ready call is supposed remove any uncertainty about the need to hold short. There have been instances in the past, in which a Tower response of "Roger" or "Copy" was mistaken as authorization by Tower to enter the runway.

Runway Incursions

Crossing a runway's hold short line, without authorization, is known as a runway incursion. A runway incursion is a big deal because it creates a potential for a collision with another airplane that has been authorized to use the runway. To avoid a runway incursion, never enter a runway without first hearing one of these key phrases from ATC:

"Cleared to cross Runway XX."

"Cleared for takeoff, Runway XX."

"Cleared to land, Runway XX."

"Cleared to taxi down Runway XX."

"Cleared to back taxi down Runway XX." (The ICAO phrase for this clearance is "Cleared to back track on Runway XX." It means the same thing as "back taxi." I'll explain back-taxiing later.)

"Runway XX, line up and wait."

With one exception, all of these clearances begin with the word "Cleared." All of the clearances specify the runway for which the clearance applies. This is a very important distinction. When ATC tells you to do anything in regard to a

runway, pay very close attention to which runway ATC is
applying a clearance. I'll explain why.

Some airports have two or more runways that parallel each
other. Each parallel runway is labeled by its position in relation
to the others. For example, at Los Angeles International Airport
(KLAX), there are two parallel runways on the south side of the
airport and two parallel runways on the north side of the
airport. As you face west, the left runway on the north side of
the airport is called Two Four Left (24L), and the right runway
is called Two Four Right (24R). (See the airport diagram for
KLAX. Note Hot Spot 1, labeled HS 1, on the diagram for the
high-speed taxiway turnoff for Runway 24R.)

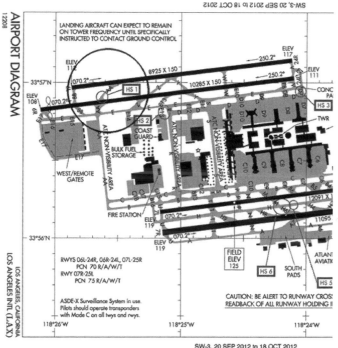

SW-3, 20 SEP 2012 to 18 OCT 2012

Here's where the problem occurs. When jets land on 24R they
turn off the runway to the left because the airport passenger
terminals are to the left. Runway 24L, generally used for
takeoffs, stands between 24R and the terminals. Runway 24R is

separated laterally from 24L by only a couple of hundred feet. Jet aircraft exiting 24R after landing are still moving at a pretty good rate of speed as they turn off the runway. They can cover that short taxi distance to 24L with a lot of momentum.

Here's the deal. When LAX Tower tells a pilot, "Cleared to land, Runway Two Four Right," that is authorization to land on and use 24R. It is not authorization to cross or use 24L. However, in the past, jets have exited 24R with so much speed, that they taxi up to 24L before the tower controller can say, "Hold short of Runway Two Four Left." Pilots have mistakenly let their jet's momentum carry them right on to 24L without authorization. This is a very dangerous type of runway incursion. It involves a large airplane mistakenly crossing a runway used by other large jets. The potential for catastrophe is huge.

Today, if you look at the airport diagram for LAX, you will see the standard warning about hold short and runway crossing clearance across the bottom of the page. The Los Angeles International Airport ATIS also makes this same warning. The landing runways have hotspots to remind pilots of the need to use caution as they exit the runway. All hotspots in the U.S. are depicted on airport diagrams. The hazards for each hotspot are described, by airport, in the Airport Facility Directory. (See the Airport Facility Directory excerpt below.) None of this would be necessary if pilots simply applied the rule to not enter any runway without authorization.

LOS ANGELES

| **LOS ANGELES INTL (LAX)** | **HS1** | **Pilots sometimes fail to hold short of Rwy 24L when exiting Rwy 24R at Twy AA.** |

From the Airport Facility Directory.

Intersection Takeoff

"Baron Four One Zero Mike Oscar," says Town and Country Tower, "Runway One Eight, cleared for takeoff." The pilot of the Beechcraft Baron acknowledges this radio call and rolls past us on the runway.

Tower says, "Mooney 5573 Quebec, Town and Country

Tower, traffic will depart from Foxtrot. Runway One Eight, line up and wait." To our left, we can see a Mooney Ranger taxi into position at Runway 18's threshold. Then we hear, "Cessna 9130 Delta, the Mooney will be holding in position. Fly runway heading. Runway One Eight at Taxiway Foxtrot, cleared for takeoff."

I answer, "Cessna 9130 Delta, runway heading. Runway One Eight at Foxtrot, cleared for takeoff." It's very important that I acknowledge this clearance as, "Runway One Eight at Foxtrot, cleared for takeoff." By saying "at Foxtrot," I'm acknowledging we will be completing our takeoff from the intersection.

Had the Mooney not occupied the runway at the threshold, we could have taxied onto the runway opposite the direction of takeoff and headed for the threshold. This process of taxiing from an intersection, back to the threshold for takeoff, is called "Back taxiing."

If the tower controller does not specifically clear us to depart from an intersection, we could back taxi on our own initiative and use the full runway length to takeoff. Of course, we would be numbskulls to try and do this with the Mooney already at the intersection. Tower's clearance to takeoff from intersection Foxtrot means we are not authorized to back taxi and must depart from abeam Foxtrot. To summarize, if Tower doesn't clarify, we could back taxi. If Tower specifically says takeoff from the intersection, take off from the intersection and acknowledge that clearance verbatim. If there is any doubt in your mind about what Tower wants you to do, ask the controller: "Tower, do you want Cessna 9130 Delta to take off from the intersection, or may we back taxi?"

In this case, we are cleared to depart from Foxtrot, so let's light the afterburner and blow this popsicle stand. After liftoff, we'll fly runway heading per Tower's clearance. The runway's heading, as printed on the airport diagram is 184 degrees magnetic. We'll hold that heading on the gyro compass. Let's talk about this for just a second, because it may need a little clarification.

What to Fly After Takeoff

Today, the wind is blowing from 190 degrees, which is almost directly down Runway 18. When we fly runway heading after liftoff--184 degrees magnetic--our airplane will probably track directly over Runway 18's extended centerline. How would this be different if the wind was blowing from 270 degrees at 20 knots?

With a strong crosswind, after takeoff, our airplane would begin to drift well left of Runway 18's centerline. Though we would fly 184 degrees on our compass, the crosswind would likely cause us to track a path over the ground of about 160 degrees, give or take a few degrees.

Here's why I'm talking about this distinction. When ATC tells you to fly a heading after takeoff, that means fly the heading on your compass. It does not mean fly that path over the ground. If the heading ATC clears you to fly causes your airplane to drift well right or left of the runway's extended centerline, so be it. If ATC really wanted you to track the runway's extended centerline after liftoff, the controller would give you a heading that compensates for the crosswind.

In our example, if the wind was 270 degrees at 20 and you were taking off from Runway 18, ATC might tell you to fly a heading of 200 to get your airplane to track the centerline. Simply fly what the controller tells you to fly, and let him worry about drift. There is one exception to this rule. (See the illustration below.)

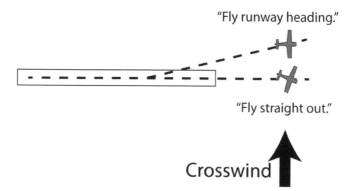

If Tower tells you to depart "straight out," or "straight ahead," then he wants to you to select your own heading to compensate for the crosswind component. You would crab into the wind after takeoff and attempt to track outbound on the runway's extended centerline. Today, the controller told us to fly a heading, so let's do that, and get back to our regularly scheduled program, already in progress.

Tower knows we want to depart the traffic pattern to the northwest because we passed that request to Clearance Delivery controller a while ago. Still, we have to comply with Tower's instructions to maintain runway heading. Tower probably needs us to maintain this heading to avoid other aircraft in the airport traffic pattern.

"Cessna 9130 Delta, traffic is a single-engine Cessna at your two o'clock and three miles at 2,000 feet," says Tower. There's the Cessna, right where Tower said it would be.

"Cessna 9130 Delta, traffic in sight," I answer.

Switching

Tower: "Cessna 9130 Delta, roger. Right turn out of traffic approved. Contact Departure."

Me: "Cessna 9130 in a right turn and switching." Tower said we can turn, so let's turn 90 degrees to the right to exit the traffic pattern. I'll flip the radio to 134.6 because that is the frequency Clearance Delivery told us to use for Departure Control.

Oh good, I see you pre-tuned Departure Control into the standby side of your radio. It's always a good idea to have the next known radio frequency tuned into the standby window of your primary communication radio. That way, when you are busy flying, all you have to do is flip the pre-tuned frequency from the standby to the active side of your radio.

"Town and Country Departure, Cessna 9130 Delta, passing one thousand, seven hundred for six thousand, five hundred, VFR." Whenever we check in on a new frequency with a radar controller, we always state our current altitude and our intended or cleared altitude. We state the current altitude so the radar controller can compare what we say to the altitude readout he sees on his radar display.

A terminal radar, one that is used by approach and departure controllers, makes a complete 360-degree sweep of the sky about every 4 seconds. That means a terminal radar interrogates and gets a reply from our airplane's transponder about every 4 seconds. The altitude we are currently passing should be fairly closely matched to what the radar controller sees on his display because of the quick pace of radar sweeps.

When we are talking to an enroute center controller, the enroute radar sweeps our airplane about every 12 seconds. That means an enroute controller's altitude readout for our aircraft might be slightly greater or less than our actual altitude as we climb or descend. This slight mismatch is due to the longer intervals between altitude readout updates produced by the 12-second sweep of an enroute radar.

Enroute controllers are aware of this lag, and less likely to be concerned about the mismatch when an airplane is climbing or descending. In level flight, if the controller sees an altitude readout that differs by 300 feet or more from what the pilot says is his current altitude, the controller will pass an updated altimeter setting to the pilot and ask the pilot to re-check his altitude. Here's the reference in the Air Traffic Controller Manual:

5-2-17. VALIDATION OF MODE C READOUT

a. Consider an altitude readout valid when... [i]t varies less than 300 feet from the pilot reported altitude....
b. When unable to validate the readout, do not use the Mode C altitude information for separation.

c. Whenever you observe an invalid Mode C readout below FL 180: Issue the correct altimeter setting and confirm the pilot has accurately reported the altitude.

PHRASEOLOGY-
(Location) ALTIMETER (appropriate altimeter), VERIFY ALTITUDE.

If the altitude readout continues to be invalid:

(a) Instruct the pilot to turn off the altitude
reporting part of his/her transponder and include
the reason; and

(b) Notify the operations supervisor-in-charge of
the aircraft call sign.

Off Altitude

Sometimes with crossing traffic within a 1000 vertical feet of
the airplane with the mismatched altitude, ATC will have even
less tolerance for a pilot being off an assigned altitude. In Class
C airspace controllers can maintain a minimum vertical
separation of 500 feet between VFR and IFR aircraft. This
conforms to a VFR pilot maintaining altitudes in 1000-foot
increments, plus 500 feet. Ex. 2,500.

Don't blame an air traffic controller if he becomes stern about
making sure you are exactly on your assigned altitude. Air
traffic controllers have to deal with a computer system they've
sarcastically nicknamed the Snitch. This system automatically
monitors the altitudes of all aircraft within a controller's sector.
If the systems anticipates a vertical or lateral separation
between 2 aircraft that is less than the legal minimum for the
airspace in use, the system will set off an alarm at the
controller's station. If there actually is a violation of the rules for
separation between aircraft, the controller is supposed to fill out
a report documenting the loss of separation. The report is
reviewed by the controller's supervisor to determine whether
follow-up action is necessary.

You need to be concerned about Snitch too. If an
investigation proves there was loss of separation, and it was not
the controller who was negligent, guess who is going to take
the blame for the loss of vertical separation. That's right. The
pilot who was not on his assigned altitude is going to take the
heat from the FAA.

Departure

Back to our flight. The departure controller says, "Cessna
9130 Delta, Town and Country Departure, radar contact,
climbing to six thousand five hundred. Maintain VFR and

advise me if you change altitude." Simply acknowledge this
radio call with your call sign.

From this point, Departure Control will provide traffic
advisories in the same way an enroute center controller
provides traffic advisories during flight following. Departure
Control will maintain its radio and radar connection with your
aircraft until you approach the outer area of the Class C
airspace.

First, here is the full definition of Class C airspace, quoted
directly from the AIM:

> Although the configuration of each Class C airspace
> area is individually tailored, the airspace usually
> consists of a 5 NM radius core surface area that
> extends from the surface up to 4,000 feet above the
> airport elevation, and a 10 NM radius shelf area
> that extends no lower than 1,200 feet up to 4,000
> feet above the airport elevation.

(See the illustration of Class C airspace because a picture may
not be worth a thousand words, but it probably won't put you
to sleep like the definition of Class C in the AIM.)

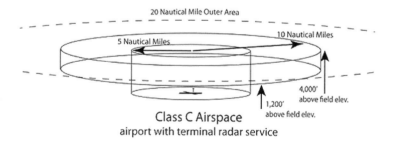

Class C Airspace
airport with terminal radar service

The outer area of Class C airspace is also defined in the AIM.
(Nap time again.):

OUTER AREA (associated with Class C airspace): Nonregulatory airspace surrounding designated Class C airspace airports wherein ATC provides radar vectoring and sequencing on a full-time basis for all IFR and participating VFR aircraft. The service provided in the outer area is called Class C service which includes: IFR/IFR-standard IFR separation; IFR/VFR-traffic advisories and conflict resolution; and VFR/VFR-traffic advisories and, as appropriate, safety alerts. The normal radius will be 20 nautical miles with some variations based on site-specific requirements. The outer area extends outward from the primary Class C airspace airport and extends from the lower limits of radar/radio coverage up to the ceiling of the approach control's delegated airspace excluding the Class C charted area and other airspace as appropriate.

In a nutshell, the radar controller will continue to provide traffic advisories and safety alerts until you fly about 20 miles away from the departure airport. At that point, Departure Control will hand your aircraft off to the adjacent or overlapping sector for an enroute control center and say, "Cessna 9130 Delta, for further flight following, contact Atlanta Center on one two eight point two. Good day."

You may respond to that call with your call sign, or, if you need verification, repeat the frequency to the controller along with your call sign: "Cessna 9130 Delta, one two eight point two."

From here, we'll check in with Atlanta Center and then activate our VFR flight plan with Macon Radio. Let's do that in the next chapter. Put the airplane on motion freeze until you have a chance to flip the page. I'll meet you there.

Take Action

Pick an airport on your sectional map that is surrounded by Class C airspace. Chair fly the radio calls you would make to Clearance Delivery, Ground Control, Tower, and Departure Control. (Use the radio conversations you just read about in this chapter to guide your practice.) Then, switch hats and play the air traffic controller at each of these positions. If you can, find the airport diagram for the airport before you play the various air traffic controller roles. Try to make the kinds of radio calls you would expect Clearance, Ground, Tower and Departure would say to your aircraft as it taxis from its parking area to the runway and then takes off.

Chapter 15: Out with Old Habits and In with New

"Atlanta Center, Archer 561 Golf Sierra, with you at eight thousand." Let's give Atlanta Center a chance to respond to that guy, then we'll check in. While we are waiting, I would like to blow off a little steam about that radio call we just heard.

I looked in the books--the Aeronautical Information Manual and the Air Traffic Controller Manual. Guess what? "With you" ain't in there.

Here's why it's not in there: What does "With you" mean? What does it add to the conversation? To answer, let's put it into context.

"Atlanta Center, Archer 561 Golf Sierra, with you at eight thousand."

Hmm. If I were the controller at Atlanta Center, and the pilot of Archer 561 Golf Sierra is reporting to me at eight thousand, obviously he's with me. Where else would he be? On another frequency but sending a message to me by mental telepathy? Of course he's with me, so why say it?

Because it sounds cool. "Professional" pilots say it, and they know everything. Let's imitate the pros and be cool like the pros.

Give me second to stop gagging. Okay. Better. The truth is, many pros have a lot of bad habits. These bad habits are passed from one generation of pilots to another, and no one ever questions why they persist.

You've heard that expression "What's learned first is learned best"? I absolutely agree with that. Flying is all about building habit patterns through repeated experience. Fortunately, or unfortunately, depending on the outcome, once a habit pattern gets established, it's very hard to unlearn.

If you are just starting your flying career or your flying avocation, now, right now, is the very best time to build good habits on the aircraft radio.

I've been thinking about this problem lately because I've been hearing a lot of crap on the aircraft radios. Bear in mind that I spend most of my time flying an airliner, which means I'm generally sharing radio frequencies with other airline pilots-- professionals who should know how to speak correctly on the aircraft radio.

Truth be told, many pro pilots do a fine job on the radios. Still, there are quite a few who "garbage up" the radios with all kinds of bad habits: speed talking, mumbling, dropping call signs, nonstandard phrasing, and non-essential verbiage that does nothing but take up extra time on the frequency.

Once you get to be a high-time pilot, no one is going to tell you that you sound like crap on the radios. You might hear a controller state "Say again," but if your bad habits are well established, that "Say again," won't give you the big clue bird that your radio technique sucks.

Old timers are hopeless on the radio, in the same way a lousy car driver will always be a lousy driver. The old dog can be taught new tricks, but no one has the nerve or the enthusiasm to try teaching the old dog. So the old dog keeps repeating the same old lousy routine.

Now, right now, as you are learning the ropes of flying, is the single best time in your life to get your radio phrasing, pacing, and enunciation right. It's important. Just ask a pilot who could have been saved from an altitude bust or a runway incursion had the controller been able to understand the pilot's read back.

Piloting, by its nature, is a collection of habits. That's how we produce consistent and safe results flight after flight. Habits are so important to safe flight that we have checklists that require us to run through a series of habits during each stage of flight. It's just so damn difficult to form good habits when the majority of pilots are setting the wrong example.

You really need to be a rebel, odd as it sounds, to overcome the bad influence of others. You have to make up your mind that you are going to carve your own path and use standard phraseology on the radio, despite what you hear from others.

With that, I'll stop. My rant has kept us from checking in with Atlanta Center. I'll make that radio call now.

Roger, I Understand

"Atlanta Center, Cessna 9130 Delta, passing five thousand, eight hundred for six thousand, five hundred. VFR to Chattanooga."

ATC: "Cessna 9130 Delta, Atlanta Center, roger. Maintain VFR and advise me of any altitude changes."

"Cessna 9130 Delta, wilco," I reply. The term "wilco," is a contraction for "will comply." Also, notice how Atlanta Center used the word "roger." A lot of pilots have the wrong idea about the meaning of "roger." Let's explore that for a sec. Here is a made up conversation that helps illustrate how incorrectly using the word "roger" in place of "affirmative" can confuse an air traffic controller:

Pilot: "Washington Center, Baron 219TU, passing 7,000."

ATC: "Baron 219TU, Washington Center, verify the previous controller gave you 9,000."

"Baron 219TU, roger."

ATC: "Baron 219TU, you are climbing to 9,000?"

"Baron 219TU, roger. 9,000."

ATC: "Baron 219TU, did the last sector controller assign you 9,000? I need an 'affirmative,' indicating yes he did, or a 'negative' indicating he didn't."

Here are the various forms of "roger" and their meanings.

"Roger" means: "I understand."

"Roger that" means: "I understand."

"That's a roger" means: "I understand."

Roger never means "yes," "okay," or "will comply." The aviation terms for those words are: "affirmative," "okay," and "wilco" respectively. Roger that?

Crossing Sectors

It looks like we are comfortably set up in cruise now. Let's tune Comm Radio 2 to Macon Radio and activate our VFR flight plan. As I look for the frequency on our sectional chart, I want to briefly cover how we would handle switching radio frequencies if we only had 1 communication radio on board.

With only 1 comm radio on board, we would have to check with Atlanta Center before leaving the frequency. The reason we do this is two-fold.

First, we need to give Atlanta Center, or any controller we happen to be talking to, an opportunity to look ahead for traffic conflicts with our aircraft. It would not be smart to simply leave the frequency just prior to Atlanta Center issuing a traffic advisory or safety alert to us.

Second, we might be approaching the edge of the center controller's sector. That means the controller might be about to hand us off to the controller in the next enroute sector. Think of an enroute center's layout like a jigsaw puzzle. Each controller has responsibility for one piece of the puzzle. As our airplane travels from piece to piece in the puzzle, the current controller will hand us off to the controller who owns the next puzzle piece we are about to fly into. It would be unwise to leave the frequency on other business just as the current controller is about to hand us off to the next.

When leaving the controller's frequency to attend to other business, we should advise the controller about how long we think we will be off of his frequency. This gives him a time frame he can use to judge how far we will travel before he hears from us again. He can look ahead for that distance and see if we might reach the boundary of his sector, or if we might cross paths with another airplane. Our radio call would sound something like this:

"Cessna 9130 Delta needs to leave your frequency for two minutes." Atlanta Center would reply, "Cessna 9130 Delta, frequency changed approved. Report back in two minutes." Or, if the controller projected we would be entering the next control sector in two minutes, he would say, "Cessna 9130 Delta, frequency change approved. When you return, contact Atlanta Center on 125.32."

The controller could also say, "Cessna 9130 Delta, before you go, traffic will be a Seneca at your eleven o'clock and one zero miles, opposite direction, one thousand feet above you." You would reply either, "Cessna 9130 Delta, traffic in sight," or, "Cessna 9130 Delta, searching." Then the controller would approve your request for a frequency change.

Earlier, I said each enroute center's sector is similar to a jigsaw puzzle piece. Like all jigsaw puzzles, there is a finite size to the overall puzzle. Eventually, you will fly to the edge of the puzzle, which means you will approach the limit of the enroute center's radar and radio coverage. There is usually some overlap in coverage between sectors. The boundaries are set so you never completely leave the radio and radar coverage of one controlling agency before being acquired by the radio and radar coverage of the next controlling agency.

Within the land mass of North America, the outer edge of every enroute center touches the border of another enroute center. As you exit off the edge of one center's airspace, you fly into the boundary of an adjacent enroute center. For example, as you reach the northwest limit of Atlanta Center's coverage, you enter the southeast edge of Memphis Center's coverage. As you depart Minneapolis Center at its northeastern corner you enter the airspace of Toronto Center at its southwestern corner. As you exit Houston Center to the south over Texas, you enter the northern edge of Monterrey Center.

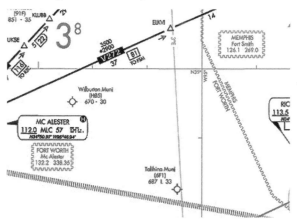

Adjacent sectors of Fort Worth and Memphis Air Route Traffic Control Centers (ARTCC). Note the "postage stamp" boxes showing the frequencies for each sector.

From a pilot's perspective, it really doesn't matter when you exit one enroute center's boundary and enter another enroute center's boundary. All of the controllers on the edge of one center coordinate with their counterparts working the edge of the adjacent center. Your airplane will be handed off from enroute center to enroute center in the same manner you get handed off from sector to sector within the same center.

The only time handoffs get interesting is when you fly across gaps in radar coverage between enroute centers. For example, if you were to fly across the Gulf of Mexico between New Orleans and Merida, Mexico, you would fly far enough out over open water where there is no radar coverage.

You would drop off Houston Center's radar coverage, and it would be awhile before Merida Center could pick your airplane up on radar. In this case, there would be no radar handoff between Houston and Merida. The last air traffic controller you speak to at Houston Center as you travel south would ask you for your estimated time of arrival over a published point on the boundary to Merida Center. The Houston controller would then get on the landline and pass your estimate to the receiving controller at Merida Center. When your airplane reached the published point on the boundary to Merida Center, the Mexican controller would be expecting you. You would check in with Merida on the radio and the controller would let you know when you were back in radar contact.

Flight Service Check In

As I said, all this is conjecture because today, we have two communication radios in our airplane. That means we can communicate with Atlanta Center on Comm Radio 1 and talk to Macon Radio on Comm Radio 2. With two pilots, like we have today--that's you and me--one of us can pay close attention to Atlanta Center while the other talks to Macon Radio. When you are flying solo, or when you are the only pilot with passengers who don't know how to speak on the radio, you might find it easier to tell Atlanta Center you will off of his frequency for a couple of minutes. If you think you can effectively manage communications on two radios simultaneously, go for it.

Most pilots find it pretty difficult to effectively listen and talk on two radios at the same time. Even if you are a super talker and listener, don't let your silver tongue and golden ears draw your attention away from maintaining aircraft control. Stick with the mantra, "Aviate, navigate, communicate," in that order of priority.

I'm looking at our sectional chart and I see the frequency box for the Rome VORTAC. Just below the frequency box, there is a bracket that says "Macon." That means the flight service specialist identified as Macon Radio works the area around the Rome VORTAC. Just above the Rome VORTAC frequency box, there is a bolded blue frequency of 122.3. That's the frequency the flight service station uses in this area. (See the sectional map below.)

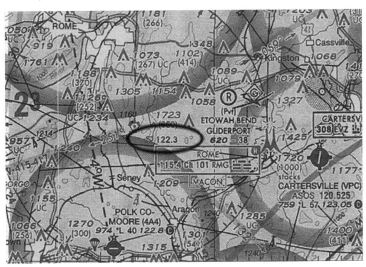

Near the Rome VORTAC, you may contact FSS on frequency 122.3.

When I say 'the flight service station,' I'm talking about one of only a few stations that cover the entire continental U.S. (CONUS), Puerto Rico, and Hawaii. At the time I write this, Lockheed Martin Corporation operates Automated Flight Service Stations (AFSS) from 3 hub stations and 3 satellite stations in the CONUS. The FAA still operates 3 hub stations in Alaska, plus 14 satellite facilities in that state. Even though you are calling Macon Radio, you are probably talking to a flight service station special sitting in a hub facility in Raleigh-Durham, North Carolina.

Make no mistake. Automated Flight Service Stations are operated by people, though the term "automated" might conjure up an image of a robot running the show. The automation comes from a computer system that helps the people operate the AFSS over a very wide area of responsibility.

By the way, if you want to get the skinny on Flight Service, you can glean information out of various chapters in the AIM. Chapter 7, Meteorology, covers Flight Service weather reports in detail. There is also a small blurb in paragraph 4-1-3 Flight Service Stations, but it doesn't say much. The website http://www.afss.com has some pilot tips, but it largely draws from information readily available in the AIM. If you really want to get geeky about flight service, you can crack open J.O. 7110.10 (online in .pdf format) to read the Flight Service Station Manual.

I'll spin 122.3 into the standby window of Comm Radio 2 and then hit the flip flop switch to move the frequency into the active window. We'll keep the listen buttons pressed for Comm Radio 1 and Comm Radio 2 so we can hear incoming transmissions on both radios. I'm going to flip the radio transmit selector to Radio 2 so I can talk to Macon Radio. If Atlanta Center calls us, I'll tell the flight service specialist to standby. I'll then flip the transmit selector back to Radio 1 so we can answer Atlanta Center.

"Macon Radio, Cessna 9130 Delta, on one two two point three." Let's give the specialist a half-minute to reply. Sometimes those people are pretty busy working with pilots on other frequencies. In a distress situation, which this is obviously not, we could get the flight service specialist to answer our radio call immediately by preceding our call with "Pan, pan, pan," as I discussed earlier.

"Aircraft calling Macon Radio, say your call sign and request," the specialist answers. This is fairly typical. If the specialist was very busy, he might have heard the incoming radio call from us, but missed our call sign.

Me: "Cessna 9130 Delta, one five miles south of the Rome VORTAC at 6,500. We would like to activate our VFR flight plan to Lovell Field, Chattanooga."

FSS: "Cessna 9130 Delta, Macon Radio copies one five miles south of the Rome VORTAC at 6,500. We will activate your flight plan at one seven three niner zulu. Do you have time for a pilot report?"

Me: "Cessna 9130 Delta, affirmative. At 6,500 MSL, the sky is clear. Estimated visibility is two zero miles. Outside air temperature is plus five Celsius. Smooth ride."

FSS: "At 6,500 MSL, clear skies. Visibility estimated two zero miles. Outside air temperature plus five Celsius. Smooth ride. Is there anything else I can do for you?"

Me: "Cessna 9130 Delta requests an update on the current and forecast weather for Lovell Field," I answer.

FSS: "Cessna 9130 Delta, the latest weather for Lovell Field is four thousand scattered. Visibility seven miles. Temperature one eight. Dew point one zero. The wind is three three zero degrees at eight knots. Chattanooga altimeter three zero zero one.

"The terminal forecast from now until two zero Zulu is five thousand scattered, visibility seven. From two zero Zulu until zero one Zulu, three thousand scattered, ten thousand broken. Do you need the NOTAMs for Lovell Field?"

Me: "Cessna 9130 Delta, negative. That's all we need. Thank you."

FSS: "Macon Radio, copies. After landing, you may close your flight with Nashville Radio on 122.2 or 123.65. Have a good flight. Macon Radio is clear at one eight zero three Zulu."

And that, as they say, is that. I'll rotate the radio transmit selector back to Comm Radio 1 so all transmissions will go out to Atlanta Center. I'm going to leave the listen button for Comm Radio 2 switched on. I'm putting frequency 121.5 in the active window of Comm Radio 2 so we can monitor Guard.

Let's double-check the communications panel setup:

1. Transmit selector set to Comm Radio 1.

2. Comm Radio 1's active window set to the current frequency for Atlanta Center.

3. Comm Radio 2's active window set to 121.5.

4. Listen buttons for both Comm Radio 1 and Comm
    Radio 2 switched on.

I run through this quick review of the radio setup every time
I switch to the secondary radio to accomplish a task. It only
takes a few seconds and it's time well spent. Deliberately
double-checking the radio panel setup reduces the chances you
will transmit or receive on the wrong radio.

As we approach the Rome VORTAC, the air traffic controller
says, "Cessna 9130 Delta, for further flight following, contact
Atlanta Center on one two eight point six."

Chattanooga Chatting

"Cessna 9130 Delta, one two eight point six." We switch
frequencies and say, "Atlanta Center, Cessna 9130 Delta, six
thousand, five hundred. VFR."

ATC: "Cessna 9130 Delta, Atlanta Center, six thousand, five
hundred. Maintain VFR and advise me of any altitude changes.
Where'd you come up from today?"

Me: "We flew out of Town and Country."

"Oh yeah. I heard they did some big upgrades to that place. I
haven't had a chance to go there and check it out though," the
controller says.

"Yep. They hit the big time. It's a pretty good airport."

"Roger that." Sometimes, when an air traffic controller doesn't
have much going on his sector, he might chat you up just to kill
time. Here's the deal on that. Let the controller lead the
conversation. Only he knows what is going on in his sector.
That means, only he knows whether the two of you can use
precious radio air time for casual conversation. Don't let a
controller's invitation to speak freely be a license to make long
speeches on the radio. Keep your replies short and to the point.
When the controller stops making conversation, let that be a
cue to go silent and return to business.

If you even need to ask a controller something that does not
concern your last clearance--a general question--ask the
controller if he has time for a question. Don't start blabbing on

the radio without the controller's approval. When the controller approves your request to ask a question, get right to the question in as short a sentence as possible. Don't make a speech that hogs the radio. When you eat up radio time with a speech or a joke, you might be preventing someone else from making a critical transmission.

The Radio is No Joking Matter

We've all been to websites that feature funny conversations between pilots and air traffic controllers:

ATC: "123YZ, say altitude."

123YZ: "ALTITUDE!"

ATC: "123YZ, say airspeed."

123YZ: "AIRSPEED!"

ATC: "123YZ, say cancel IFR."

123YZ: "Eight thousand feet, one hundred fifty knots indicated."

Most of the time, these exchanges are fictitious—the product of a good imagination. Occasionally, in real life, someone grabs the aircraft mic and pretends he's the featured act at Caesar's Palace: "Just flew in from the coast, and boy are my arms tired." When you let one rip on an aviation frequency, are you lightening everyone's day, or are you gumming up the works?

Let's talk about radio discipline, and then you can decide for yourself. I'm not going to sit here and tell you joking around on the radio is dangerous. I don't have the facts to back it up. No one has done a definitive study on the subject. I am going to say, based on my own experience, that as the radios go, so goes the flight.

Here's what I mean. When your radio work is sharp and to the point, air traffic controllers respond in kind. Your radio transmissions set the tone, and almost always, everything else follows that tone. In the military, we placed such a high emphasis on razor sharp radio work that it was thoroughly discussed in every preflight briefing. Woe unto the sloppy wingman who did not check in on the radio promptly and crisply. You've heard this at airshows:

"Thunderbirds check-Two-Three-Four-Five-Six!"

Why is the check-in on the radio by each wingman so fast and sharp? It sets the tone for the precision flying that is about to come.

I propose the following, and you might not agree. When you try to be entertaining on the radio, you may get a chuckle from others sharing the frequency.

You may also disrupt a busy air traffic controller's train of thought.

You may tie up the radio frequency longer than necessary.

You may create a moment of confusion in which a critical piece of information is either lost or misinterpreted.

None of that may happen, but here is what I know will happen. The conduct of your own flight will be taken down a notch. The long slide down a slippery slope begins with a mis-step. Though it may be tempting at times to go for a laugh on the radio, I strongly urge you to rein it in and avoid temptation.

Here's a related topic about chatting on the radio. Occasionally, you might recognize the voice of a friend on the radio. It would be nice to talk directly to your friend on ATC's radio frequency. Don't do it. There is an alternative.

Ask the controller to tell your friend to meet you on 122.75, the aviation chat frequency. Bear in mind, your friend will probably hear this request and know what to do. You should still relay your request through the controller as a courtesy. You can then use your secondary radio to talk to your friend on the chat frequency. Use the same listen and talk techniques we already discussed for using Comm Radio 2 while working with ATC on Comm Radio 1.

Speaking of chatting, we have talked our way through most of the flying time to Chattanooga. The airport is only 40 miles away. We know the outer area of the Class D airspace that surrounds Lovell Field is only 20 miles ahead. Let's get our poop in a group before we are told to contact Chattanooga Approach Control. We will cover the game plan in the next chapter.

Take Action

Design your own personal checklist for switching back and forth between your primary communication radio and your secondary communication radio. Make sure your checklist accommodates the radio configuration for your aircraft. Keep the checklist short and easy-to-memorize. You are more likely to use a checklist if it's manageable.

Practice simulated radio transactions with Flight Service for the following scenarios:

- Initial contact with flight service.

- Activating and closing a flight plan.

- Making an inflight position report.

- Requesting updated current and forecast reports for your destination.

Chapter 16: Landing at a Busy Airport

Before we brief the particulars of Lovell Field at Chattanooga, let's talk about what we can expect from Approach Control. If you look at the Aeronautical Information Manual under 4-1-8. Approach Control Service for VFR Arriving Aircraft, the information is pretty skimpy:

a. Numerous approach control facilities have established programs for arriving VFR aircraft to contact approach control for landing information. This information includes: wind, runway, and altimeter setting at the airport of intended landing. This information may be omitted if contained in the Automatic Terminal Information Service (ATIS) broadcast and the pilot states the appropriate ATIS code.

NOTE
Pilot use of "have numbers" does not indicate receipt of the ATIS broadcast. In addition, the controller will provide traffic advisories on a workload permitting basis.

b. Such information will be furnished upon initial contact with concerned approach control facility. The pilot will be requested to change to the tower frequency at a predetermined time or point, to receive further landing information.

c. Where available, use of this procedure will not hinder the operation of VFR flights by requiring excessive spacing between aircraft or devious routing.

d. Compliance with this procedure is not
mandatory but pilot participation is encouraged.

The real description appears later in Chapter 4 of the AIM:

4-1-18. Terminal Radar Services for VFR Aircraft

a. Basic Radar Service: In addition to the use of
radar for the control of IFR aircraft, all
commissioned radar facilities provide the following
basic radar services for VFR aircraft:

(a) Safety alerts.
(b) Traffic advisories.
(c) Limited radar vectoring (on a workload
permitting basis).
(d) Sequencing at locations where procedures
have been established for this purpose and/or
when covered by a Letter of Agreement.

Vectoring service may be provided when requested
by the pilot or with pilot concurrence when
suggested by ATC.

There is a contradiction between the AIM and Air Traffic
Control Manual J.O. 7110.65. While the AIM says vectoring
service is provided upon pilot request, or when the pilot agrees
to the service, the ATC Manual puts it a different way:

c. Radar sequencing to the primary airport, when
local procedures have been developed, shall be
provided unless the pilot states that the service is
not requested. Arriving aircraft are assumed to
want radar service unless the pilot states "Negative
radar service," or makes a similar comment. (J.O.
7110.65, 7-6-2 Service Availability).

My experience has been that Approach Control will
automatically provide sequencing unless you tell the controller

you don't want it. I also believe you should take advantage of everything Approach Control has to offer. You are going to be placed in sequence with other arriving aircraft when you contact Tower, so why not let Approach Control do the same work earlier? By having your place in line for the runway arranged before you contract Tower, there will be less maneuvering and speed changes as you enter the airport traffic pattern. It's like the difference between "Please seat yourself" at a crowded diner, and having a maitre'd lead you to a reserved seat in a fine restaurant.

In Sequence with Wake Turbulence

I already hinted at what ATC means by sequencing, but let's look at their definition in their manual:

7-6-7. SEQUENCING

a. Establish radar contact before instructing a VFR aircraft to enter the traffic pattern at a specified point or vectoring the aircraft to a position in the approach sequence. Inform the pilot of the aircraft to follow when the integrity of the approach sequence is dependent on following a preceding aircraft. Ensure visual contact is established with the aircraft to follow and provide instruction to follow that aircraft.

b. Direct a VFR aircraft to a point near the airport to hold when a position is not available in the approach sequence for the runway in use. The aircraft may be vectored to another runway after coordination with the tower.

The AIM expands on sequencing by Approach Control with this:

5. The purpose of the service is to adjust the flow of arriving VFR and IFR aircraft into the traffic pattern

in a safe and orderly manner and to provide radar
traffic information to departing VFR aircraft. Pilot
participation is urged but is not mandatory. Traffic
information is provided on a workload permitting
basis. Standard radar separation between VFR or
between VFR and IFR aircraft is not provided (*AIM
4-1-18*).

The ATC Manual says, when sequencing you behind other
aircraft, controllers will maintain the separation minima
specified in the manual for wake turbulence avoidance (*J.O.
7110.65 5-5-4*):

> e. Separate aircraft operating directly behind, or
> directly behind and less than 1,000 feet below, or
> following an aircraft conducting an instrument
> approach by:
>
> NOTE-
> When applying wake turbulence separation criteria,
> directly behind means an aircraft is operating
> within 2500 feet of the flight path of the leading
> aircraft over the surface of the earth. Consider
> parallel runways less than 2,500 feet apart as a
> single runway because of the possible effects of
> wake turbulence.
>
> Heavy behind heavy-- 4 miles
> Large/heavy behind B757-- 4 miles
> Small behind B757-- 5 miles
> Small/large behind heavy-- 5 miles

Here are the definitions of the various types of aircraft
classes, as presented in the Pilot/Controller Glossary of the
AIM:

> AIRCRAFT CLASSES- For the purposes of Wake
> Turbulence Separation Minima, ATC classifies
> aircraft as Heavy, Large, and Small as follows:
>
> a. Heavy- Aircraft capable of takeoff weights of

more than 255,000 pounds whether or not they are
operating at this weight during a particular phase
of flight.

b. Large- Aircraft of more than 41,000 pounds,
maximum certificated takeoff weight, up to 255,000
pounds.

c. Small- Aircraft of 41,000 pounds or less
maximum certificated takeoff weight.

Don't fall asleep while in the hands of Approach Control,
because as the AIM puts it, "The pilot has the ultimate
responsibility for ensuring appropriate separations and
positioning of the aircraft in the terminal area to avoid the wake
turbulence created by a preceding aircraft" (AIM 7-3-4 para. 5).

When I have flown in trail of a Boeing 777 or a 747, ATC is
careful to create at least the minimum spacing between my
aircraft and the flying apartment building ahead. Even with the
letter of the law met, more than once, my aircraft has managed
to find the wall of the tumble dryer created by wake
turbulence.

ATC's separation standards are based on wake turbulence's
tendency to descend, spread out, and dissipate behind the
aircraft that created the wake turbulence. While ATC's
separation standards for wake turbulence usually work well,
the winds at altitude sometimes hold wake turbulence in place
longer than predicted. When the winds aloft are holding wake
turbulence in place, the minimum separation behind a wake-
producing aircraft may not be enough to keep your airplane out
of harm's way.

Encountering the wake of a heavy jet is real wake up call if
you have ever been there. The day before I wrote this, I was
flying a Boeing 757 into the Atlanta Hartsfield-Jackson
International Airport. We were following another 757 to the
runway. The other 757 was so far ahead of us, I couldn't even
see it. We had more than the ATC-standard separation for wake
turbulence. Even so, our jet passed through the persistent wake
of the preceding aircraft. The wake rolled our 195,000-pound
airplane so hard and so quickly to the left, the autopilot was
incapable of keeping the jet upright. I had to disconnect the
autopilot and hand fly the jet back to level flight. If a 100-ton

Boeing 757 is thrown around like a rag doll by the wake of another jet of the same type, imagine what that wake might do to a small light aircraft.

My best advice? Stay alert, because the minimum required separation for wake turbulence is not always adequate. Your flight instructor can provide techniques for avoiding or escaping wake turbulence.

Prepping for Arrival

That's quite a bit of information on working with wake turbulence and with Approach Control. We'll see some, if not all of it put into action after we contact Chattanooga Approach. Speaking of which, it's almost time to get handed off to the approach controller. Atlanta Center will tell us when to switch.

If we were on our own, and not in radar contact with Atlanta Center, we would be responsible for getting in touch with the approach controller. The best time to do this is 25 miles out from the airport. This would put us in initial contact with the approach controller 5 miles before we entered the outer ring of his working area.

Let's get the ATIS for Chattanooga before we are handed off to Approach. I'll dial that in to Comm Radio 2. Here's the recording:

> "Chattanooga Information Echo, one eight five three Zulu weather. Few at three thousand. Five thousand scattered. Visibility seven miles. Temperature two six. Dewpoint one eight. Wind three four zero degrees at eight knots. Altimeter two niner niner niner. Landing and departing Runway Two. Runway Three Three. Notices to Airmen, Taxiway Zulu is closed. Use caution for men and equipment working between Taxiway Hotel and Runway Two. Advise the controller on initial contact you have received information Echo."

It sounds like, given the wind direction, we could be

assigned either Runway 2 or Runway 33. The approach controller should give us our expected runway assignment after we make contact. That's one of the good things about working with Approach. You get an earlier indication of where you will be going, and how you will get there, than if you waited to contact Tower only 10 miles out from landing.

That's not to say our runway assignment is set in cement. We could request a particular runway, if we needed it for operational reasons. Our operational need would override, in almost all cases, the needs of ATC. We can't simply tell Approach we want to land on a runway that is different from the one assigned to us without having a good reason to switch.

What's an operational need? Let's say we were flying a large airplane that needed a minimum runway length on which to land. If ATC assigns a landing runway that is shorter than our airplane requires, we can say we need a longer runway for operational reasons. That would suffice.

ATC can, and will, change your runway assignment at any time. Controllers at some airports are notorious for runway changes. Take Dallas-Fort Worth International, please. That airport that has, at last count, 8 runways. A runway change is almost inevitable. Count on it at any airport with more than one runway. You won't be surprised if it happens.

Think of a runway change as you would think of picking a line at a fast food joint. You look at all the lines leading to the counter, and try to find the one that is not only the shortest, but also looks like it is moving the fastest. Perhaps you choose the first line on the left and then see that the next line to the right is a little shorter. So you switch lines. That choice is one of the reasons ATC uses to change your runway assignment. Wind direction, the mix of aircraft on final, the current length of the line of aircraft on final, and your final approach airspeed relative to other aircraft on final, may all be reasons to change your assigned runway.

At some airports, ATC will ask you where you plan to park after landing. They might make your runway assignment contingent on your parking choice to minimize your taxi distance. Don't expect this type of red carpet service at all airports, and certainly do not demand it from the controller. Treat it as a pleasant surprise when it happens.

The point is, when you prepare to land at an airport with

multiple runways, take the time to consider all your options. As Forrest Gump might have said, "A multi-runway airport is like a box of chocolates. You never know what you are going to get." I'm not sure that is exactly how he would have put it, but you get the idea.

Let's get down to business and look at the airport diagram for Chattanooga. (See the airport diagram below.)

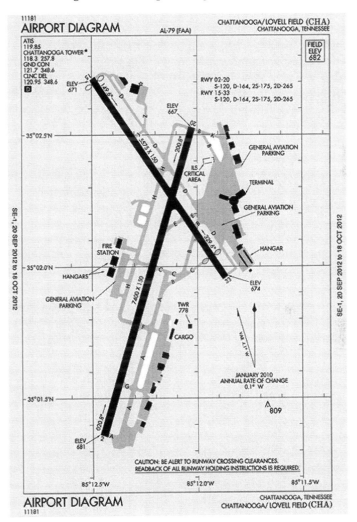

The ATIS said we can expect to land on either Runway 2 or Runway 33. If I were betting, I'd bet on Runway 33 for us, because it is the shorter runway. I'm guessing they will use the longer runway for large aircraft and the shorter runway for small aircraft, like us. As I said, we'll be ready for either runway.

The big deal on Runway 33 is that displaced threshold, about 750 from the approach end. From there, the first available taxiway turnoffs are Bravo, which appears to be 750 feet from the threshold, and Echo, which appears to be 1000 feet from the threshold. Let's forget about Bravo because it's too close to the threshold. Echo might be doable without romping on the brakes, but let's not blow a tire trying to make the turnoff.

If we roll past Echo, I'll ask Tower if we can turn off onto Runway 2. When landing, we are authorized to roll through intersecting runways, but we may not use them for taxi without authorization from ATC. Here's the quote from the AIM:

4-3-20. Exiting the Runway After Landing

a. Exit the runway without delay at the first available taxiway or on a taxiway as instructed by ATC. Pilots shall not exit the landing runway onto another runway unless authorized by ATC.

While we are on the subject, we may turn off at any high-speed taxiway. High-speed taxiways are ones that are angled relative to the runway. The angle required to turn, which is always less than 90-degrees to the runway, allows us to exit the runway while still decelerating to taxi speed. They are not a license to turn the corner on two wheels, but they do allow a slightly quicker exit than a 90-degree turn off the runway. A high speed taxiway is always usable as long as the turn off angle takes less than 90 degrees of turn to exit. If the high speed taxiway is oriented so it presents more than a 90-degree turn off the runway, ATC calls it a "reverse high speed." (See the illustration, next page.)

The reason I'm attempting to bore you with this discussion of high-speed and reverse high-speed turn offs has to do with ATC approval. While you may use any high-speed taxiway to turn off the runway, you must get approval from Tower to use a reverse-high speed turn off after landing. Using a reverse-high speed is not standard procedure, so ATC is not usually expecting it. That's why you need ATC's approval to do it.

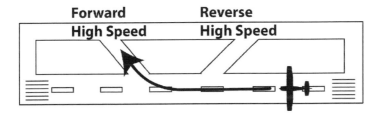

High Speed Turnoff Taxiways

The high speed turnoff. Note the turnoff requires less than 90 degrees of turn to exit the runway. A reverse high speed turnoff requires more than 90 degrees of turn.

Getting back to our scenario: If we land a little long, or if we have too much momentum to turn off prior to Runway 2, and Tower does not approve a turnoff onto Runway 2, we can turn off on to Taxiway Hotel, or roll to the end of the runway. Sometimes, Tower will say "Roll to the end," to fit the landing airplane into the flow of traffic taxiing near the runway.

Rolling to the end of the runway is always an option. It's a good idea to advise ATC of your intent to do this as early as possible so the controller can plan for it. If another airplane is landing shortly after your landing, ATC would like a heads up that you plan to be on the runway longer than anticipated. By all means, if you need to the full runway length to slow to taxi speed, use the full runway length. If, after slowing to taxi speed, you want to use the remaining runway as a taxiway, advise ATC.

After landing on Runway 33, we will plan to taxi to the general aviation parking area on the east side of the airport. So let's plan on using Taxiway D to get there. That's all I have for that runway. Let's look at landing on Runway 2.

If we are assigned Runway 2 for landing, we'll have plenty of turnoff options before we reach the intersecting runway. Notice, on Runway 2, you can turn off to the left or to the right. We would prefer to turn off to the right, since that is the direction of our parking space. We will listen up to Tower and not brain-lock on turning off to the right. Tower may want us to exit to the left to fit into the taxi flow.

Here's another option for us if we land on Runway 2. The runway is over 7,000 feet long, far longer than we need. We could intentionally land beyond the runway's touchdown zone, but we need to alert the Tower controller of our intention to do that. Unless we speak up, Tower expects us to land in the first 3,000 of the runway, or, for runways shorter than 3,000 feet, in the first half of the runway. Our radio call to land long would be, "Cessna 9130 Delta would like to land long." Tower would probably say, "Cessna 9130 Delta, approved as requested." If a long landing is not approved, don't do it.

Tower may also ask us to land on Runway 2 and hold short of Runway 33 for traffic landing on Runway 33. They will only do this when the weather permits VFR operations; the runway is clear of any contaminants such as snow, slush, or rain; and, your aircraft type is on the airport's list for land and hold short operations (LAHSO) for the available landing distance.

You may read about the particulars of the LAHSO program in J.O. 7110.65 if you want to be bored to death. The AIM has information about LAHSO that is more relevant to pilots. When taken as a whole, the AIM says, as pilot-in-command, you have the ultimate authority on when to accept or decline a clearance to land and hold short of an intersecting runway. The AIM says you should do a preflight study of the airports LAHSO program, comparing your aircraft's landing performance to the available landing distances in the program. For further information on LAHSO, refer to AIM 4-3-11: Pilot Responsibilities When Conducting Land and Hold Short Operations (LAHSO).

If you look at the airport diagram for Runway Two, you can see we will have about 6,000 feet of available landing distance before reaching Runway Three Three. That's obviously more than enough landing distance for our aircraft, and there is no appreciable downward slope to Runway Two. I feel confident we could land on 2 and hold short of 33.

We did not do a thorough pre-flight study of Lovell Field's LAHSO program as stated in the AIM. If Tower says, "Cleared to land, Runway Two. Hold short of Runway Three Three," we will say, "Cessna 9130 Delta, we're unable land and hold short." Our refusal to land and hold short might irritate the Tower controller. I'm sorry for that, but our first responsibility is flight safety, not an air traffic controller's best laid plans.

What you Must Do vs. What you Can Do

Let's be careful to not be flippant in our attitude towards air traffic control. We pilots need to operate with respect and courtesy when speaking to air traffic controllers. I believe we should do everything we can to cooperate with ATC. After all, ATC's mission is to help keep us safe as we fly.

Our goal is to fly safely and to work with ATC. ATC does not always have all of the information about our flight that we have. While most air traffic controllers are perceptive by nature and training, they cannot possibly know everything about our individual capabilities as pilots. A maneuver that may be well within the capabilities of one pilot may be beyond the capabilities of another pilot. That's why we pilots have to make the final call on safety when it comes to the conduct of our own flight.

When we make a decision in the interest of safety, that decision may not always help a controller with his plan for the flow of traffic in his section of airspace. As presidential candidates on the campaign trail say, "Let me be clear on this." When ATC gives you a legal clearance, you are required to comply with that clearance. You may not pick and choose which clearances you care to follow based on a whim. ATC clearances are legally binding according to CFR 91.123:

> (a) When an ATC clearance has been obtained, no pilot in command may deviate from that clearance unless an amended clearance is obtained, an emergency exists, or the deviation is in response to a traffic alert and collision avoidance system resolution advisory.

Notice there is a way out in this paragraph of the reg. If you obtain an amendment to your clearance, you may deviate from the original clearance. You then become obligated to adhere to the instructions given in the amended clearance.

A request or suggestion by ATC is different from an ATC clearance. When ATC makes a request or a suggestion, you have the option to refuse. You know you are dealing with a request when it presented either as a question, or a conditional statement. Examples:

ATC: "Cessna 9130 Delta, are you able the next high-speed?" This is a question Tower might ask. It means "Can you slow down in time to turn off of the runway at the next high-speed taxiway?"

ATC: "Cessna 9130 Delta, if able, make the turnoff at the next high-speed." This is a conditional statement that gives you the option to not turn off at the next high-speed if your speed is too high to turn safely.

A suggestion by ATC will include the word "suggest." For example, ATC might say "Cessna 9130 Delta, for traffic avoidance, suggest a heading of zero six zero." As we discussed earlier in the section on flight following, if you have a better idea of how to avoid the traffic you are not required to follow ATC's suggestion.

Again, just to be clear, if ATC says do "A," you have to do "A" unless you get an amended clearance that allows you to do "B." Here is an example of how that would sound:

ATC: "Cessna 9130 Delta, make the next right turn onto the high-speed."

You (before reaching that taxiway): "Cessna 9130 Delta will be unable the next high-speed."

ATC: "Cessna 9130 Delta, continue down the runway and make the right turn off at taxiway Bravo."

Notice the difference? ATC gave you a clearance to turn off at a high-speed taxiway. You must comply with that clearance unless you are able to get an amended clearance. Get the amended clearance before you deviate, and then follow the amended clearance. Get the amendment before it applies. For example, don't zoom past your assigned taxiway turnoff and then get an amended clearance. This procedure applies to any flight situation, on the ground or in the air.

While we have been talking about deviations from ATC

clearances, there are some cases where you can avoid an entire ATC program. One example would be acceptance of sequencing by Approach Control in Class C airspace. You may accept or deny ATC sequencing in Class C airspace as you wish. Once you accept the service, you are required to comply with all ATC clearances given during that service.

Approach Control

"Cessna 9130 Delta," the controller at Atlanta Center says, "contact Chattanooga approach on one two eight point three five."

"Cessna 9130 Delta, one two eight point three five." I'm switching the frequency to Chattanooga Approach.

Me: "Chattanooga Approach, good afternoon. Cessna 9130 Delta, six thousand, five hundred, VFR, with information Echo."

Approach: "Cessna 9130 Delta, Chattanooga Approach, verify you are landing Lovell Field." Why would he say this? We could be planning to transition through the Class C airspace without landing, or, we could be planning a landing at another airport inside the controller's airspace. In this case, we are landing at Lovell Field.

"Cessna 9130 Delta, affirmative," I say. Notice I didn't have to preface my radio call to the controller with "Chattanooga Approach." Once we have established radio contact with each other, I don't need to use the controller's call sign anymore. While there are many airplanes in the area, there is only one Chattanooga Approach controller on this frequency. That's why calls going out to individual aircraft must be distinguished with a call sign in every transmission. Calls inbound to the controller do not require the addition of the controller's call sign.

Approach: "Cessna 30 Delta, roger. Expect Runway Two at Lovell. Maintain your present heading and advise me of any altitude changes." Notice the controller changed to our abbreviated call sign.

"Cessna 30 Delta, Runway Two. Maintain present heading," I answer. Technically, I don't have to repeat the runway assignment since that part of Approach's transmission is an advisory. I repeated the runway so the controller could quality check my read back.

We are now 20 miles from the airport. The airport's traffic pattern altitude is 2,300 feet MSL. From out current altitude of 6,500 we have about 4,000 feet of altitude to lose in about 17 miles because we want to be at traffic pattern altitude before entering the pattern. On a 3 to 1 glide ratio, it's time to descend. I'll advise the controller.

"Cessna 30 Delta is descending to traffic pattern altitude."

Some pilots feel they must wake the controller up with his call sign any time they will be providing ATC with new information. For example: "Chattanooga Approach, Cessna 9130 Delta?"

Approach: "Cessna 9130 Delta, Chattanooga Approach go ahead."

Some pilots like to say, "Chattanooga Approach, Cessna 9130 Delta, request."

Approach: "Cessna 9130 Delta, go ahead with your request."

These types of transactions are wasteful and unnecessary. Sure, there is a chance the controller is temporarily not listening because he is talking on his landline, but so what? As a technique, make your request without the introduction. If the controller didn't hear you because he was distracted, he'll say, "Aircraft calling, say again. I was on the landline." No big deal. Just repeat your request.

In our case, the controller hears our statement that we are descending and replies, "Cessna 30 Delta, roger." Then he says, "Cessna 30 Delta, turn right, heading zero five zero, radar vectors for sequencing."

The controller will always give you a reason for the initial heading change. The words "for sequencing" means he intends to put us in line with other aircraft inbound to the airport. Alternatively, he might say, "Radar vectors to final," or, "Radar vectors to the downwind."

"Cessna 30 Delta, heading zero five zero," is all we need to say. No need to repeat the advisory part of his message.

Approach: "Cessna 30 Delta, turn left, heading three six zero."

Me: "Cessna 30 Delta, left, heading three six zero."

Approach: "Cessna 30 Delta, when you roll out of that turn, traffic will be a Cessna 210 at your twelve o'clock and four miles, northeast bound. Report that traffic in sight."

Let's look to our 10- to 11-o'clock now, while we are still in this turn. "Cessna 30 Delta," I transmit, "searching."

Ahh. There's that Cessna traffic. See him? I'll tell Approach. "Cessna 30 Delta has the Cessna Two-Ten in sight."

Approach: "Cessna 30 Delta, follow the traffic to a straight-in approach to Runway Two."

Me: "Cessna 30 Delta, we'll follow the traffic for a straight-in to Runway Two."

Approach: "Cessna 30 Delta, you are 10 miles south of the airport. Contact Lovell Tower on one one eight point six. Good day," the controller says.

"Cessna 30 Delta, one one eight point six," I say. No need to repeat the rest. It's all advisory. There's Tower's frequency in the active window of Comm Radio 1. Here's the call.

Over to Tower

"Lovell Tower, Cessna 9130 Delta, nine mile straight-in for Runway Two." Notice, since we changed frequencies, we have to go back to using our full call sign.

Tower: "Cessna 9130 Delta, Lovell Tower. Continue. You are number three for the airport, following a Cessna 210 on a 4 mile final."

"Cessna 9130 Delta, continue." I answer. Even though Approach sequenced us behind the Cessna 210, apparently there is another airplane ahead of the 210. Yes, see that airplane on a right base leg for the runway? He's at our 12:30 and slightly low. He must be number 1 for the runway.

Tower: "Cessna 581 Uniform Zulu, cleared to land, Runway Two. Traffic is a Piper Arrow turning base to final," Tower says.

Other Pilot: "Cessna 581 Uniform Zulu, cleared to land, Runway Two." That must be the Cessna 210 in front of us. The Piper is definitely the aircraft rolling out on final approach now.

We had better slow down to give the 210 time to land and get clear of the runway.

The Piper has landed and is turning off the runway. It looks like the Cessna 210 is just crossing over the approach lights for Runway 2. He must be on about a half-mile final approach.

"Cessna 9130 Delta, cleared to land, Runway Two. Traffic is over the approach lights," says Tower.

Me: "Cessna 9130 Delta, cleared to land, Runway Two." All right! Make it a greaser, Bubba. The 210 is just touching down now. He'll be off the runway well before we cross the threshold.

Sure enough, the 210 is turning off the runway to the right. The runway is all yours, Bubba.

Nice landing. Okay, it looks like we will be able to comfortably turn off to our right at the next taxiway.

"Cessna 9130 Delta," says Tower, "if able, make the next right turn off the runway at Taxiway Charlie."

Me: "Cessna 9130 Delta can make Charlie."

"Cessna 9130 Delta, right on Charlie. Left on Bravo. Hold short of Runway Three Three on Bravo. Stay with me," says Tower. I repeat those instructions to Tower.

Notice how Tower didn't switch us to Ground Control as we exited the runway? We still need to cross Runway 33. Sometimes Ground will handle control of aircraft crossing runways. In this case, Tower retains control of airplanes until they cross all intersecting runways. Once there are no more runways to cross, Tower will hand us off to the ground controller.

Who controls what at each airport depends on local procedures and the overall workload. The process really doesn't matter to us. All we need to do is follow instructions and switch frequencies when we are told to switch.

You know what? Let's terminate this flight right here. That's right, Bubba. We've beat the daylights out of Class C operations. I'm going to hop out. You are on your own, and for good reason. The rest of the airport operation is exactly as we did it at the home drome.

I'll meet you at the airport diner for lunch. We can talk about operations in Class B airspace over a burger and fries. Sorry, I don't mean your burger and fries will be contained within Class B airspace. I mean we will discuss the details of operating in Class B while we eat a burger and fries. Pardon? You'd prefer tofu, sprouts and edamame? Suit yourself. Either way, you're buying.

Take Action

Plan a cross-country to a busy airport within Class C airspace. Try to plan your arrival for a peak traffic period. Peak traffic usually occurs about the same times of day as the morning and evening rush hours on the highways of big cities.

Be sure to do a thorough preflight study of your chosen destination. Chair-fly your actions and radio calls to ATC for different arrival scenarios. Pay particular attention to all of the possibilities for how your aircraft might be handled after landing. Think about runway turnoff options, and the taxi clearances you might receive after landing.

Participate in the airport's radar sequencing program. Although Approach Control's radio frequency will be very busy, you will be surprised how much easier it will be to fit into the flow of traffic with Approach's help.

Chapter 17: Class Bravo and the Odd Duck

When speaking of airspace, the B in Class B stands for "Boy, oh boy, are you not getting in here." It's pretty difficult--if not nearly impossible--to penetrate most Class B airspace under VFR. The reason is simple. Class B surrounds the nation's busiest airports. By "busy," I mean jam-packed with IFR traffic.

Air traffic controllers are usually so busy working with enormous volumes of IFR traffic in Class B, that they rarely have the time or the desire to add to that workload by mixing in VFR traffic. Occasionally, you might be able to pass through Class B if it's an off hour, when traffic volume is very low. At some of the busiest airports, such as the Hartsfield-Jackson International Airport in Atlanta, the only time the airspace isn't packed with IFR traffic is between midnight and just before dawn. The rest of the time? Fuggedaboutit. Actually, in North Georgia, we might say, "T'aint happnin'." Either way, you aren't getting in.

Let's say you happen to arrive at the perfect time to enter Class B airspace under visual flight rules. First there are some personal requirements to enter. You must hold at least a private pilots license. If you are a student pilot you must meet the requirements stated in CFR 61.95. The reg says you must, within the past 90 days, have received ground and flight instruction on Class B operations from your supreme being, a.k.a. flight instructor. You must also have an endorsement in your logbook from your all-knowing-one verifying you have received this instruction.

To operate in Class B, your airplane must have an operable transponder with altitude reporting capability (Mode C). (There are exceptions to the requirement for Mode C. You can find these in the Aeronautical Information Manual under Class B airspace requirements.)

Prior to entering Class B, whether for landing or for transiting through the airspace, you must obtain a clearance from ATC. This requirement is a little bit different than the requirement for Class C airspace.

To enter Class C, all the controller has to do is acknowledge your initial radio call. Even if all the controller says, on initial contact, is "Standby," that fulfills the requirement for establishing radio contact. Unless the controller says, "Remain clear of Class C," you are authorized to enter.

Not so with Class B. Prior to entering Class B airspace, a pilot must hear from the controller, "You are cleared to enter the Class Bravo." If you don't hear "Cleared to enter," stay out. Even if the controller says "Radar contact," or acknowledges your initial call with "Roger," you are not cleared to enter until the controller specifically tells you so.

Unlike Class C, operation in Class B is strictly controlled. Participation in radar service is mandatory for VFR and IFR flights. All VFR aircraft will be given sequencing and standard radar separation from other aircraft operating in the Class B airspace. That means you may be given specific altitudes to maintain, airspeeds to hold, and headings to fly. You might even be given a specific rate of descent to apply. For example, "Cessna 9130 Delta, maintain at least one thousand five hundred feet per minute in your descent."

For radar separation, you can expect to be separated from all other VFR and IFR traffic that weigh 19,000 pounds or less, by:

- Target resolution, or

- 500 feet vertical separation, or

- Visual separation.

Target resolution means the air traffic controller must see "green between," or some clear space between the radar blips for two aircraft.

For radar separation from all VFR and IFR traffic weighing more than 19,000 pounds, or from turbojet aircraft, expect to be separated by:

- 1-1/2 miles lateral separation, or

- 500 feet vertical separation, or

- Visual separation.

These numbers come straight out of the AIM, Chapter 3 Para. e., ATC Clearances and Separation. Even though you are flying VFR, your aircraft is given the same radar handling as an IFR aircraft. The only difference between the two types of handling has to do with weather avoidance. While IFR aircraft can penetrate clouds and low visibility, you are still required to maintain at least 3 miles inflight visibility and clear of clouds inside Class B airspace. If ATC gives you a heading or altitude that would cause you to violate the regs for VFR cloud clearance or inflight visibility, you should tell the controller what you will need to do to maintain VFR.

Get your advisory into the controller as early as possible so he can plan for your deviation around clouds. Then, do what needs to be done to maintain VFR. Never let a controller's instructions cause you to violate the regs for VFR.

A controller would not intentionally try to cause you to violate the regs for VFR. The controller cannot see clouds or inflight vis from his position in the radar facility, so he has no way of knowing whether his headings or altitude assignments will put you in cloud or put you too close to a cloud. Even the weather observation data for the airports in his airspace only tell him the cloud layers and visibility at each airport. He cannot see the weather around each airport. You have to do all of the cloud spotting and maneuvering to maintain VFR. You also have a responsibility to keep the controller advised of your plan.

The AIM also cautions you that the procedures for radar separation in Class B airspace do not relieve you of the duty to continually watch for traffic conflicts, wake turbulence, terrain, and ground-based obstacles. Put another way, don't relax and say to yourself, "My life is in ATC's hands now." Your responsibilities as pilot in command are never turned over to ATC, no matter where you are flying.

Here is something to be particularly aware of when operating in Class B. Air traffic control will frequently assign an altitude to you that is not standard for VFR operations. For example, you might enter Class B at a standard VFR altitude of 5,500. Upon entering the airspace, ATC may say, "Cessna 9130 Delta, descend and maintain 4,000."

It's likely, as long as you remain inside Class B airspace, ATC will have you fly at whole altitudes. For example, 3,000; 4,000; 5,000; etc. At some point, particularly when you are about to exit Class B, ATC will say to you, "Cessna 9130 Delta, resume appropriate VFR altitudes." At that point, you should pick a whole altitude, plus 500 feet, such as 4,500, and fly to it. Of course, let ATC know about your targeted altitude before you climb or descend.

There is a Way In

Earlier, I said there are many locations where it is unlikely ATC will let you enter Class B during peak traffic hours. There are some Class B structures where it is possible to enter VFR along a specific, charted transition route. These routes are designed to allow VFR traffic to pass through Class B airspace without disrupting the flow of IFR traffic. Transition routes, set up around airports such as Seattle, Phoenix, and Los Angeles, were instituted so VFR aircraft would not have to detour long distances around Class B airspace.

To use a VFR transition route, refer to the terminal area chart that depicts the Class B airspace you would like to pass through. Note the name of the transition route and position your aircraft at the end of the route. Then make your radio call to ATC:

"Phoenix Approach, Cessna 9130 Delta at the south end of the East/West Route, 4,500 VFR. Request a transition northbound."

If your timing is good, ATC should clear you to enter the Class B airspace on the requested transition route immediately with an assigned altitude. If not, remain clear of the Class B and circle the area. Be sure to clear for traffic, because the entry and exit points for a transitions route are gathering areas for VFR traffic.

Once you receive clearance to enter Class B, follow the route as depicted on your chart. Pay close attention to any modifications, including altitude assignments, given by ATC.

While on the route, clear vigorously for traffic. Many other VFR aircraft will be squeezed in along the narrow route. Approach control should call out traffic to you. If Approach is very busy handling IFR traffic, the controller may miss a traffic advisory, so clear, clear, clear.

When you reach the exit point of the transition route, advise ATC. Don't expect a handoff to the next controller. It's likely you will have to make your own arrangements on the radio to pick up flight following by the next controller outside of Class B airspace.

Flying into LaGuardia

Tell you what. Let's throw your airplane inside the Class B airspace for a VFR approach and landing at New York's LaGuardia Airport. For some reason, you decided to pay the landing fee necessary to use LaGuardia. Perhaps you want the privilege of parking next to Donald Trump's black and gold Boeing, rather than landing at the more accessible Teterboro Airport in New Jersey, or at Islip Airport on Long Island.

So there you are, approaching the southern edge of New York's Class B airspace at 5,500. You have been working with New York Center. LaGuardia's ATIS tells you the airport is using Runway 22 for landing, and Runway 13 for departures. The surface wind is 170 degrees at 10 knots and the ceiling and visibility are unlimited.

I can tell you right now, there is no way New York Approach is going to try and insert your 115-knot Cessna 172 into the flow of turbojet and turboprop traffic lining up for LaGuardia. Approach will more likely keep you out of the way, below and off to one side of the general flow of traffic. The controller will build a slight gap between the jets and turboprops, and then sneak you in via a very short approach to Runway 22. (See the illustration of your probable flight path next page.)

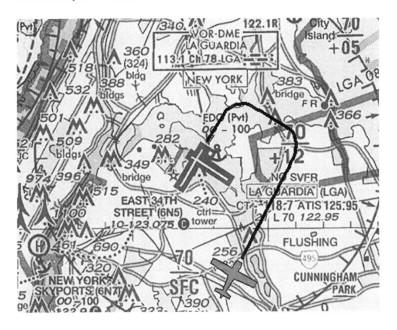

ATC is going to set you up for a short approach to Runway 22 from the east side of the airport.

While the big jets will be heading up the Hudson River at 4,000 feet to a base leg 7 to 10 miles from the airport, you will likely be kept down low and told to fly to a downwind leg east of the airport. From there, Approach will set you up for a left base leg by having you cut across Flushing Bay. Here is what it might sound like:

You: "New York Approach, Cessna 9130 Delta, 6,500, VFR with information Charlie."

Approach: "Ha, ha, ha. Is that you Ralph? C'mon, quick joking around. We're kinda busy over here."

"Cessna 9130 Delta is a Cessna 172, landing LaGuardia," you answer.

"You're kidding, right?" says New York Approach.

You: "Cessna 9130 Delta, negative. We have a landing slot at LaGuardia for 2210 Zulu."

Actually, I made up this whole joking-around conversation to prove a point. New York Approach controllers are consummate professionals and would never joke like this. What comes after this is closer to reality, if reality included you actually getting permission to land at LaGuardia, which it wouldn't, unless you were a major player. If you were a major player, you would probably arrive in a Gulfstream V on an IFR flight plan.

Approach: "Cessna 9130 Delta, roger. You're cleared to enter the Class Bravo. Descend and maintain 5,000, VFR."

You: "Cessna 9130 Delta, 5,000."

Approach: "Cessna 9130 Delta, maintain your maximum forward airspeed. Turn right heading zero four zero, vectors to Runway Two Two."

You: "Cessna 9130 Delta, maximum forward speed. Right, heading zero four zero."

Approach: "Cessna 9130 Delta, fly heading zero two zero. Report the airport in sight."

You: "Cessna 9130 Delta, heading zero two zero and we have the airport in sight."

Approach: "Cessna 9130 Delta, copy. Expect a short approach."

"Cessna 9130 Delta," you answer. A short approach is exactly what it sounds like. You can expect to be turned to a base leg that puts you on a short final approach. Bear in mind, New York Approach is used to handling heavy iron. Their definition of a short approach for the big jets is a 7- to 10-mile final. In your case, it would be safe to assume New York is going to set you up for a 1- to 2-mile final. Their objective is to have you on final approach for as little time as possible. Your airplane's airspeed is so incompatible with the big jets that there is no other way to mix you into the traffic flow.

Approach: "Cessna 9130 Delta, descend and maintain 3,000. No delay through 4,000 for traffic."

You: "Cessna 9130 Delta, descend and maintain 3,000. No delay through 4,000." When Approach says, "No delay," it means the controller wants you to immediately initiate your descent and maintain the highest rate of descent possible for your aircraft's performance and potential configuration.

First, never set up a descent rate that would cause your airplane to exceed its maximum allowed airspeed for its configuration. If your aircraft's flaps are up, then your max allowable speed would be VNE . If your flaps were extended, your max allowable airspeed would be your flap limiting speed or VFE. In either case, descend as rapidly as possible while still keeping airspeed comfortably within structural limits.

Second, if your airplane has drag devices, such as speed brakes, that allow it to descend at a higher rate of descent than it would in a clean configuration, you should extend those drag devices. If you have retractable landing gear, you could even extend the gear to add drag. Some drag devices have a maximum allowable airspeed for extension. Make sure your airspeed is below any applicable limit before extending a drag device.

An ATC instruction to make a maximum rate descent should not compel you to exceed 1,000 to 1,500 feet per minute descent during the last 1,000 feet of your descent prior to level off. For example, if ATC tells you to expedite your descent to 3,000 feet, as you pass 4,000 feet, you should reduce your descent rate to 1,500 feet per minute or less.

When ATC instructs you to make a maximum rate descent, or to expedite your descent, you should do what you can within safe limits to comply. Never let an ATC clearance push you to fly outside the limits of safety.

You reach the north end of Queens. The New York Mets Citi Field is just off to your right. Flushing Bay is straight ahead. New York Approach says, "Cessna 9130 Delta, turn right, heading zero four zero. I'll have base leg for you in two miles."

"Cessna 9130 Delta, right, heading zero four zero."

When the airport slides to your 9:30 position, Approach says, "Cessna 9130 Delta, turn left heading three one zero. Descend and maintain one thousand, five hundred."

You reply, "Cessna 9130 Delta, left, heading three one zero. Descend and maintain one thousand five hundred."

Approach: "Cessna 9130 Delta, contact LaGuardia Tower one one eight point seven."

You: "Cessna 9130 Delta, one one eight point seven." You make the frequency switch and say, "LaGuardia Tower, Cessna

9130 Delta, left base, Runway Two Two."

LaGuardia Tower: "Cessna 9130 Delta, LaGuardia Tower, cleared to land, Runway Two Two. Traffic will depart off Runway One Three prior to your arrival. Traffic is a Delta MD-88 on a seven mile final for Two Two."

"Cessna 9130 Delta. Cleared to land, Runway Two Two." Sure enough, you look to your 2:30 position and see an MD-88 on final approach. Time to get on the ground.

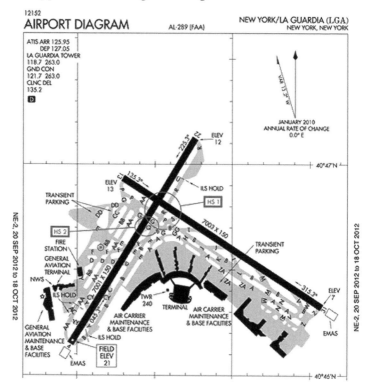

Here's the deal. I see this all the time at the big airports where light, general aviation aircraft are mixed in with faster moving commercial jets. General aviation pilots feel obligated to do their best to not get in the way of jets by flying as fast as possible. I often see the pilot of a light airplane try to land from a final approach flown at cruise airspeed. The result is not good. At the last moment, the pilot tries to pull back power, lower flaps and land. The nonstandard approach results in a long float in ground effect down the runway and a landing beyond the touchdown zone. This can be unsafe. At the very least, the time wasted floating in ground effect negates any time saved by flying final approach faster than normal.

Listen up. When Tower tells you to fly a short approach because a jet is barreling down on you from your 6 o'clock, do your best, but stick to your normal approach speed and landing procedures. If air traffic control puts a faster airplane in line behind you, it's ATC's problem to make the spacing work.

If the jet following you has to discontinue the approach and go-around, because it was about to get too close to your aircraft, then that's how it has to be. I guarantee you, when that jet comes around for its second landing attempt, ATC will take great care to make sure there is plenty of room for the jet to approach the runway and land. (Um, maybe. One time, many years ago, on a very busy night at LaGuardia, when I was flying MD-88s, we had to go around twice for inadequate spacing behind another jet landing on Runway 22.)

After your landing, you will be switched to LaGuardia Ground Control and told to taxi to the general aviation parking ramp. There, you may park next to The Donald's black and gold Boeing jet. I hope the thrill is worth the high landing fee you paid for access to LaGuardia Airport.

What's a Tersa?

Before we wrap up our riveting discussion of operations in radar controlled airspace, we ought to give a head nod to the Terminal Radar Service Area, or TRSA (pronounced "Tersa" in most places). A TRSA is the crazy family member no one acknowledges. No one seems to know how to classify it or apply any rules to it.

At one point, the FAA wanted to re-designate all TRSAs as Airport Radar Service Areas and slap all kinds of restrictions on them. The process became so difficult and mired in regulation that the idea was eventually abandoned. (Yes, it's true. Sometimes the government does decide it is over-regulating a system and then backs off.) It was eventually decided to leave well enough alone and let TRSAs continue as they are: a way to use radar service around an airport without a lot of restrictions.

A TRSA gives you the same benefits of Class C approach and departure control service for VFR aircraft. You get radar sequencing with other aircraft on arrival to, or departure from the airport(s) within the TRSA. Aircraft separation priorities are the same used for Class C airspace:

* Visual separation;

* 500-foot vertical separation;

* Target separation, also known as a "green between" gap between radar targets when broadband radar is in use.

Participation in radar sequencing and separation for VFR aircraft is strictly voluntary. If you don't want it, tell the controller, "Negative radar service." In response, the controller will tell you to switch frequencies to the tower at your destination airport.

Even though this sounds like Class C radar service, a TRSA looks a bit different than Class C airspace. You will find TRSAs depicted on sectional charts and terminal area charts as black rings around the primary airport they serve. The 5-nautical mile radius around the primary airport within the TRSA boundary is still Class D. The rest of the airspace that makes up a TRSA is Class E airspace, which is a catch-all term for any controlled airspace that isn't Class A, B, C, D or G.

Class E airspace begins at 700 or 1,200 feet above the ground and has no upper limit. Oddly, some TRSAs have core areas that begin at the surface inside the primary airport's Class D airspace, but have extensions down to the surface that extend outside the Class D perimeter of the airport. This conflicts with the definition of Class E which always begins at a minimum of 700 feet above the ground. As I said earlier, there are no published regulations for TRSAs in Part 71 or Part 91 of the CFRs. TRSAs, unlike true Class E airspace, have an upper limit as well. The upper limit of a TRSA is depicted on sectional and terminal area charts.

Most TRSAs look like the classic upside-down wedding cake associated with Class B structures. The floor of the TRSA begins at the surface for a certain radius around the primary airport. There are concentric rings, with successively larger circumferences, around the primary airport. Each ring has a base, the lowest of which begins between 700 and 1,200 feet above the ground. As the rings progress outward, the base level of each ring increases in height. (See the Macon, Georgia TRSA below.)

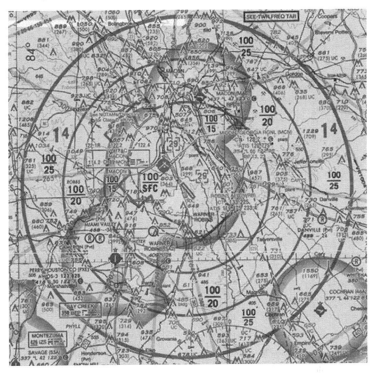

The TRSA surrounding Macon has a ceiling of 10,000 feet. Base layers step from 2,500 down to the surface around Macon Airport and Warner-Robbins Air Force Base.

The height of the top of the TRSA varies widely. The top of the TRSA in Macon, Georgia, is 10,000 feet MSL. Nearby, at Montgomery, Alabama, the TRSA tops out at 6,000 feet MSL. The radar facilities for both TRSAs control a mix of high-performance military aircraft, airliners, and general aviation aircraft. Macon's TRSA has a footprint over the ground that is about 33% larger than the TRSA serving Montgomery. Considering each TRSA serves the same type of traffic mix, your guess is as good as mine why one is so much larger than the other. Somebody who used to work at the FAA, and is now retired, probably knows the answer, but do we really care?

We do care about how to operate in a Terminal Radar Service Area. The method is the same one you would use for operating in Class C airspace:

Listen to the ATIS or AWOS/ASOS for the airport you will using. If on the ground, get a pre-departure clearance from ATC. Be sure to tell ATC your intended direction of flight after departure. For VFR, your clearance will include a transponder code to squawk and a departure frequency to contact after airborne.

- If in the air and inbound for landing, contact the approach controller about five miles before crossing the boundary for the TRSA.

- If you were receiving flight following from an enroute controller at an ARTCC, expect a handoff to Approach Control before entering the TRSA.

- If you want radar service, follow the approach controller's headings. If you do not want radar service, tell the controller, "Negative radar service," or, "I don't want radar service."

- Maintain VFR at all times, and advise the controller if he gives you a heading to fly that would make you unable to maintain VFR cloud clearances and inflight visibility.

- Advise the controller when you make any altitude changes.

- Listen up for traffic advisories, or suggested headings to fly to avoid a traffic conflict.

- Advise the controller when you have your destination airport in sight, or when you have the aircraft you are supposed to follow in sight. ATC will point these out to you when they become relevant.

- Switch to the tower frequency when told to do so. Then follow the tower controller's instructions, as you would for operations in any Class D airspace.

A Terminal Radar Service Areas is one of those good deals for pilots flying VFR. You get all of the bennies of a radar controller helping you fly safely past traffic, and safely over terrain, without any of the restrictions of Class B or Class C airspace. You will still need a radio to communicate, and a transponder to let the radar controller get a read on your airplane, but you call the shots on altitude, airspeed, and whether you even care to participate. ATC will line you up for the airport with a nice sequence relative to other arrivals. There really is no downside, so take advantage of the good deal.

And that, my friend, is all there is to operating into and out of airports busy enough to warrant a Terminal Radar Approach Control facility. The key takeaways for operating in a TRSA, or in any radar controlled airspace are:

- Maintain VFR, even if that means advising the controller you will not be able to follow his directions.

- Otherwise, follow the controller's instructions exactly as they are given. There is no such thing as participating halfway. You are either all in, or you are out.

- See and avoid other aircraft. Radar control does not guarantee ATC will point out every conflict.

- Repeat the controller's instructions like a parrot, but don't repeat advisory information.

What's left? A few loose ends that we'll tie, or snip, or smash in the next chapter. Bring snacks. I'll bring the beverages. It should be fun.

Take Action

If your home airport is based within a manageable flying distance from Phoenix, Los Angeles, Seattle, or New York, plan a VFR cross-country flight that requires the use of a Class B transition route. Fly to any of the entry points for a VFR transition route.

Prior to contacting ATC, rehearse the radio call you would make to ATC: Who you are, where you are, and "Request the transition through Class Bravo." Then contact the approach control serving the Class B airspace.

When cleared to enter the route by ATC, clear diligently for other aircraft on the route. Listen carefully to ATC for any amendments to your clearance, including changes in your assigned altitude.

If you cannot fly to any of the airports listed above, take a look at the paper edition or online edition of the terminal area chart for Los Angeles. Study the many VFR transition routes depicted on the chart. Practice simulated radio calls to Socal Approach, requesting transition routing from various points around the Class B airspace.

Chapter 18: What You Know Now that You Didn't Know Before

Where was your head when you started this book? No, not on your shoulders! I mean, what was your perception of air traffic control? Did you believe:

ATC is a big, complicated bureaucracy, devoted strictly to high-time pilots flying IFR.

ATC is a hindrance on the freedom of flight you enjoy when operating VFR.

ATC is a watchdog, ready to pounce on you the second you make a mistake while flying.

ATC provides nothing you cannot do on your own as a competent pilot.

ATC is an opponent, not a partner in flying.

Air traffic controllers will not adjust their clearances to accommodate your piloting skill level.

You wouldn't be able to speak fast enough when talking to ATC.

You might say the wrong thing to ATC and embarrass yourself.

You wouldn't be able to absorb and retain rapid-fire instructions from ATC.

You wouldn't be able to understand what ATC wanted you to do.

Where is your head now? Can you clearly see that, while not perfect, ATC does a good job of helping you fly safely?

With only a very few exceptions, ATC handles all pilots on a first-come, first-served basis. ATC does not rank order your priority by aircraft size or by type of flight plan--IFR vs. VFR.

The rules of ATC are clearly spelled out and they rarely change. Once you understand the system it is very reliable and predictable. With repeated exposure, the system will not seem complicated at all.

ATC puts no restrictions on VFR flight. Go where you want to go and do what you want to do, as long as it conforms to VFR and the general regulations for flying. Nothing changes.

ATC is a watchdog, but it's a watchdog that guards you. ATC watches out for your safety and works with you to resolve inflight problems.

ATC helps you see and hear more than you would when flying without ATC's assistance.

ATC's mission is to set up to work with you, not against you. Your mission is their mission: get from A to B safely and within the flying regs.

Air traffic controllers are trained to accommodate your level of flying skill.

You don't have to, and shouldn't talk fast to ATC.

At one time or another, all pilots have said the wrong thing on the radio. As long as you make a correction and clear up any misunderstandings, it's no big deal.

If ATC talks faster than you can absorb and retain, ask the controller to slow down, and he will.

The most important part of communication with ATC is understanding. They know it. You know it. Ask for clarification or a repeat of anything you don't understand, and you will get it.

Let's expand on this list just a little bit more. The clarification will be worth it.

It's Predictable

Air traffic control is a predictable system. From moment to

moment you should be able to anticipate what is coming next from ATC. This is because the rules for air traffic control are clearly spelled out and followed. The reason controllers are able to handle large volumes of traffic is because, in general, they do the same procedures over and over again in habit patterns. Once you understand those patterns, you will be able to predict what is coming next.

Even the language of air traffic control, the "phraseology" as we call it, is clearly spelled out. No matter where you fly in the world, air traffic controllers use the same language. Once you have a firm grip on that language, you can travel far and wide and expect to understand air traffic control wherever you find it.

It's true that controllers have to improvise and occasionally give instruction in plain language, but those instructions must come on the heels of standard phraseology. In other words, controllers use other words to clarify the standards. Of course, if you don't understand something a controller says, all you need to do is ask for clarification and you will get it, guaranteed, at no extra cost to you.

While admittedly still stuck in the 20th century, ATC does have some technology that you might not have in your own aircraft. This technology is designed to give you safety benefits without the cost of carrying it around in your own airplane. For example, some airports have fairly sophisticated windshear detection systems that can give you an early warning of danger ahead. A similar system, installed in your own aircraft would cost tens or even hundred of thousands of dollars. I know, because we have it installed in the Boeing 757 and it ain't cheap. The same goes for ATC's low altitude alert system, a component that warns you before you might hit the ground. Ground proximity warning systems in aircraft, using radar altimeters, are heavy and costly.

So yes, there is a lot going on when you connect to ATC. Once you understand the system and get familiar with it through repeated exposure, the perception of complexity goes away. You are left with a fairly sophisticated system at your disposal that gives you far more benefits than you could afford on your own.

Freedom

The FAA understood if it set up a system that put shackles on you when you fly VFR, you would not volunteer to use that system. Wherever and whenever possible, the FAA made Basic Radar Service for VFR Aircraft as user-friendly as possible.

When you connect to an air traffic controller while flying under VFR, you get all of the benefits of radar service with none of the inconvenience. VFR flight following gives you a wider field of view of the airspace around you. Basic radar service does not place any restrictions on where you go or how you get there.

When using basic radar service, you can even pick and choose which parts of the service you want to use. For example, if you don't want low-altitude alerts from ATC, don't request them. You can even fly right through a radar service area while refusing radar service. All you have to say is, "Negative radar service." The controller will pass you off to the tower controller at your destination, or leave you alone entirely as you pass through her airspace.

With the exception of Class B airspace, you can accept radar advisories but refuse radar sequencing within radar controlled airspace. Even when you get radar advisories, you don't have to follow the controller's advice. For example, if the controller sees a traffic conflict ahead, he will give you a suggested heading to avoid that traffic. You don't have to take his suggestion. You can fly a different heading, or climb or descend to avoid the traffic. Whatever you do, the controller will try his best to accommodate you. He is at your service.

All of this doesn't mean you can completely disregard an air traffic controller or treat the controller with disrespect. Pilots are expected to work in partnership with ATC to keep air traffic moving safely. A legal clearance from ATC should be followed, except in an emergency, or to avoid a collision, or to stay in compliance with a flying regulation.

For example, if ATC gives you a heading that would cause your airplane to fly closer to clouds than allowed by Visual Flight Rules, you should advise the controller and do what is necessary to maintain VFR. Controllers are well aware of your obligation to maintain VFR under all circumstances. That is why you will hear every controller remind you, "Maintain

VFR," when making initial contact with you.

Initial contact has two meanings. There is the meaning in the Aeronautical Information Manual, which says initial contact happens each time you contact a new controller. I believe there is a secondary definition of initial contact. My definition describes the moment you check in with the first air traffic controller in the chain of contacts you will make with ATC. Once you make contact with the first radar controller, you are plugged into the ATC system. Radar handoffs from controller to controller means the basic information about your flight is being passed along. It reduces your workload because you don't have to make position reports and do all of the other work involved in setting up contact with each subsequent controller.

Assistance

Once you are in the ATC system, your workload should go down, not up. ATC can provide assistance with almost anything you need that does not exist, or is not carried in, your aircraft. Almost anything. ATC cannot fly your airplane for you, but a controller can provide a lot of assistance with emergencies. ATC can also fetch weather information for you when you are too busy or not equipped to get it yourself.

The information relay does not stop with weather data. Basically, if you need almost any type of information pertaining to your flight, Air Traffic Control can likely get it for you. All you have to do is ask.

Be aware that controllers get overloaded as well. Sometimes they will be too busy to do anything beyond controlling traffic. We pilots understand this. For us, basic aircraft control always takes priority over everything else. For controllers, keeping traffic safely separated takes top priority. If an air traffic controller is too busy to accommodate your request, take a breath and let it go.

Requests and updates on the radio travel in both directions. You can help ATC by providing pilot reports, including everything from flight conditions to observed bird activity near your flight path. You can also help out an air traffic controller by updating him on changes to your flight plan as far in advance as possible before taking action. With information flowing freely between you and ATC, you and your controller can work together as a team to get your aircraft safely from here to there.

It's What You Say *and* How You Say It

How and when you exchange information with ATC depends on your skillful use of the radios. The more clearly and succinctly you speak on the radio, the better ATC will be able to understand you. Clarity on the radio begins with practice and evaluation. You will produce the clearest transmissions by making a conscious effort to be clear. Correct microphone positioning, careful enunciation of each word, and proper timing with the microphone key are all good areas to concentrate effort.

Pacing your words on the radio is also important. If you default toward a pace you would use in relaxed conversation, you are heading in the right direction. The notion that you have to talk fast on the radio is not only incorrect, it's a set up for failure. Though other pilots do it, speed talking on the radio can be extremely wasteful. As in a stall recovery, you want to make your first attempt at a radio transmission count. It is better to say something once at a clear, even pace and be understood the first time. If you speak too fast to be understood, you will have to repeat your transmission. Multiple transmissions to get your point across is a time-waster, not a time-saver.

Similarly, if an air traffic controller is burning up the radio with speed-talking, ask him to repeat his last transmission more slowly. Sometimes speed talking is simply a bad habit. Pilots and controllers may not even be aware they are doing it. A wake up call from you should fix the problem.

It doesn't matter how slowly a controller speaks if you don't understand the message. If a controller says something you cannot grasp, for whatever reason, don't worry about the reason. Focus on understanding. Ask the controller for a repeat or for clarification. A controller is obligated to repeat or clarify anytime you ask, and for as many times as you ask. There is no limit on what it takes to get you to understand a clearance.

If you have problems remembering a clearance, don't try and remember it. Write it down, with caution. Never give up aircraft control in favor of writing a clearance. You'll spend less time concentrating on writing if you keep your written notes to short scribbles that jog your memory. Your notes only have to work for you, so don't write a book for someone else's benefit. Write just enough to help you remember.

Here's another great thing we know about ATC. Air traffic controllers are trained to adjust the pace and length of their clearances when working with student pilots. Even if you are not a student pilot, you will probably hear an adjustment to a controller's delivery if the controller thinks you sound inexperienced on the radio.

This is nothing to be embarrassed about. We all had to start somewhere. No one comes into the world of air traffic control with knowledge of every nuance of radio communication. Controllers and pilots understand the process it takes to mature on the radio. If a controller ever forgets that, a simple reminder of "Say again, slowly," should be enough to get what you need.

ATC does have a hear back program that is supposed to catch errors in your read back. It works most of the time, but most of the time is not all of the time. If you don't understand something, or you didn't get the full clearance the first time, you know what to do: ask for a repeat or clarification.

If you are concerned you won't be able to find the right words to use with ATC, your best tactic is to parrot what the controller said to you. Rather than trying to spin the controller's words into your own poetic expression, simply repeat the controller's clearance word for word. Technically, you don't and probably should not repeat advisory information, but no one will flog you if you do. Be an ATC copycat on the radio and you won't go wrong. Later, as you get more experienced, you will learn what does and does not have to be repeated.

Anticipation

As I said at the outset, ATC is a system that works in predictable patterns. Once you learn those patterns, coping with ATC clearances becomes easy. You will be able to anticipate what is coming next. Never let your anticipation cloud over what is actually said on the radio. If you anticipated hearing the controller tell you to descend to three thousand, but the controller actually tells you to descend to one three thousand, don't let your expectations override listening. Remember, there is a big difference between hearing and listening. Listening is a conscious act. Stay conscious to stay out of trouble.

Opportunities

As a pilot flying VFR, you are never obligated to use ATC's service, as long as you remain outside of controlled airspace. In most areas, there is plenty of open sky where you can easily avoid controlled airspace. Sooner or later, if you fly long enough and seek out new experiences, you will eventually reach a place where you have no choice but to enter controlled airspace. It would be a shame if, after flying many years, your first encounter with ATC arrived because you had no choice.

Knowing that at some point in the future, your flying adventures are going to put you in touch with air traffic control, get a jump start on ATC communication right now. Like all other skills in aviation, practice improves your performance. You can almost always get away with low-level radio skills when working with ATC. Your flight will go smoother and be so much more enjoyable if you approach ATC communication as an opportunity, not as a thing to avoid.

If I leave you with only one lasting impression from this book it is this: Seek out opportunities to work with ATC. I believe you will be pleasantly surprised at how much benefit you gain. You will also discover that most, if not all of the pre-conceived notions about how difficult it is to work with ATC, turn out to be false or overblown. While partnering with ATC may not be as thrilling as flying a low level route over a beautiful valley, or as much of a rush as pulling G's in a aerobatic airplane, it is an activity that is well worth your time.

We pilots know aviation is a lifelong learning experience. Part of that experience can be getting in touch with your local air traffic controller and having a conversation. Do it. You will be a better, more well-rounded, and safer pilot as a result.

Take Action

Stay in touch. As you fly and work with ATC, questions are going to come up. You have a great resource that answers most questions about radio work at:

http://ATCcommunication.com.

Most of the information at ATCcommunication.com is derived from the Aeronautical Information Manual, the Air Traffic Controllers Manual, and the ICAO Air Traffic Management Manual. All are available online. If you cannot find what you are looking for at the website or in the manuals, send an email to me at jeff@ATCcommunication.com. If I don't have the answer you need, I will know where to direct you to get the answer. I look forward to hearing from you.

Be well and fly safe.

About the Author

Jeff Kanarish is an airline pilot, author, and host of the website ATCcommunication.com. He lives in Atlanta with his wife and 2 dogs. His first book, Clearance Magic: Copy IFR Clearances with Ease and Accuracy Every Time, is available at IFRclearance.com.

Alphabetical Index

Made in the USA
San Bernardino, CA
18 January 2013